THE GUIDANCE NURSERY SCHOOL

Books from the Gesell Institute

PARENTS ASK
Frances L. Ilg, M.D., and Louise Bates Ames, Ph.D.

THE GESELL INSTITUTE PARTY BOOK
Frances L. Ilg, M.D., Louise Bates Ames, Ph.D., Evelyn W.
Goodenough, Ph.D., and Irene B. Andresen, M.A.

CHILD BEHAVIOR
Frances L. Ilg, M.D., and Louise Bates Ames, Ph.D. (with a
Foreword by Arnold Gesell, M.D.)

YOUTH: *The Years from Ten to Sixteen*
Arnold Gesell, M.D., Frances L. Ilg, M.D., and Louise Bates
Ames, Ph.D.

THE CHILD FROM FIVE TO TEN
Arnold Gesell, M.D., and Frances L. Ilg, M.D., in collaboration
with Louise Bates Ames, Ph.D., and Glenna E. Bullis

INFANT AND CHILD IN THE CULTURE OF TODAY
Arnold Gesell, M.D., Frances L. Ilg, M.D., and Louise Bates
Ames, Ph.D. in collaboration with Janet Learned Rudell, Ph.D.

THE FIRST FIVE YEARS OF LIFE
Arnold Gesell, M.D., Frances L. Ilg, M.D., Louise Bates Ames,
Ph.D., Henry M. Halverson, Ph.D., Helen Thompson, Ph.D.,
Burton M. Castner, Ph.D., and Catherine S. Amatruda, M.D.

IS YOUR CHILD IN THE WRONG GRADE?
Louise Bates Ames, Ph.D.

STOP SCHOOL FAILURE
Louise Bates Ames, Ph.D., Clyde Gillespie, A.B., John W.
Streff, O.D.

DON'T PUSH YOUR PRESCHOOLER
Louise Bates Ames, Ph.D., and Joan Ames Chase, Ph.D.

THE GUIDANCE
NURSERY SCHOOL

A Gesell Institute Book for
Teachers and Parents

REVISED EDITION

By *Evelyn Goodenough Pitcher, PH.D.*

Professor, Eliot-Pearson Department of Child Study,
Tufts University

and *Louise Bates Ames, PH.D.*

Co-Director
Gesell Institute of Child Development

HARPER & ROW, PUBLISHERS
NEW YORK, EVANSTON, SAN FRANCISCO, LONDON

Designed by Lydia Link

Library of Congress Cataloging in Publication Data

Pitcher, Evelyn Goodenough.
The guidance nursery school.
Bibliography: p.
1. Nursery schools. 2. Child study. I. Ames,
Louise Bates, joint author. II. Title.
LB1140.P52 1975   372.21'6   74–1848
ISBN 0-06-013352-X

75 76 77 78 79 10 9 8 7 6 5 4 3 2 1

Contents

Acknowledgments

Sincere thanks are due Dr. Frances L. Ilg, who from the time in the 1930s when she was in charge of the nursery school at the Yale Clinic of Child Development to the present day has had so strong a part in determining the practices and policies of education for young children. Dr. Ilg has also been of substantial help to the writers in the editing of the final manuscript.

Irene Andresen Scatliff, formerly co-director of the Gesell Institute Guidance Nursery, provided much of the material dealing specifically with 4-year-olds.

Preface

Preschool, or early childhood, education has been a matter of considerable interest and concern in this country for many years, and its popularity is increasing. Private nursery schools continue to serve the largest number of preschool children. However, day care facilities for the very young are mushrooming. And there are some who even feel that preschools should be part of our public education system. Whether they attend from necessity, from community custom, or merely from their parents' choice, most children are ready to benefit from and to enjoy a group or school type of situation long before they are old enough to attend kindergarten.

When nursery schools were first begun, there was a tendency in many to think of a "right" and a "wrong" way to treat young children. Some schools appeared to consider that the teacher's way of handling them was right; the parents' way, all too often wrong. Thus in some schools children were kept for both a morning and an afternoon session, including lunch, five days a week. Parents often were allowed to observe the teacher's methods, apparently in hopes that they would learn from her how to handle their children.

Most schools, however, came to realize that a child's behavior in school with his teacher was often extremely different from the same child's behavior at home with his mother. Thus, though certainly a mother might pick up many clues about handling young children, the difference between a mother's and a teacher's relation to a child was clearly recognized.

It was also recognized that the teacher had much to learn from the parent. Schools increasingly came to stress the guidance that comes from communication between teachers and parents, and to consider the nursery school experience as an adjunct to, rather than as a substitute for, home experience.

Though every nursery school is inevitably influenced in its procedures by the personality and point of view of its teachers and administrators, from 1940 until quite recently in this country a more or less uniform point of view tended to prevail. Nursery school has been considered as a place for young children to play and grow and learn to live with others. It has been thought of as a place where they could express themselves at their own level of behavior or performance, but could be helped on toward more mature, cooperative, or effective ways of behaving. It has been a place where children, through play with a wide variety of multisensory materials and numerous relations with peers, could solve many of the problems of growing up and relating to others. It has been a place for learning in all areas.

In 1944 the faculty of the Nursery Training School of Boston (the precursor of the present Eliot-Pearson Department of Child Study at Tufts University) set forth the following fundamental principles as guidelines for the students.

1. Children are persons.
2. Education should always be thought of as guidance (teaching) which influences the development of persons (personalities).
3. Maturing and learning must go hand in hand in the process of development.
4. It is important that personalities be well balanced. Therefore, in guiding children, we should aim to help them develop

balancing traits at the same time we try to supply what they need for self-realization. Some of the balancing traits considered are security and growing independence; self-expression and self-control; awareness of self and social awareness; growth in freedom and growth in responsibility; opportunity to create and ability to conform.

These principles are still suitable as goals for today's programs for young children.

A well-run nursery school can provide for almost any child the most ideal school situation he may ever experience. This is true because in a nursery school that supports the principles just listed, more than in any group or grade that comes after, the school adapts itself to the child—to his individuality and to his level of maturity. Though certain demands and expectations, certain rules and regulations are maintained, at this level of education school exists to suit the child.

Very often in higher grades these principles are sublimated or lost, and there is a deplorable effort to force the student to fit the curriculum. But in good nursery schools the curriculum modifies itself to meet the child's needs and abilities. Teachers are not entirely permissive—they have quite definite hopes and expectations as to what school may provide for every child and as to how he may be helped to react—but both their hopes and their timetables can, when occasion demands, be extremely flexible.

In recent years a certain number of preschools have changed their emphasis. Some now lay a great deal of stress on what they call "cognitive development." They attempt to teach academic subjects even to 3- and 4-year-olds, believing that if children are thus instructed in the preschool years they will become brighter, will mature faster, and will thus perform more effectively in kindergarten and in the years which follow, than if they are permitted to "just play."

We ourselves do not separate the so-called cognitive from the rest of behavior, nor do we separate work and play. Dr. Arnold Gesell has often stressed that "mind manifests itself . . . in whatever the individual does." Work and play should not be distinguished in the learning process of children because play is a child's way of learning. And the child is a person, whose mind, body, emotions, spirit are interdependent and always influenced by his own unique personality.

Though this book is written primarily for teachers in the hope that the information it contains will help them set up and run their own nursery schools more effectively and more enjoyably, it is also written for parents to help them understand what their own child's nursery school is all about and how they can get the greatest possible benefit from it, for themselves and for their children. Nursery schools are, we believe, here to stay. How effective they will be depends on teachers and parents alike. We hope that this book will help.

LOUISE BATES AMES
EVELYN GOODENOUGH PITCHER

ONE

The Child

1

The Developmental Point of View
—Age Levels

BEHAVIOR CHANGES

The developmental point of view is concerned primarily with behavior changes which accompany age changes in the physical structure of the organism. It considers also of primary importance the individual differences which exist from child to child, differences also primarily determined by the inherent physical structure of the organism. Third, it is concerned with the effect of environmental forces as they play on the individual organism at any particular stage in its development.

Thus, in fact, those adults whose philosophy may be termed "developmental" are actually interested in the same three forces as are other students of human behavior: age, individuality, environment. But their emphasis is quite different from that of those who are primarily concerned with the effect of the environment, especially the emotional environment, on the organism.

A developmental philosophy—within which the present volume is written—will lead the nursery school teacher to take as much account of the individuality of any given child as her knowledge permits, but to place her primary emphasis on the developmental level at which that child is functioning. Thus she

3

will need first of all to be familiar with behavior patterns characteristic of each of the preschool levels. And she will then need to be able to recognize at least roughly at which level each of her young charges is operating. She will then treat him according to his developmental or *behavior* age, not according to his chronological age in months or years.

There follows a brief description of some of the most outstanding behavior patterns which characterize each six-month age level between eighteen months and five years of age. The reader will note that behavior does not necessarily improve steadily as the child grows older, but rather that ages of equilibrium tend to alternate with ages of disequilibrium; ages of inwardized or focal behavior seem to alternate with ages of outwardized or expansive behavior. Thus, when a child's behavior suddenly takes a turn for the worse, the reason for this turn may not necessarily be that something has gone wrong in his environment, or that he is just naturally "bad." It may simply be that a stage of equilibrium has been succeeded, as will often be the case, by a stage of disequilibrium. Thus 2-year-old equilibrium quite normally breaks up and behavior becomes "worse" at two-and-a-half. The good 5-year-old becomes the explosive Six.

We can try to smooth over the child's "worst" stages, curb some of his extreme expansiveness, or try to spread him out a little when he is in a too "close-to-home" stage. But even the most skilled handling does not appear appreciably to affect the rhythmic alternation of stages of equilibrium and disequilibrium, of focal versus peripheral behavior.

Before describing, somewhat specifically, the behaviors which outstandingly characterize the preschool age levels, we should perhaps give several warnings, lest the reader apply the information which we give too literally and too dogmatically.

First of all, it is important not to take this "timetable" too literally. Do not try to match any given child exactly to it. We are here describing more or less representative behaviors for each age level. That is, when we describe something as being typical 4-year-old behavior, we mean that of any one hundred presumably normal 4-year-olds, approximately half of them may be behaving in the manner described, when they are four years of age. Approximately one-quarter of them will already have gone past this kind of behavior. One-quarter will not yet have reached it.

Thus any one child may, quite normally, be a little ahead of or a little behind the behavior described as being typical of his age. He will in all probability go through the stages which we describe in the order given, but his rate of growth will be his own. It is not remarkable, then, if he is a little faster or a little slower than the given average.

The important thing is not so much to compare a child with the "average" or representative picture, as to compare him with himself—as he has been in the past and as he might be in the future. Our age sketches are not absolute norms of behavior that every child "ought" to exhibit exactly at a given moment. Rather they aim to help show the probable *direction* of the changes that may be expected as a child matures.

As most readers will realize, any description of age levels is inevitably a gross oversimplification. When we describe characteristic behavior for any given age, we do not mean that all children of that age will behave just that way all of the time. In fact, some may behave that way very little of the time.

It is the *order* in which these stages follow each other which is most important—far more important than the exact age at which any certain child reaches any one of the stages. And each child gives his own individual twist to these age sequences. Thus among the many possible exceptions to our suggestion that behavior in general, around four years of age, tends to be out of bounds, could be the following.

A child may quite normally reach the 4-year-old out-of-bounds stage a little ahead of time or a little behind time. He may be of such a gentle nature that even at his worst he does not go far out of bounds. Or he may be of such a vigorous nature that at *every* stage he is more or less out of bounds. Furthermore, even at a rather disorderly stage, there may be moments when his environment fits especially well with his own personal needs, when his behavior is quite calm. And lastly, though four may in many be an age when there is considerable disequilibrium between the child and his environment, some children seem to be relatively in harmony and at peace within themselves even at ages when their behavior is quite disturbing to those around them.

Actually it might be more accurate, and might avoid some error in application, should we refer to the different stages simply as Stages A, B, C, rather than as Age Two, Age Two-and-a-Half, etc. However, satisfactory as this might be from a scientific point of view, most parents and most teachers would find it cumbersome and impractical to refer to a child as being at the A, B, or C stage of development. It seems much more practical in everyday usage to be able to say that a child is at a 2-year-old or a 3-year-old stage of behavior.

A further misunderstanding to be avoided is this. Some people believe that when we describe some unattractive behavior as being typical of a given age, we mean that there is nothing that can be done about it. That we are advising them just to sit back and do nothing, thinking, "Oh that's just a stage!" Far from it. Knowing that any unattractive behavior is in all probability "just a stage" may help parent or teacher to feel more relaxed about it. But it can also, we hope, help him to cope with this behavior more successfully than might otherwise have been the case. Sometimes an undesirable behavior can be brushed over. At other times other interests should be substituted. At still other times its occurrence might have been prevented. Sometimes, however, it must be dealt with, directly and firmly.

There follows a brief descriptive summary of outstanding and characteristic behavior changes as they occur in the young human organism in the age range from eighteen months to five years, the age range dealt with in the present volume.

EIGHTEEN MONTHS

The 18-monther walks down a one-way street, though this one-way street can be rapidly reversed. And this street more often than not seems to lead in a direction exactly opposite to that which the adult has in mind. Asked to "Come here, dear," the 18-monther either stands still or runs in the opposite direction. (He may even like to walk backward.) Ask him to put something into the wastebasket, and he is more likely to empty out what is already in it. Hold out your hand for the cup which he has just drained, and he will drop it onto the floor. Give him a second sock to put on, and he will more likely than not remove the one which is already on his foot. His enjoyment of the opposite may be the reason why it works so well, if he is running away from you, to say, "Bye-bye," and walk away from *him.* Then he may come running. Not only does he not come when called, he seldom obeys any verbal command. "No" is his chief word.

It is not so much that the 18-monther is bad as that there are so many abilities he has not yet mastered. He has not yet reached the place where he can wait. "Now" is the one dimension of time which he has in his repertoire. Thus efforts to get him to wait a minute are for the most part doomed to failure, and he cannot stand any frustration. (Unfortunately, no matter how much you try to protect him in the way you set up the environment, he cannot seem to keep from frustrating himself.)

His interpersonal relations are almost completely dominated by ideas of taking, not of giving. Actually, except for his parents, he may treat other people, especially other children, more as if they were objects than people. He will as likely step on a friend as walk around him. He not infrequently resorts to the experimental poking, pulling, pinching, pushing, and sometimes hitting of other children. He has not even a beginning concept of sharing or of give-and-take or cooperative play with another child.

In the nursery school situation, if an 18-monther is introduced into such a setting (and this is the exception rather than the rule in most schools), he shows himself to be nowhere near ready for group play. Much of his time will be spent in solitary and often very active play. He covers a lot of ground, briefly contacting one thing after another. His manipulation of any single object, however, is neither elaborate nor long continued. He may drop the handle of a cart which he is pulling, forgetting that he was pulling it. He seems almost to think with his feet, moving rapidly from place to place. Often it appears that he notices an object after he has touched it, rather than moving about with any purpose or plan.

Eighteen months is not one of the "better" ages if we measure goodness in terms of minding, responding to commands, keeping within reasonable bounds. However, if we can appreciate the immaturity—in motor ability, language, and emotions —of the 18-monther, it can be fairly easy to keep his behavior within reasonable limits.

Thus if the adult would like to have him move from wherever he is to wherever she is, he can be lured or picked up and carried. But, for best results, not called. He is simply not mature enough to respond, in most instances, to a verbal command.

If it is desirable for him to stay away from certain areas, for best results make it physically impossible for him to get to those areas. Physical barriers work better than verbal prohibition.

When words are used, they should be kept short and simple: "Coat-hat-out" is about as complicated a command as the average 18-monther can follow.

It is important in dealing with an 18-monther to keep in mind at all times that he is an extremely immature little creature. He understands more words than he can say, but even his understanding is extremely limited. He can walk and even run and sometimes climb, but his balance is very unsteady. And with his quick temper and his need to have everything "now," his emotions are as immature as any other part of him.

If very little is expected of him, if demands that he "mind" are kept at a minimum, and close and rather constant physical supervision is provided, he may get on very well. He needs plenty of outlet for his boundless physical energy. Stair climbing is one of the best.

TWO YEARS

The child's behavior at two years of age is so much better organized than earlier, from the adult's point of view, that we sometimes fall into the trap of expecting a steady improvement from here on and are thus unhappily surprised when the customary difficulties of Two-and-a-Half make their appearance.

At any rate, regardless of what may come after, here at two comes a brief breathing space for the child as well as for the adult taking care of him. For two is in most children, compared to the ages which immediately precede and follow, an age of rather marked equilibrium. Things are much smoother with respect to nearly every field of behavior. Added maturity and a calm willingness to do what he can do and not to try too hard to do the things he cannot manage largely account for this greater smoothness.

The 2-year-old is much surer of himself motorwise than he was at eighteen months. He is less likely to fall. He runs and climbs more surely. Thus he no longer needs to be so much preoccupied with keeping his balance and getting around, and can turn his attention to other things. Also, the adult does not have to be so much on guard to protect him.

He is also surer of himself in language. Not only does he now understand a surprising amount of what is said to him, but he himself can, as a rule, use language with remarkable effectiveness. Being able to make his wants known and being understood by others relieves much of the furious exasperation which he felt earlier when he could only point or cry and hope that someone who knew his ways and wants would be on hand to interpret. At eighteen to twenty-one months a wrong spoon or a wrong bib could cause a long crying spell, until a perceptive mind-reading adult was able to produce the desired object without any real clue other than the child's crying and a knowledge of his possible wants.

Emotionally, too, he finds life easier. His demands are not quite as strong as they were. His ability to wait a minute or to suffer slight or temporary frustration if necessary has tremendously increased.

Furthermore, people mean more to him than they did earlier. He likes, on occasion at least, to please others; and he is often pleased by others. Thus he can, as the 18-monther could not, occasionally do things just to please people; he can occasionally put another person's wishes above his own. Though he cannot as yet share with other children, he will on occasion, if so directed, be willing to find substitute toys for these other children. This marks a whole new dimension in social relations over those of six months earlier. In fact, his aptitude for and interest in interpersonal relations helps to make nursery school, for many 2-year-olds, a practical and interesting experience.

Two's awareness of and interest in other children may exceed his ability to get along with them, it is true. Play at this age is primarily solitary, but 2-year-old approaches to other children are much more personal and friendly than those of eighteen months. Now instead of poking, pushing, and hitting, as earlier, the child is likely to hug and pat.

Two-year-olds like to watch each other's activity, to play near each other, and even occasionally for brief periods to imitate each other. Their interest in any given object or activity lasts longer than it did at eighteen months. It often lasts long enough to permit considerable exploratory manipulation of various play objects. Several may join briefly in domestic doll play which, while it will probably not involve real cooperative activity, may briefly keep two or more children together.

Two is, on many occasions, demonstrative and affectionate. He can be warmly responsive to others. This, along with his increased good nature, makes him, in home or nursery school, a much easier person to deal with than he was when younger. Much can be, and often is, said in praise of the 2-year-old. He is a loving companion and often a real joy.

TWO-AND-A-HALF

This is an age about which parents and teachers may need warning, because so much that the child now does naturally, almost inevitably, is directly contrary to what the adult would like to have him do. The 2½-year-old is not, temperamentally, an easily adaptable member of any social group.

The change in behavior which takes place between two and two-and-a-half can be rather overwhelming, perhaps to child as well as to the adults who surround him. Two-and-a-half is a peak age of disequilibrium. Adults often complain that they can't do a thing with the child of this age. Actually, once they understand a little about the structure of behavior at this time, they often find that, awkward as it may be, it does make sense. Working *around* the behavior characteristics of Two-and-a-Half is often much more successful than trying to meet them head-on.

Some of these outstanding characteristics:

First of all, Two-and-a-Half is rigid and inflexible. He wants exactly what he wants when he wants it. He cannot adapt, give in, wait a little while. Everything has to be done just so. Everything has to be right in the place he considers its proper place. For any domestic routine, he sets up a rigid sequence of events which must always follow each other in exactly the same manner.

Second, he is extremely domineering and demanding. He must give the orders. He must make the decisions. If he decides, "Mummy do," Daddy cannot be accepted as a substitute. If he decides, "Me do it myself," then no one is allowed to help him, no matter how awkward or incapable he himself may be.

Two-and-a-half is an age of violent emotions. There is little modulation to the emotional life of the child of this age.

Furthermore, this is an age of opposite extremes. With no ability to choose between alternatives (it is almost impossible for Two-and-a-Half to make a clear-cut choice and stick to it), the child of this age shuttles back and forth endlessly between any two extremes, seeming to be trying to include both in his decision. "I will—I won't," "I want—I don't want," "Go out —stay in." If someone doesn't cut into his back-and-forth shuttling, he may go on with it for upward of an hour. The decision of what clothes to wear may usurp a whole morning for a conflict-ridden 2½-year-old girl. Any caretaker of a 2½-year-old will need to streamline all routines, make the decisions herself, try to avoid situations where the child himself takes over.

Another characteristic of this age is perseveration—that is, the child wants to go on and on with whatever he is doing. Not only right at the moment but from day to day. If you read him four stories before bedtime yesterday, he wants four stories— and the same ones—today. It is very difficult with many a child of this age to introduce new clothes, new pieces of furniture, new things to eat. He wants things to go on just the way they have always been or at least wants to hold on to the old as new things are added.

Total all these characteristics and you have a child who is not easy to deal with. Vigorous, enthusiastic, energetic, the typical Two-and-a-Half may be. But he is not an easy person to have around. Great patience, a real understanding of the difficulties of the age, and a willingness to use endless techniques to work around rigidities and rituals and stubbornness are all necessary in dealing with the 2½-year-old effectively.

In school he pays considerably more attention to other children than he did when he was only two. But it is not a primarily friendly or cooperative attention which he exhibits. For the most part he attends to other children chiefly for the purpose of protecting any object which he himself is using, has used, or might be going to use.

Two-and-a-Half's demands are strong. His ability to share, wait, take turns, give in is very limited. He is interested in other children, it is true, but he seems much of the time to consider them as actual or potential rivals rather than as partners, collaborators, or friends.

In nursery school, oddly enough, the child of this age may be much more docile than at home. He is more ready to separate from his parent than he was at two. He is ready for this new experience. Often he seems quite different at school from the way he acts at home. His response to his parent as he is being picked up, however, reveals his other side. He may refuse to leave and may even have a temper tantrum.

There was a time when the teacher was apt to criticize the parent, feeling that the parent lacked control. But with increased understanding of the 2½-year-old stage of development she has come to realize that the transition of leaving nursery school is hard for the child. Also, he can explode with his mother but rarely does so with his teacher. It is then the teacher who needs to step in to help the child in this new step, and to make the parent feel comfortable in her role of sounding board.

THREE YEARS

Things quiet down, briefly, at three for most children. Two-and-a-Half seemed to love to resist. Three seems to love to conform. The typical 3-year-old uses the word "Yes" quite as easily as he formerly used the word "No."

Two-and-a-Half seemed to be all "take." Three likes to give as well as to take. He likes to share—both objects and experiences. "We" is a word which he uses frequently. It expresses his cooperative, easygoing attitude toward life in general.

Three is for the most part in good equilibrium with people and with things around him, perhaps because he is in better equilibrium within himself. He no longer seems to need the protection of rituals, of doing everything always the same way. Greater maturity has led him to feel much more secure—secure within himself and secure in his relations with others.

Not only has the need for rituals dropped out, but almost every other aspect of 2½-year-old behavior which made trouble for him and those about him seems to have disappeared, or at least diminished. The child is no longer rigid, inflexible, domineering, grasping. No longer does everything have to be done *his* way. Now he not only can do it *your* way, but can enjoy the doing.

People are important to him. He likes to make friends and will often willingly give up a toy or privilege in order to stay in the good graces of some other person—something of which he was incapable earlier.

Increased motor ability allows daily routines and other necessary activities to be gotten through with minimal difficulty. It also allows him to carry out successfully play activities which earlier baffled and enraged him.

But above all, his increased ability with and interest in language helps him to be a delightful companion, an interesting member of a group. His own vocabulary and ability to use language have increased tremendously in most cases. His own appreciation of the language of others has increased similarly. Now he not only can be controlled by language, but can be entertained and can himself entertain. He loves new words, and they can often act like magic in influencing him to behave as we would wish. Such words as "new," "different," "big," "surprise," "secret" all suggest his increased awareness of the excitement of new horizons. Such words as "help," "might," "could," "guess" are active motivators to get him to perform necessary tasks.

The 3-year-old's increased interest in and responsiveness to other children and his decreased need to protect himself and all of his possessions and to have everything for himself, plus his improved language ability, combine to make him enjoy play with other children. He not only takes considerable pleasure in elementary "cooperative" play (rather than parallel play as earlier), but he gets into fewer arguments and quarrels over materials. He not only is beginning to be able to take turns, to share, or to accept substitute toys, but he can even in a simple way use these "techniques" himself on other children.

Thus simple cooperative play, as with blocks or other construction materials, or in domestic play in the doll corner, enables children to play more elaborately and more enjoyably, as well as more smoothly than earlier, with other children.

Two-and-a-Half seemed often to resist just as a matter of principle. It was safer. Three goes forward positively to meet each new adventure.

THREE-AND-A-HALF

Temporarily at three many children reach what most parents and teachers consider to be a delightful stage of equilibrium. The child's wishes and his ability to carry out those wishes seem, for a while, to be in remarkably good balance. Three-year-olds, for the most part, seem to be well pleased with themselves and with those about them, and the feeling tends to be reciprocal. They seem also, so far as their outward behavior shows at least, to feel secure within themselves.

At three-and-a-half there comes, in many, a tremendous change. It is as though, in order to proceed from the equilibrium of the 3-year-old stage to that which is usually attained by five years of age, the child's behavior needs to break up, loosen up, and go through a phase of new integration. All of this comes to a head in many at three-and-a-half years of age—a period of marked insecurity, disequilibrium, incoordination.

This poor or new coordination may express itself in any or all fields of behavior. It may express itself only temporarily and very lightly in some children, for a considerably longer period and much more markedly in others. It is so characteristic of this particular age period that, though certainly environmental factors may exaggerate it, in many cases we can fairly consider that it is caused by growth factors alone. Certain by-products of behavior started at this period, such as stuttering, may continue longer than desirable within the more usual course of growth.

Thus one may look for incoordination in any or in all fields of behavior. Motor incoordination, for example, may express itself in stumbling, falling, fear of heights. A child who has previously shown excellent motor coordination may go through a period of extreme motor disequilibrium. Though the total body is often involved in this incoordination, the hands alone may be involved. Thus a child whose hand and arm movements have up till now been strong and firm may suddenly draw with a thin, wavery line; may build with a noticeable hand tremor. Language may be involved. Stuttering very often comes in at this period in children who have never stuttered before.

Ears and eyes may be included. Parents are often worried by the temporary crossing of the eyes which comes in here. Or the child may complain that he "can't see," or that he "can't hear."

Tensional outlets are often exaggerated in this 3½-year-old period. Thus the child may blink his eyes, bite his nails, pick his nose, exhibit facial or other tics, masturbate, suck his thumb excessively.

And lastly, along with motor and verbal difficulties often come tremendous difficulties in relations with other people. The 3½-year-old expresses his emotional insecurity in crying, whining, and frequent questioning, especially of his mother: "Do you love me?" Or perhaps in complaining: "You don't love me." He is also extremely demanding with adults: "Don't look!" "Don't talk!" "Don't laugh!" Or he may demand that all attention be focused on himself, and thus become extremely jealous of any attention paid by members of the family to each other.

With his friends, too, he shows considerable insecurity and great demand for their exclusive attention. The emotional extremes which he expresses (very shy one minute, overboisterous the next) also make him an uncertain contributor to any social situation.

Three-and-a-Half seems to feel so insecure that he must protect himself by holding tight, not so much to his possessions, as at two-and-a-half, as to his own way of doing things. Many at this age are as ritualistic and rigid as they were earlier at two-and-a-half. Thus any, or all, routines—eating, sleeping, dressing—can present areas of great difficulty for the adult in charge. Many Three-and-a-Halfs get through the smooth stretches between routines without too much difficulty, but any routine may end in a temper tantrum or tears.

In school, children in the 3½-year-old group often actually get along less smoothly in their interpersonal relations than they did six months earlier. At three years of age many children are able to enjoy simple cooperative play with others of the same age. Relationships may perhaps be a trifle superficial and not particularly intense, but group play often proceeds very harmoniously.

By three-and-a-half, relations are less smooth, and oddly enough the reason often seems to be that relationships are more important. Thus the child of this age is capable of, and interested in, forming strong friendships. "My friend" is an important person to him. But, as in so many other areas of behavior, the child often goes about the business of forming friendships in a somewhat backward manner. He emphasizes his liking for certain children by excluding and refusing to play with certain others.

Thus among a group of 3½-year-olds there is likely to be a good deal of discriminating against, keeping out, refusing to play with, demanding, commanding. Harsh words are uttered, and even the use of physical force against enemies is often resorted to. Group life at this age can on occasion be extremely stormy.

If the adult in charge knows in advance that all of this uncertainty, insecurity, incoordination quite normally marks the three-and-a-half age period, it can help considerably. First of all, it can keep him from blaming various aspects of the environment for any or all of the different incoordinations. It can stimulate him to try to fit the demands of the environment a little more to the abilities and inabilities of the age. It can help him to understand and sympathize with Three-and-a-Half's somewhat stormy relations with other children. And it can help give patience to provide the child with the extra affection, the extra understanding, which he so desperately needs at this age.

One of the more positive aspects of behavior at this age is the child's play with imaginary companions. A good many children at this age enjoy themselves immensely in their play with imaginary animals or people, which in many reaches its peak at this time.

Others now become the animal—the cat with paws—or the fireman or cowboy or other hero of the moment. The teacher and parent can go along with this imaginative play, treating the child within the framework of his role.

FOUR YEARS

For every age it seems possible to discover a key word or words which describe the structure of behavior at that time. If we can find and remember these words, it often helps tremendously to understand and appreciate the child of that age.

For Four, the key word is "out of bounds." If we can remember this, and smile sympathetically when we say it, it can be of immeasurable aid in helping us to deal with any 4-year-olds who may come our way. For the 4-year-old, almost more than the child of any other age, is out of bounds in almost every direction.

Thus he is out of bounds motor wise. He hits, he kicks, he throws fits of rage. "You make me so MAD," he will tell you.

Verbally he is almost more out of bounds than in any other way. The language of a typical 4-year-old can be almost guaranteed to shock anybody except perhaps a hardened nursery school teacher. Profanity (where did he ever hear such awful language?) is rampant. Bathroom and elimination words come into common use. He uses them not only incidentally or where they might be appropriate, but may dwell on them and rhyme with them—accompanying his rhyming with much silly laughter which shows that he fully appreciates their inappropriateness or appropriateness, according to his feelings.

And in interpersonal relations with adults he is quite as out of bounds as anywhere else. He loves to defy adult commands. In fact, he seems to thrive on being just as defiant as he dares. Even severe punishment may have little chastening effect. A terrible toughness has seemed to come over him—he swaggers, swears, boasts, defies.

With other children he tends to get on much better than he did six months earlier. He is less sensitive, less vulnerable, less demanding. He can now enjoy his friendships more positively, with less need to exclude others. However, even within his friendships there is much out-of-bounds behavior, much boasting—"I'm bigger (better, smarter, stronger) than you are"; "I have bigger ones at home"; "My father can do it better." Names are called and threats are uttered. However, not all of this need necessarily be taken seriously by the adult. Fours just naturally behave this way and probably recognize such behavior as normal and relatively harmless in their contemporaries.

Four's imagination, too, seems at this time to have no "reasonable" limits. This new-found expansion through imagination, so strong at three-and-a-half years, continues in his enjoyment of imaginary companions. Most parents accept this fairly well. Four's tall tales, particularly when they strike the adult as just plain lies, are less well accepted. Yet to the average 4-year-old the line between fact and fiction is a very thin, flexible line. He may not actually be telling falsehoods. It's just more interesting that way, and he may come to believe his own imaginings, which become very real to him.

How firm a stand the parent or teacher takes toward all these out-of-bounds behaviors is up to him. Certainly there are limits. Even the very simple social situation of a nursery school group requires a certain toning down of 4-year-old exuberance.

Home life requires perhaps even more.

A good deal of firmness is needed in dealing with the average 4-year-old. But he can be dealt with more effectively if parent or teacher keeps in mind that behaving in an out-of-bounds manner is not only an almost inevitable but a probably necessary part of development. The 3½-year-old was, certainly, too insecure for practical purposes. Four seems to most overly secure and too brashly confident of his own abilities. He is so secure that now he not only can stand his ground but can thrust out against the environment. Nature seems to have this awkward way of going to opposite extremes as the child develops. Eventually the swings of the pendulum become less extreme and settle down to a narrower range as the individual's basic personality is less swayed by age changes.

The 4-year-old needs to be allowed to test himself out. He is surprisingly responsive if he has been allowed some initial expansion. The reins of control can be held loosely, but there are always those moments when they need to be pulled up, short and sharp.

FOUR-AND-A-HALF

The 4½-year-old is beginning to pull in from his out-of-bounds 4-year-old ways. He is on his way to a more focal five, when life is more matter-of-fact and not so deep.

He is trying to sort out what is real from what is make-believe, and he does not get so lost in his pretending as at three-and-a-half and four years, when he really *was* a cat or a carpenter or Roy Rogers. "Is it real?" is his constant question. Making a *real* drawing of an airplane, he includes a long electric cord so the people can plug it in. However, he can still become quite confused as he tries to straighten out what he pretends, what happens on TV, and what is real.

This mixture of reality and imagination can be quite exasperating to parents. Thus when one mother, completely out of patience, threatened that the Sandman would come and get him —we don't recommend this—her 4½-year-old considered and replied, "O.K., well, I think I better take my cowboy boots and shirt. Will you get down my suitcase?"

Four-and-a-half-year-olds are a little more self-motivating than they were earlier. They start a job and stay on the same track much better than at four years, and with less need of adult control. When they start to build a farm with blocks, it ends up as a farm, not, as at four years, becoming first a fort, then a truck, then a gas station.

Four-and-a-half-year-olds are great discussers. Reading a book about fires might lead to a long discussion of the pros and cons of fires. They often have a surprising wealth of material and experience to draw upon, and seem to be prompted by an intellectual, philosophizing sort of interest. They are interested in details and they like to be shown. Their desire for realism is sometimes entirely too stark for adults—they seem sometimes almost too frank as they demand the details about death, for example.

Children of this age are improving their control and perfecting their skills in many ways. Their play is less wild than at four; they are better able to accept frustration.

Their fine motor control as expressed in drawing is markedly improved, and they will often draw on and on. They show a beginning interest in letters and numbers, and may count quite well, though skipping certain numbers.

Four-and-a-Half shows a beginning interest, too, in seeing several sides of the picture. He is aware of front and back, of inside and outside. (One child wanted to know what her back looked like.) They may even draw a man on one side of a paper, and then turn it over and draw the back of his head on the other side.

Four-and-a-Half, with its increased control and its interest in improving and perfecting skills, is a "catching up" time with children, especially with boys who have been slow in motor or language development; or it may be an age of rapid intellectual growth for those who have already caught up.

FIVE YEARS

Most children have already "graduated" from nursery school before they get to be five years of age. However, since some Fours do turn five in the spring of their last year in nursery school, we shall describe 5-year-oldness briefly.

Five years of age marks, in many children, a time of extreme and delightfully good equilibrium. "He's an angel," say many mothers of Fives, in awe and wonderment. "He's almost too good!" worry others.

Five is indeed a good age. Gone is the out-of-bounds exuberance of the 4-year-old. Gone is the uncertainty and unpredictability of four-and-a-half. The 5-year-old tends to be reliable, stable, well adjusted. Secure within himself, he is calm, friendly, and not too demanding in his relations with others.

He seems secure and capable because he is content to stay on or near home base. He does not seem to feel the need to thrust out into the unknown, to attempt that which is too difficult for him. Rather he is content to live here and now. He tries only that which he can accomplish, and therefore he accomplishes that which he tries.

His mother is the center of his world, and he likes to be near her. He likes to do things with and for her; likes to obey her commands. He is usually well satisfied with his teacher, too. He likes to be instructed and to get permission. To be a good boy is not only his intention, but is something which he usually can accomplish. Therefore he is satisfied with himself, and others are satisfied with him.

Many parents wish, when the customary 5½- to 6-year-old

breakup of behavior comes, and when their "good" little 5-year-old turns into an often less-than-good little Six, that they could have their docile 5-year-old back again. Looking backward in this way is, of course, fruitless. It is like wishing that the 18-monther, when he gets around the house too briskly and gets into too many things, were once again in the precreeping stage. Five is, in most children, an enjoyable age for everybody while it lasts. But a growing child needs more than 5-year-old equipment to meet the world. He needs to branch out, as he does at six. Unfortunately, in branching out, he often thrusts into areas which cause a good deal of difficulty for all concerned. That is the difficulty of six. But that is another story.

THE GROWTH OF INTELLIGENCE

Piaget's theories are helpful in understanding the developmental process in the growth of intelligence.[1] Piaget's work differs from Gesell's in that Piaget is primarily a theoretician, though there is striking agreement between the two points of view. Piaget believes that intellectual development, which passes through a series of maturing stages, results from an interplay between internal and external forces. He distinguishes between two major stages of intellectual development: sensorimotor (birth to two years), and conceptual (two years to maturity). These stages are further elaborated by him in terms of specific sequences.

Piaget's theory, as a whole, reveals the young child as quite different from the adult in his intellectual functioning. He is different in his approach to reality, his views of the world, his

1. The reader who wishes to explore his work in more detail is referred to an excellent introduction to Piaget by H. Ginsburg and S. Opper, *Piaget's Theory of Intellectual Development: An Introduction* (Englewood Cliffs, N.J.: Prentice-Hall, 1969).

use of language. Intelligence grows through the *activity* of the child, as he manipulates and explores objects, as he engages in verbal interactions with others.

The educational implications of Piaget's theory are manifold. For the preschool child they suggest that his environment must provide a wide range of multisensory experiences: feeling, tasting, hearing, seeing. Materials should be abundant and easily available, inviting children to touch, to try, to test. The way to learning moves from the concrete to the abstract, from manipulation to symbolization. Premature symbolization violates developmental processes and therefore accomplishes no sound educational objectives.

Piaget's theories, like Gesell's, embrace a developmental point of view, since he shows, on the basis of children's responses to his experiments, that intellectual development seems to follow an ordered sequence. At each stage of development a child is capable of certain forms of thought. As age progresses, he acquires certain ideas of reality. Teachers and parents need to be aware of a child's current level of intellectual functioning, realizing that there are definite limitations in what the child can learn and that intellectual development is a progressive process involving assimilation and accommodation, with new ways of responding fitting into the old ones and expanding them as a child grows.

2

Individuality

DIFFERENT PHYSICAL TYPES

"Perhaps we shall never know how to treat children until we have learned to tell them apart." This cogent statement by William Sheldon applies very well to children at the preschool level, particularly in the nursery school setting. In the home, most parents do tell their children apart very effectively, in many cases without much formal intellectual differentiation of their personalities. They know, for instance, that it is "just no use" pushing Danny once he makes up his mind that he won't do a thing. They know that Laura gets too excited when there is company. They know that Jimmy always has to be warned in advance, and goes to pieces if you spring surprises on him.

Hours of daily contact, year in and year out, have built up their knowledge. A nursery school teacher, presumably equally interested in and alert to individual differences, will need to make many decisions about, and many moves in relation to, most children before she has time to come to know them fully. Some general theoretical understanding of personality differences can be of great help in her initial contacts with a new group of children, as well as in subsequent work with them. A theoretical or systematic understanding of individual differences should never be used either in school or at home to take the place of careful, intuitive observation of individual children.

But it can offer real shortcuts to such knowledge and can sharpen such observations all along the way.

The system of classification which we have found most effective and the one used by us at the Gesell Institute is that set forth by Sheldon.[1] According to this system, behavior is a function of structure, and the human individual behaves as he does largely because of the way he is structured. Remaining reasonably consistent throughout the life span, the actual physical structure of the body can be a clue as to what kind of behavior one can and cannot expect of each individual.

Though there do not actually exist different distinct "types" of body build, we can identify three chief physical components. Each person actually represents a combination of these three different components, but in most people one or the other tends to predominate. Thus we often loosely speak *as if* there were three types of individual. These three components are—endomorphy, mesomorphy, ectomorphy.

The person in whom endomorphy predominates is referred to as an *endomorph.* These individuals have large stomachs and livers, that is, large digestive viscera. They float high in water and are usually fat. They are soft and spherical in shape. Their behavior is characterized by extreme relaxation and love of comfort. They are sociable, love food, love people, and are gluttons for affection.

The *mesomorph,* in contrast, has big bones, a well-developed heart and circulatory system, and heavy muscles. He is hard, firm, upright, and relatively strong. Blood vessels are large and the skin is relatively thick, with large pores. In his behavior, muscular activity and vigorous bodily assertion predominate.

1. William H. Sheldon, *Varities of Physique* and *Varieties of Temperament* (New York: Hafner, 1970. This chapter is an adaptation from *Varieties of Temperament.* For a simplified description of the behavior of individuals of the several somatotypes, see Frances L. Ilg and Louise B. Ames, *Child Behavior* (New York: Harper & Row, 1955).

He loves exercise and activity, loves to dominate.

The *ectomorph,* in extreme contrast, is the thin, fragile, linear person, flat of chest and with long, slender, poorly muscled or "pipestem" arms and legs. His behavior shows restraint, inhibition, oversensitiveness, and a desire for concealment. He shrinks from even ordinary social occasions.

Each of these three types of individual, because of his own special physical structure, has different drives, different responses, different interests, from each of the others. Sheldon sums up these differences by saying that the endomorph exercises and attends in order to eat; the mesomorph eats and attends in order to exercise; and the ectomorph eats and exercises in order to attend.

It is very important to keep in mind that no one individual is *purely* one thing or another. In most individuals, one component or the other predominates and largely determines behavior, but we are each a combination of these three elements.

TECHNIQUES FOR DEALING WITH DIFFERENT KINDS OF CHILDREN BASED ON THEIR PHYSICAL TYPES

From all that we have said it will be appreciated that children are by no means all alike. At school as at home, we can deal with them most effectively if we do not try to treat them alike. At the Gesell Nursery School we have discovered that an understanding of and a respect for temperamental differences based on the different kinds of physical structure lead us to have quite different expectations of, and to make quite different demands of, the endomorph, the mesomorph, and the ectomorph.

The *endomorphic* child in nursery school often presents less of a problem than do children in whom either of the other two physical components predominate. Good-natured and cheerful, the plump little endomorph often asks nothing better than to follow along cozily where a more dominant friend may lead. An experienced nursery school teacher will usually feel that there is nothing damaging to personality in the fact that a child like this is happier to follow the leader than to initiate behavior himself. The true endomorph is a born follower. He not only enjoys following, but usually feels more comfortable that way. He would rather have peace and harmony than have things all his own way. It is not essential to help him get free of his more dominant friends, or to try to push him to strike out on his own.

Most endomorphic children love humor and are very responsive to a humorous approach, but they are not always too discerning in this respect. They may simply repeat a joke with which somebody else has gotten a laugh. Or they may laugh as heartily as anybody else when the joke is actually on them.

The endomorph likes people and likes to have them like him. But, if not too perceptive, he may even enjoy attention which is not entirely friendly. An endomorphic child in our nursery once took great pleasure in a game in which several of her 4-year-old friends were planning to "blow her up with dynamite."

Whatever the role somebody else might plan for him, the endomorphic child is usually glad to fit in and play the way the others want him to. If, as also is often the case, he plays his part awkwardly and not too effectively, he fills in the gaps with pleasant giggling.

Interested in food, and liking to do what is expected, the plump endomorph often is one of the easiest children to guide through midmorning milk and crackers and other domestic routines. The skinny ectomorph may be too diffident (or not hungry); the mesomorph too busy or too active to bother about the simple routines which the morning schedule usually demands.

Warm and friendly, very responsive to personal approaches,

endomorphic children, though they may cry easily, also laugh easily, express all emotions easily. The teacher does not have to watch them closely for secret signs of distress, carefully concealed. Happy or sad, they let everyone know it. Under ordinary circumstances they are more often happy than sad. But if they do give way to tears, they can easily and quickly be comforted by close physical contact. A teacher can take them on her lap, as a mother would, and can express sympathy and friendliness. Or she can give them something to eat. Food, useful in solving problems with almost any kind of child, is especially effective with the endomorph.

A good deal depends, with the endomorphic child, on what other physical components are included in his makeup. If a child is extremely endomorphic without mesomorphy, he may be poor athletically and may be clumsy. Also he may be lazy and fearful in climbing and in other athletic activities. If there is considerable mesomorphy combined with endomorphy, the child may be expected to have hearty, warm relationships with others. If the secondary component is ectomorphy, he may prefer to watch and to laugh. In the nursery school we do not as a rule seem to see as much extreme endomorphy as extreme mesomorphy or ectomorphy. This may be because it is not always easy to differentiate baby roundness from endomorphy. At any rate, endomorphy does not seem to affect behavior in the nursery school child as much as do the other two components, and less allowance seems to have to be made for it.

The endomorphic child perhaps above all loves comfort, so if out-of-door play is too uncomfortable because of dampness or cold, he will complain. Otherwise he will accept it, as he accepts most things, agreeably and without too much question. Endomorphy, in the nursery school as elsewhere, makes for comfortable, easygoing relations with other people, and in all phases of nursery school activity.

The typically *mesomorphic* child expresses himself through

almost constant vigorous, noisy, energetic gross motor activity. He is almost constantly in motion, covers a great deal of ground, and cannot seem to keep his hands off anything. Because of his energy and roughness, the things he touches often break, the children or animals he touches are often hurt. It is difficult for him to sit still, or to obey orders and do things in the way that someone else wishes.

However, in the nursery school, as in any other play group situation, this need present no insurmountable problem provided that there are not too many mesomorphs in any one group. And provided that the teacher understands the mesomorphic individual and makes allowance (and provision) for the way he will almost inevitably behave. It is the motor-driven mesomorphic child who poses a problem in nursery school as well as in the home.

First of all, the teacher will recognize that it is very difficult for this kind of child to sit still for any long period of time. Thus she will provide him with many opportunities for active play and will make few demands on him to sit still for more than brief snatches of time. Whenever any long sitting still may be necessary, she will provide him with a good opportunity to blow off steam afterward.

She should realize that children of this type are hard to handle, and that they make great demands on a teacher's time, energy, patience. Such children need to be handled with consistent firmness. They question, more than do other children, what the rules are and who is in authority. They test the limits more than do other children. A teacher thus needs to be consistently firm, but at the same time she will need to make allowance for the exuberance and aggressiveness which this kind of child exhibits. She should not jump on him every single time he goes out of bounds.

Two extreme motor-driven mesomorphs in the average-sized nursery school are ordinarily as many as the group can absorb and the teacher can stand. We once had an extremely mesomorphic little boy in our nursery school, and when he moved out of town it was found possible to include three new children in his place.

Teachers must accept the fact that many mesomorphs (especially young ones) seem to be just naturally destructive as well as loud and vigorous. They cannot seem to keep their hands out of things. They are insatiable touchers, handlers, explorers. But their ever-active hands are often not particularly skillful. What they touch is, therefore, likely to be dropped, bent, broken. Since this natural destructiveness is seldom intentional badness, a teacher should try—when she cannot prevent it—not to penalize it too severely. She may have to "not see" much that a child like this does. Otherwise she may find herself engaged in a constant series of head-on collisions, the very thing she wants to avoid. Rerouting, preplanning, substitutions, watchful supervision all aimed to prevent the worst disasters can be more effective in dealing with a child like this than a heavy-handed and direct frontal attack.

Where climbing and other athletic activities are concerned, a teacher may need to be even more watchful than with other kinds of children. However, she should recognize both that the mesomorph is unlikely to fall and that, even should he fall, he is not likely to hurt himself. Not only are these children very secure and sure of themselves motorwise, but they often seem almost impervious to physical pain. A bruise on hand or knee for them can often be healed by a kiss. It is not so much that they are a good deal braver than other children—rather that they seem much more sturdy and apparently less susceptible to pain.

Along with trying to protect a child of this type, a teacher will need to protect his playmates, any animals which may turn up in his vicinity, or even herself. With animals the true mesomorph is loving but apt to be very, very rough. More or less impervious to pain himself, he often has little idea that he is actually hurting an animal. Other children, too, may need to be protected from the advances of the mesomorph, who in anger, in play, or just out of sheer exuberant curiosity may really hurt another child. Even teacher herself may need a little protection, particularly when she is attempting discipline. Such a child is not above kicking or striking out at a disciplining adult. Often this type of response indicates that the child has overstayed his time. Difficulties are most apt to occur after 11 A.M. Therefore a wise teacher could arrange that this type of child be picked up by 11 A.M. or even earlier if he gives evidence that his tolerance threshold has been reached.

It is wise to recognize that, in playing with other children, mesomorphs need to be leaders. This is a real need, and leadership is a role which they fill effectively. Thus a teacher should help them to be in situations where they can lead.

Furthermore, the fact that to the mesomorph approval of contemporaries is important can be utilized. What the other children will think, or that he may be "bothering" the other children, can often be used in steering a mesomorph's behavior from nonacceptable to acceptable.

The discipline of any mesomorph requires constant firmness. However, since a teacher cannot jump on such a child every time he goes out of bounds, her disciplinary policy will need to include a judicious combination of firmness and reasonable allowance for his exuberance and aggressiveness. She should not be afraid to use humor—even rather rough and noisy humor—since this appeals tremendously to the mesomorphic child, and often can do more than anything else to smooth over difficult spots.

Out-of-door play is usually much enjoyed by mesomorphic children and presents little problem. They love climbing, riding, jumping, and other athletic activities and seem quite impervious to rain, cold, snow down their necks, or whatever the weather may offer. On the jungle gym or on other climbing apparatus, this type of child is an enthusiastic, active, and secure climber, nearly always knows what he is doing, has good control, and even if he tumbles a lot seldom minds any but major physical hurts.

The shy, thin *ectomorph* makes an entirely different response to the nursery school situation. The teacher will probably need more techniques, and will be more aware of the need for techniques, with him than with any of the other children. And the techniques needed will be quite different in many ways from those used with the others. With the mesomorph a teacher uses techniques to subdue the child and to keep him in hand; but with the ectomorph she will often use techniques to bring him out and to help him, as time goes on, to take a confident though special part in the daily activities.

One of the most important considerations, in effectively dealing with an ectomorphic child in nursery school, is to realize that he must be given time to warm up. Not just hours or even days—but in some cases it will be weeks before he is ready to take part fully in group activities. Till then he must be allowed to go his own slow way. And even once he is warmed up it is important not to expect too much exuberance. Much of the ectomorph's preferred activity consists in watching and talking. Within reason this must be permitted, but a teacher must guard against these being his only activities. Often such a child will prefer association with teachers, and thus must be helped to have good dealings and relations with other children.

This slow warming up repeats itself over and over again. Thus, even after such a child has become adjusted to the nursery school as a whole, he may continue to express reserve and reluctance whenever a new activity presents itself. Ectomorphs are likely not to want to do a thing at all unless they can do it well, which adds to the slowness of their approach to any new situation.

Children of this type tend to be oversensitive, and therefore care has to be taken not to hurt their feelings. The smallest things—any slight failure or harsh word—may make them unhappy. They are likely to go to pieces if too much attention is focused on them. For instance, it may embarrass them to take their turn at a group song, though they may be very much hurt if a turn is not offered. Since they cannot, like others, ask for a turn, the teacher often seems to be walking a tightrope between seeing that they receive enough attention, and protecting them from too much. Such children may need to be given permission for even very small, unimportant things.

The ectomorphic child tends to be extremely vulnerable in almost every respect. He is particularly vulnerable about misunderstandings—even things that he misunderstands in stories that are being read. His total adjustment often breaks down because of some very minor thing which has gone wrong, and then the teacher may have to start at the beginning again. If such a child is in trouble, he may best be comforted through discussion and distraction on an intellectual level—he often refuses to be picked up or touched or comforted in ordinary physical ways. Actually such a child needs a lot of attention from the adult, but this attention often needs to be oblique. The ectomorph much more than the others seems to make his adjustment to school through a teacher.

These children have to be helped and encouraged to any physical activity. For the most part they do not care much for climbing, running, fast riding, violent jumping, or sliding from high places. And outdoor play is not fun for many. They tend to stand around with their hands in their pockets, feeling cold, or wet, or hot. A teacher should try to stimulate them to some activity but should be ready to bring them in ahead of the others. They could stay happily indoors all morning.

Such children may enjoy best purely imaginative activities —having different personalities, playing different roles, or playing with imaginary friends or animals. They greatly enjoy gentle humor—as the use of funny words or amusing ideas in a story.

Even more than with other preschoolers, the belongings of the ectomorph and the things he has made seem to be a part of him. He loves to bring things with him from home—might carry around a little china animal or a tiny flower throughout the entire school session. And he is very anxious to take home paintings or clay products which he has made. These things are important to him. He usually takes very good care of them, and if they are lost or destroyed he is very much distressed.

Perhaps more than children of other temperaments, the ectomorphic child is often misjudged in nursery school by those teachers who do not understand and respect his personality makeup. He is also misjudged by those who do not realize that it not only takes him a long time to warm up, but that his participation may never be as socially warm and friendly as that of the endomorph, or as confidently active as that of the mesomorph. The ectomorphic child who merely stands and watches, for relatively long periods of time, may in his own way be getting as much out of the school experience as is the more actively participating child.

OTHER WAYS OF LOOKING AT INDIVIDUALITY

There are of course many other ways of thinking about individual differences than those proposed by Sheldon. Chess, Thomas, and Birch[2] have isolated eight temperamental attributes observable in children from birth on through the years that follow. They identify them as follows:

Activity Level. From birth on, babies vary in their amount

2. Stella Chess, Alexander Thomas, and Herbert G. Birch, *Your Child Is a Person* (New York: Viking Press, 1965).

of activity. Some babies are almost constantly and vigorously in motion, even when asleep. Others are very placid and move very little.

Regularity. Some children are born with what seem like better biological clocks than others. Some wake up every four hours almost to the minute for their feedings, for example. These babies naturally do well on the self-demand schedule. They are usually easy to toilet-train. Others are more irregular and vary in their self-imposed schedules and in their demands from day to day. You never know what to expect of them.

Adaptability to Change in Routine. Some babies accept a change in schedule easily. You name it, they like it. With others, even the slightest change in scheduling is bitterly resisted, and it can be a real fight to change bedtime, or feeding time, or a carriage-ride time, by even a few minutes. Clearly some babies are highly conservative by nature. They adopt the principle that nothing new should be tried for the first time.

Level of Sensory Threshold. There are some children who could sleep if a brass band were playing in their room. Others will awake with a start if you merely whisper in the next room, "Shh! You'll wake the baby."

Positive or Negative Mood. Some babies and children have a predominantly negative or complaining mood. As one mother reported, "Susie cries when she wakes up. She cries when she is put down. She cries if the door bangs." Others are basically cheerful and good-natured no matter what happens.

Intensity of Response. "When he is hungry, he lets you know it," a perceptive mother of three children once commented to her pediatrician, above the sounds of loud, furious bellowing issuing from her 4-month-old infant. Others seem to have a very low energy level, and all their responses are mild, even when they are angry.

Distractability. Some infants and some children are highly distractable. The sound of a typewriter or conversation in the next room or a branch scratching against a window may make it impossible for some children to study. Others can work or may even seem to work better with radio *and* TV on in the same room.

Persistency. This is the quality of stick-to-it-iveness. Give one child a clothespin or even an old leaf or a piece of string, and he will play with it for hours. A less persistent child may need constant distraction. One child will refuse to give up until he has solved a problem or finished a game or task. Another will leave a stream of half-finished tasks or activities behind him as he goes restlessly searching for something new.

According to Chess, Thomas, and Birch, though a child's way of functioning depends to a large extent on the organization of these characteristics, a critical factor which must be considered is the environment's reaction to each of any child's temperamental traits. Persons inside and outside the family are constantly reacting to the child; and some temperaments are easier to live with than others. The results of the interaction of child with environment cannot be underestimated.

Some children need more structure; others, more freedom. Some have patterns of temperament more vulnerable to environmental influence than do others. In some instances serious behavioral disturbances come from intrafamilial and extrafamilial circumstances, peer group and school interactions. Temperament alone is not always the thing that produces behavioral disturbances. On the other hand, the same environment may have quite diverse effects on different individuals.

DIFFERENT PSYCHOSEXUAL EXPERIENCES

Erikson feels that any child's cognitive, social, and sexual growth is subject to a series of developmental crises.[3] Every

3. E. Erikson, *Childhood and Society,* rev. ed. (New York: W. W. Norton & Co., 1963).

child must successfully negotiate a number of crises which come in quick succession in the early years. A successful solution brings progress and integration to the personality. Failure brings regression or retardation. The issues are described in his writings as "The Eight Stages of Man." The infant is confronted with the issue of trusting or mistrusting his environment. If distrust predominates, the dilemma is an unresolved one that interferes with functioning in subsequent issues. The child may withdraw from his real environment into a world of fantasy or self-stimulation.

Other issues confronting the child are those of autonomy, initiative, and industry. Unsuccessful solution of autonomy may bring undue aggression in play situations, an inability to complete tasks, compulsive rituals, or a defiance of authority. The negative counterpart of initiative, feelings of guilt, brings extreme dependence, restricted movement, limited expression of fantasy, and limited use of conceptual language. Such a child may stick to the familiar, refusing to explore even when encouraged. The negative counterpart of industry is inferiority, involving low self-esteem, isolation, and aggression.

DIFFERENCES IN PERCEPTION

Benefits, handicaps, or any differences, however benign, in young children's environments obviously will alter their perceptions of the world.

As we are able to observe, to know, to understand, to empathize, we increase our ability to identify with a child as though we were in his situation, and to see the world in some respects as he sees it. Somehow the teacher must try to "get inside" the young child in terms of his experience, try to realize how the complicated pieces of his kaleidoscopic experiences have been joined in some sort of meaningful pattern for him. We realize this most sharply when we consider how differently life may be perceived by children of different socioeconomic backgrounds.

Is the policeman, for example, a symbol to be trusted or feared from the point of view of all children? Middle-class teachers often must make a special effort in understanding the frame of reference—so linked in many ways to what we see as "individuality"—in children from different backgrounds. A preschool teacher who is thus sensitive can communicate better the child's own perceptions, and she can also make efforts to modify a child's perceptual schemata or to enrich her own.

In fact, as we become increasingly aware of the essentially pluralistic nature of our society, we appreciate that middle-class white children need to respect other life styles. We also feel that minority group members need to share their school experience with other children like themselves in skin color and life style with whom they can easily identify, and thus enhance their self-awareness and self-esteem.

Consequently when it is practical we favor heterogeneous racial groupings in school, both for teachers and for children. We would also encourage schools to provide an abundance of good books and curriculum materials about children other than white. The history, art, music, and tradition of minority groups should be made part of the school curriculum.

SEX DIFFERENCES

Do boys and girls see the world differently, act in different ways, because they are biologically different? Or because society conventionally treats them in different ways? Most people would agree that differences in behavior do exist, and seem to believe that they arise from complex interactions between genetic and environmental variables. Maleness and femaleness are institutionalized as statuses in all cultures and as such have assumed psychological identities.

If it is true that the tendency to passivity or activity is inherent in different degrees in the male-female biology and anatomy, it is not surprising that over a broad spectrum of society and a long passage of time, training for girls has emphasized responsibility and nurture and for boys has stressed self-reliance and achievement. Such differences have presumably not been mere arbitrary customs, but adjustments to the social implications of the biological differences between the sexes.

At present, however, there is a prominent movement to bring about changes in attitudes toward sex differences, to avoid attitudes that lead to sex stereotyping. Stereotyped attitudes tend to label the male as active and intelligent, the girl as passive and less intelligent. Men are regarded as able to carry out a variety of occupational roles, whereas women are seen by some primarily in such nurturant roles as nurse, housewife, secretary, or teacher in the elementary school. There is a strong belief that more productive options in living will be available to both sexes if these stereotypes can be broken down.

The present concern with stereotyping is relatively new and reflects increased sensitivity not only to sex but also to racial stereotyping. It is only within the past decade that we have had widespread awareness of the rights of minority groups, that we have included black studies and people in our educational programs. Intelligent education interprets and reflects the essentially pluralistic nature of our society. Funded day care programs freeing women from traditional home and child care are growing, and men increasingly participate in home management, child rearing, and child care.

While major changes have been taking place to break down sex-stereotyped views and practices, it is still too early to determine their eventual effectiveness. We do not yet know whether different practices in socialization will produce different behavior in children who are biologically different.

Present research on sex differences is vast and tends to document that differences do indeed exist.[4] While we cannot here report the range of information available, we present some findings about young children, not necessarily to suggest that these differences *should* exist, but that they *do* exist, and that those who are working for change should acquaint themselves with these and other differences.

Our own studies,[5] among others, have demonstrated conspicuous differences in the early responses of boys and of girls. Girls appear, in general, to have a more personal, boys a more objective, orientation. The thinking of girls appears to be somewhat circuitous, involved in personal emotional considerations which differentiate it from the more objective, logical thinking of the male.

Interviews with parents of nursery school children indicate that these parents have very clear and consistent notions of the behavior differences observable in their sons and daughters. It seems probable that these beliefs of the parent contribute to the differences observed. Thus it seems possible that social expectancy may to some extent become self-image. Parents do seem to carry on differential reinforcement in the ongoing stream of behavior by a consistent pattern of rewards and punishments of which they are not necessarily aware. The pattern in many instances is merely a matter of interest or attention on the part of parents; children may thus be influenced to become what they are expected to be, and the expectations may hardly be perceived by either child or adult.

A second process, itself perhaps partly generated through

4. E. E. Macoby, ed., *The Development of Sex Differences* (Stanford, Cal.: Stanford University Press, 1966).

5. Evelyn Wiltshire Goodenough, "Interest in Persons as an Aspect of Sex Differences in the Early Years," *Genetic Psychology Monographs* 55 (1957): 287–323.

differential reinforcement, is imitation. The little girl, one might assume, will imitate her mother, and this assumption becomes a formative suggestion. She imitates the mother in the role that she early sees as part of the daily life at home. Suggestive assumption directs the boy just as clearly to the life pattern of the father.

However, it seems unlikely that the parental expectation of difference is the sole cause of such differences as may be observed. Many clear-cut differences do occur which it would seem rather far-fetched to attribute solely to the child's responses to social expectation. In spontaneous drawing situations, for instance, the female child, significantly more than the male, includes people in her drawings. She also more often includes both male and female persons in her drawings than does the boy, who when he draws a person at all, most often draws merely a male. Or, in a projective technique situation, as in the Lowenfeld Mosaic Test, verbalization which accompanies the test performance is quite different in preschool girls than in boys—the verbalization of girls including many digressive, irrelevant comments about themselves and other people, made in a manner quite different from the verbalization of the male.

Conspicuous sex differences in response have also been noted in the "spontaneous story" test, in which the preschooler is asked merely to "Tell a story."[6] When we analyze the themes of these spontaneously told stories, we find that girls tend to present people more vividly and realistically than do boys and to identify themselves with the personalities and experiences of others. Boys, on the other hand, speak with significantly greater frequency of things. They seem especially fascinated by vehicles of transportation and machines. They are also more interested

6. Evelyn Goodenough Pitcher and Ernst Prelinger, *Children Tell Stories: An Analysis of Fantasy* (New York: International Universities Press, 1963).

in elements of nature, such as sun, ice, rain, snow, hurricanes. The girls' interest in objects is more likely to be in personal or household equipment, or in productive nature—leaf, tree, flower. They mention relatively few objects in motion.

Among the people most prominent in the girls' stories are parent figures, and the girl is much more likely than the boy to express emotions about the parental figure, particularly about the mother. Girls seem to know, in considerable detail, what it is to be a mother. Boys more often discover masculinity and identify themselves with it in a general way—in the policeman, the fireman, the Indian. These are the masculine roles which the boy can comprehend and play at imitating as he cannot do with his father's role as factory worker, executive, lawyer, or scholar.

It also seems that the girl's early identification with her mother may influence her ideas about morality, for she is over and again more personally and emotionally involved in her judgment of what is good and bad than is the boy. The badness the girl reports is usually minor and spiteful, and the girl is skilled in planning punishment at once devastating, personally rejecting, and humiliating.

Boys, on the other hand, move into a concern for the larger social aspects of goodness and badness. For boys, the arena of evil is more often out of the house. It is the boy who matches forces of good and evil in organized warfare, who sees a responsibility for saving people or fighting from a sense of duty.

Although almost as many girls as boys speak of aggression, this expression of aggression tends to be much more violent in boys than in girls. In discussing food, or clothes, girls are much more interested in details than are boys. Furthermore, a concern with friendship and pleasure from interpersonal relationships is much more frequent in girls than in boys.

In spontaneous behavior customarily observed in the nursery school, rather clear-cut sex differences, at least some of which in our opinion may be laid to inherent factors, are observable at every age level. Among the more conspicuous are the following.

18 Months[7]

Boys are definitely interested in wheels and in cars. They like to watch car wheels, and to line up cars. They are interested in doorknobs, and in looking at and turning on lights. *Girls are more interested in dolls and in simple doll play. There is more social response and more group feeling in girls* than in boys. The girls rock together and even sometimes talk together. The boys are more likely to sit or stand around by themselves.

Girls know people's names; boys don't. Girls are already somewhat interested in the clothes that people wear.

2 to 2½ Years

Most of the differences noted at eighteen months still hold true. *Also, the girls are quieter than the boys.* Boys tend to be more dynamic and colorful. The girls as a rule have an easier time. More of the boys have adjustment difficulties.

2½ to 3 Years

The boys are noisier and more focal; the girls more peripheral. Boys need to have their activities shifted more quickly. Girls can play longer in one situation without their play deteriorating. Boys fatigue more rapidly.

Also, boys tend to have much more of what we consider typical 2½-year-old-difficulties than do girls. Girls are less rigid and stubborn, seem to give in more. The teacher finds herself planning

---

7. Most nursery schools do not start with children as young as eighteen months of age, but while we were at Yale University our youngest group was planned for children of that age. This group was small and met only once a week for a period of one and a half hours.

more around the boys than the girls, because the girls seem to be more flexible.

3 to 3½ Years

Girls and boys may be more alike in their play at this age, which is in general a period of reasonably good equilibrium, than at some of the other ages. There is more crossover of interests than at earlier or later ages. Boys' interests are not as clearly defined as later, and they are not as yet as interested in being boys and men as later. Thus many boys enjoy housekeeping play; many girls build with blocks.

3½ to 4 Years

There is a great deal of difference between the activities of the two sexes here. This is an age when girls prefer to play with other girls; boys play with boys. Friendships are especially strong between any two members of the same sex and there is much talk of "You're my friend." "You're not my friend." In any heterosexual friendships which develop, girls tend to be the aggressors.

Boys at this age like to engage in extremely masculine, constructive play, and as the year proceeds they become more and more affiliated with men and with grown-up pursuits such as being firemen, sailors, and the like. Girls continue to be most interested in their girl friendships. Girls are now more fatigable; boys hold up better.

4 Years

Boys definitely express more clearly the out-of-bounds tendencies characteristic of this age. They run away, climb fences, call names, boast, and swagger. Girls are less out of bounds, more amenable, more aware of censure, more respectful of rules.

Boys are more focal, their play is centered more on one activity, they go on longer. They repeat one pattern over and over, elaborating gradually. Girls are more peripheral and go more from one thing to another. They are also more fatigable. Boys tend to be more active in play, to become more angry, enter into more conflicts, do more hitting.

Boys' play tends to be more dramatic. They prefer play with blocks and vehicles. Girls are more all over the place—they play with blocks if they can get them, with clay, with doll corner equipment. They play house; they dance.

A teacher is definitely aware of "the boys" and "the girls" at this age, more so than earlier. They play more apart. The boys are better at spontaneous activity, the girls better at planned activity directed by someone else. The girls enter into music and rhythms better than boys do, being less self-conscious than are the boys.

There is a general and probably well-founded belief among parents that "boys are harder to raise than are girls." Certainly the referrals to a clinical service bear this out. Referrals to our own institute are in the ratio of considerably more than five boys to every one girl, and Levy[8] in an early study reported that boys, especially first boys, are more often referred for clinical help than are girls. Also if one reviews the publications on the diagnosis and treatment of young delinquents, it is impressive to note how small a number of girls appear in the samples. Thus in one study of fifty-seven children who were clinical referrals because of antisocial behavior, fifty-five of these children were boys.[9]

Teachers, also, report[10] that more than twice as many behavior problems occur among boys in the elementary school situation than among girls. The reasons for this may be multi-

8. John Levy, "A Quantitative Study of Behavior Problems," *American Journal of Psychiatry* 10 (1930–1931): 637–654.

9. Evelyn Rexford, "Antisocial Young Children and Their Families," reprinted from *Dynamic Psychopathology in Children* (New York: Grune & Stratton, 1959).

10. Norma Cutts and Nicholas Moseley, *Teaching the Disorderly Pupil in Elementary and Secondary School* (New York: Longman, 1957).

ple. Certainly one reason for the greater incidence of school behavior problems in boys than in girls may be that, with boys on the average developing more slowly than do girls, relatively more of them may be overplaced in school in the early grades. However, it also seems reasonable to suppose that at least to some extent innate personality differences cause this greater occurrence of disturbed and disturbing behavior both at home and at school.

At the preschool level we find that many of the common tensional outlets seem to occur more frequently in boys. Certainly thumb sucking seems to run a different course in the two sexes. With boys it may be more intense. Masturbating quite certainly occurs more in boys than in girls. The use of rough, violent language—a common 4-year-old tensional outlet—is more prevalent in boys.

Complicated and difficult going-to-sleep patterns (head banging, rocking, elaborate rituals which must be carried out) seem to occur most in boys, but there is some evidence that sleeping difficulties which occur during the night are observed most in girls.

One major area in which clearly defined sex differences are observable, and an area in which for the most part it is hard to believe that cultural factors play the major role, is that of *differential rates of development.* In general it appears that in the early years of life, girls tend in many functions to develop more rapidly than do boys.

Thus girls in general appear to be more advanced in language than boys. Seemingly the majority of slow-speech children who cause their parents real concern by their slow development of language are boys. Even though girls may sometimes be delayed, when speech does come in, it comes in rather suddenly and fully. Boys tend to need more speech correction than do girls, and we find more stutterers among boys than among girls. However, boys seem to be more generally advanced in gross motor behaviors.

There is some evidence that boys may be more precocious in feeding themselves, but girls are definitely more precocious in toilet training than are boys, both for bowel and for bladder control.

Girls dress themselves earlier and much more efficiently than do boys, owing to a better fine motor coordination[11] and especially to a more flexible rotation at the wrist. Some girls at two and three dress themselves so skillfully that they may dress and undress just for fun, while at the other extreme are boys of five and six years who still have difficulty in buttoning buttons and in dressing in general. The poor wrist rotation of young boys may also be observed in hand washing, and also in their inability to turn a doorknob far enough to open a door.

Girls from four to six count higher and make fewer errors in counting than do boys.

Also, current research, supported by the observation of many parents and teachers, suggests that, so far as early schooling goes, on the average girls are ready to meet the demands of first grade a good six months earlier than are boys.

Proponents of the theory that cultural expectation and impress alone are responsible for observable preschool sex differences point out that preschool girls and boys often play with exactly the same toys, until the culture steps in and emphasizes the desirability of some types of toys for girls, of others for boys. Our own observations suggest that at the earliest ages quite marked sex differences in play activity do occur. Around three to three-and-a-half it is true that boys as well as girls play with dolls and with housekeeping toys; girls sometimes play with the more masculine toys. However, it should be noted that even here, when boys do spend considerable time in play with housekeeping toys, their method of approach, their manner of manipulation, and the total type of interest and energy which

11. Arnold Gesell et al. *The First Five Years of Life* (New York: Harper & Row, 1940).

they expend on these toys tends to be quite different from that of the girls.

In general it seems that much carefully controlled research still needs to be done on this whole problem of sex differences in the early years. The nursery school is an ideal place in which to carry out such research.

INDIVIDUALITY OF THE GROUP AS A WHOLE: HOW IT CHANGES WITHIN THE DAY, FROM DAY TO DAY, FROM WEEK TO WEEK

We have been discussing the differing personalities of individual children. In our interest in individual children we should not, however, lose sight of the fact that any given nursery school group may be considered to have its own individuality as well. This is of course made up of the individual personalities of the separate children, but it is much more than just the sum of these personalities. It is, rather, all of them in action and interaction.

Complex and variable as all of this may be, it is to quite an extent predictable, and there is much that an observant, skillful teacher can do not only to recognize the more stable characteristics of her group as a group, but, through the use of effective techniques, to deal with the daily, weekly, or even seasonal changes which will take place.

This is all an extremely individual matter, and something which experienced teachers do almost instinctively. However, we can make a few suggestions which will have general applicability.

Makeup of the group, and role of the individual. The quality of any given group probably depends a good deal more on the personalities of the individual members than on their number. Thus a group of sixteen active—though not hyperactive—independent, and imaginative children may be much easier on the teacher and may be a much more interesting group to teach than a smaller group of, say, eight children who are both cling-ing and uncreative, and who can neither start nor keep going any activity on their own.

A group of vigorous, violent, high-spirited, aggressive meso-morphs is obviously going to present an entirely different teach-ing problem from that presented by a group of quiet, shy, nonparticipating ectomorphs. In the first instance, the teacher's problem will be to quiet the children down; in the second, to help them feel comfortable so that they can in their own way participate. A stable, strong group can sometimes effectively absorb one or more hyperactive mesomorphic children in such a way that they do not come to play the bold, bad role which they play with a weaker group. A strong group is not, obvi-ously, as vulnerable to the impact of any single child, no matter how difficult, as is a weaker group.

It is sometimes difficult to appreciate the extent to which a single child can make or mar a group. Or the extent to which the individual child's role is itself determined by the group in which he finds himself. Sometimes a teacher doesn't realize the extent to which one child can spoil a group or, on the other hand, can be the one who gives spark to the whole group. He may be the one on whom the others depend, and it may be only when he is absent that the teacher realizes how much he has contributed.

The role which any given child plays is not just an individ-ual matter. Sometimes it is forced upon him by the group. Thus a child who is quite a clown in a certain group might not play this role when he is with different children. Or a child who has trouble in one group might get along nicely in another which contains acceptable and accepting children.

Or a child may play quite different roles in his different years in school. Some children, as a matter of temperament, are more suited to success with a 3-year-old, some with a 4-year-old, group. With 2-year-olds, popularity is not as a rule a particularly noticeable matter. With Threes, the friendly, aggressive, silly, noisy, socially visible child tends to be the most successful. With Fours, to be popular a child needs to be energetic, creative, good at give-and-take, but also imaginative and considerate.

Group changes within the day and week. There are many changes in the responses of any group which predictably take place day after day. The teacher comes to look for and to recognize such changes, and to quite a large extent the day's routine is planned both to take advantage of such changes and to avoid any hazards which they may present.

The 2-year-old group, for example, warms up as the morning progresses. This takes place day after day. However, this is not a steadily continuing improvement, for as the morning goes on there comes a time when the children start going to pieces. They fall down, droop, and are likely to cry if their parents do not come for them right on time. A 2-year-old group tends to be at its very best from 10 to 11 A.M., when children have had time to warm up but have not yet started going to pieces.

Ideally the 2-year-old morning at school will not last more than two and a half hours. If parents do not call for the child on time, and the session lasts longer than this, Twos are likely to wilt. Not only their behavior goes to pieces, but even their physical appearance—their noses run, their clothes suddenly look dirty. It is important if possible for their morning to be terminated before all this happens.

With 3- and 4-year-olds, conspicuous and patterned changes occur more *during the week* than during any single session. With both of these groups, Monday as the first day of the week tends to be a day of more individual behavior. By the end of the week, children of both ages are more animated and more integrated as a group. This is not an improvement with the Threes, since they actually do better before they become too high-spirited and too integrated. For instance, with Threes who are attending school Mondays, Wednesdays, and Fridays a teacher would not introduce a new song on a Friday; and music and story time usually go less smoothly on Wednesdays and Fridays than on Mondays.

With Fours, however, this weekly change tends to be for the better, children of this age actually improving in their behavior as they act more cohesively as a group. Fours tend to be at their best by the end of the week. We have found that the alternate-day attendance plan which we follow at the Gesell Institute helps considerably to keep this weekly build-up from becoming too excessive in any direction. With children attending school only on alternate days, there seems to occur considerably less build-up either of boredom or of its opposite, out-of-bounds behavior.

Seasonal changes. Conspicuous changes take place in all age groups as the season progresses from fall to spring. Two-year-old groups usually have their greatest difficulty in the fall, at the beginning of the school year. Adjusting Twos, both individually and as a group, may be both wearing and wearying to a teacher. However, as a rule a 2-year-old group gets progressively better, and usually can be counted on to be both restful and delightful by spring. Improved adjustment and increasing group spirit make things go more smoothly, and children of this age do not reach the point of too great boisterousness. Individual Twos may have trouble at any point throughout the year, but total group spirit is usually good once the initial adjustments have been made.

Threes start in in the fall more easily than do the Twos. There are usually at least a few difficult adjustment problems in a group of 3-year-olds, though the group as a whole usually starts off well. As a rule there is a building up of good behavior till Christmas. There may be a slight lag after that, during which time the teacher needs to introduce new things.

By spring the group is likely to become quite high-powered and high-strung; children are crying, aggressive, hard to please. This of course may be related to the fact that many of them are around three-and-a-half years of age by then. Fortunately the group is more often out of doors by spring, with added space available.

Four-year-olds, too, usually start the fall quite easily as a group. A few may be slow to adjust—the teacher may have to work with them for a while. But most are anxious to go to school and are excited to be there. Usually the program goes quite smoothly for the first few weeks, so that problems may not be spotted right away. Then, as the year progresses, bad spells may occur for a few days or weeks. The chief difficulty may be boredom. On some days the teacher may feel that she has nothing to offer. On other days the same group will seem excited or pleased even though nothing has been changed and no new toys added.

There are days, as the year progresses, when Fours test the limits and balk against formerly accepted routines. This is a whole-group phenomenon. In the fall, most respond well to the teachers. They like school. They want to do what the teacher wants. This wears off as the year proceeds.

In the springtime there occurs a real testing of limits. Children run out of the yard, urinate outdoors, and indulge in other forbidden behaviors. They seem to be trying out the teacher and testing the firmness of the rules. A teacher may really have a hard time in the spring. She may find it necessary to introduce many new things—movies, trips, walks. The children seem to want more, and are often ready for more, than the teacher can give. Sometimes changing the room around helps—at least helps give the teacher a feeling that she is doing something about the situation. It may help her to start in with a fresh attitude. (In general, the group follows the cues of the older children, the leaders, and it is sometimes possible to improve things by bringing them into line.)

Sometimes in the spring it may be necessary to give up music time for a while, if it gets too boisterous. Or the teacher may introduce new things and new situations or give short vacations to certain children. Often there are new and exciting possibilities in home neighborhoods, and some children really benefit by a little intermission from school.

These spring changes for the worse may or may not be inevitable, but they occur commonly enough to be considered a normal part of the seasonal change and not just a sign that something has gone wrong and must be righted by mere disciplinary measures. Certainly, "bad" and excessively out-of-bounds behavior will call for some discipline, but a teacher should not just discipline and let it go at that. Rather, we feel she should consider this kind of behavior as a sign that the group is ready for something new. It can be a challenge to a teacher to see if she can satisfy the children's needs with new projects, new activities.

Day-to-day changes. The last kind of variability in group behavior which we shall consider here is the somewhat unpredictable variation which takes place from day to day. In addition to the more or less patterned changes with time which we have described, there are many ways in which any group, somewhat like any individual, may vary from day to day. Groups, like people, have good days and bad days. On good days things in general seem to go well, and the group is quick to respond to any good creative stimulus which may be offered. On bad days, the same stimuli, from children or teacher, may be there but may not be responded to.

On bad days, bad behavior seems to spread through the group. Nobody wants to be touched, and everybody wants to touch. Nobody has enough room. Or in a group of shouters, everybody wants to shout. These bad days may end up with everybody crying, getting their hands stepped on, falling down. Of course all of this builds up tension in the teachers, and then they too get keyed up. Then *their* techniques deteriorate.

Often it isn't just the first child who starts things who makes the trouble. The second one who follows the first may actually be the one who sets the group off. Thus a second child laughing at the behavior of a first may be what sets things going. Most teachers know which children to watch and which to squelch. Any group seems to be much more responsive to certain members than to others.

Weather seems to have a marked effect on the group. Rainy days can be bad, especially when there are several in succession. Humid days, however, may be worse. A good cool down-pour does not usually have as bad an effect on group behavior as does high humidity.

There are days when it works best to handle a group with verbal techniques. There are other days when words do little good. Children seem not to listen and not to hear. On such days the teacher may best make contact with children by taking their hands. At other times they may need to be lifted and carried. In an extreme situation, if they all start screaming, a teacher can sometimes go to extremes herself and ask, "Is that as loud as you can scream?" This startles them and often they will stop. This works better with younger than with older children. It may be more effective with Fours to bring the group together by some dramatic command, given to the entire group, as for instance, "I wonder if everyone can stand on his tiptoes."

Now all of this matter of recognizing the individuality of any given group, and of being aware of the changes within that group which time brings, is very similar to the matter of recognizing individuality differences in single children. It is not something of which a teacher is constantly aware. It is more in the nature of something which she senses, and responds to almost automatically and instinctively. But a conscious awareness of any such differences, even though not constant, can be of great help in planning new moves, or in planning corrective moves when things do not seem to be going smoothly. An overintellectual approach to the task of nursery school teaching is not desirable; but some intellectual understanding of what is going on in the matter of group changes can be of aid to even the most naturally gifted teacher.

3

Individuality Revealed by Observing Children

Most parents and teachers can tell a great deal about any child simply by observing him, living with him, teaching him. However, any such naturalistic observation is subject to many errors. Thus the child who is a great talker, especially if he is one who likes to talk to adults, is often judged to be considerably "smarter" than he actually is. If such a child, in spite of having unusually good language ability, has little creative imagination and very poor fine motor control so that he is not good with his hands, he is likely in school or in free play situations to become restless. In such cases parents often feel that he is "too smart" for his class—he needs something "more interesting" to stimulate him. Actually it may not be at all that he is too smart. It may simply be that he is not capable of keeping himself occupied and amused.

Or conversely, the child whose speech comprehension is excellent but who has little spontaneous language in a new situation, or in any situation outside of home, may be misjudged as not being very bright, particularly if he is a child who, in addition to having poor spontaneous language, is shy and not good at making friends with other children.

A good teacher should know how to observe, what to observe, and how to interpret what she sees. Then she should put her observations to productive use.

Teachers in the preschool usually have, and should have, a wide acquaintance with many young children. They should know the behavior of children younger and older than those in any particular classroom, thus to better assess, in a global way, the relative maturity or immaturity of any child. Teachers also need to formulate or adopt conceptual frameworks for observation. These reveal behaviors that are characteristic of preschool children at six-month intervals in four different aspects of growth—motor, adaptive, language, and personal-social development.

Utilizing the basic framework of the Gesell Developmental Schedules, a teacher can select tasks from the various categories which afford guidelines in development in four areas of growth. She should select tasks which do not require complex or standardized examining materials, but rather those which might easily be incorporated in her usual classroom activities. Insofar as she is intimately acquainted with the behavior of young children, she can add items to the list that enable her to put her own observations into age-appropriate expectancies.

An example of such a check list follows.[1]

TABLE 1: CHECK LIST FOR THE GROWTH OF TWO-YEAR-OLDS

	Fall	Spring	Final
MOTOR BEHAVIOR			
*Runs without falling			
*Walks up and down stairs alone			
*Kicks a large ball			
*Can turn pages of a book singly			

1. This list was developed by teachers at the Eliot Pearson Children's School, Tufts University.
*Regular Gesell test items.

	Fall	Spring	Final

ADAPTIVE BEHAVIOR

*Imitates a vertical stroke

*Imitates a circular stroke

*Can repeat 3–4 syllables correctly

*Can build a tower of 6–7 small blocks

*Can align 2 or more small blocks to
make a train

LANGUAGE BEHAVIOR

*Has discarded jargon

*Can speak in 3-word sentence

*Can name objects

*Can follow 4 directions with ball: take
to mother, put on chair, bring to me,
and put on table

PERSONAL-SOCIAL BEHAVIOR

In eating, inhibits turning of spoon

Dry at night if taken up

Verbalizes toilet needs fairly consistently

Can pull on simple garment

Verbalizes immediate experiences

Refers to self by name

Understands and asks for "another"

Plays with domestic mimicry (doll,
teddy bear, etc.)

In play with others, parallel play
predominates

TABLE 2: CHECK LIST FOR THE GROWTH OF 3-YEAR-OLDS

	Fall	Spring	Final

MOTOR BEHAVIOR

*Walks alone up stairs alternating feet,
and downstairs two feet to step

*Regular Gesell test items.

*May jump from bottom step   <u>Fall</u>   <u>Spring</u>   <u>Final</u>
Climbs nursery apparatus with agility
Rides tricycle and can turn wide corners
*Can walk on tiptoe
*Stands on one foot—momentary balance

FINE MOTOR ADAPTIVE BEHAVIOR

*Copies circle
*Imitates cross
Matches two or three primary colors
Paints with large brush on easel
Cuts with scissors

LANGUAGE BEHAVIOR

Large intelligible vocabulary but speech
    still shows many infantile phonetic
    substitutions
Gives full name and sex
Uses plurals and pronouns
Carries on simple conversations and verbalizes past experiences
Asks   many   questions   beginning
    "What?" "Where?" "Who?"
Listens eagerly to stories and demands
    favorites over and over again

PERSONAL-SOCIAL BEHAVIOR

Pours well from pitcher
Puts on shoes
Undresses
Unbuttons front and side buttons
Understands sharing. Willing to share
Associative play replacing parallel play

*Regular Gesell test items.

TABLE 3: CHECK LIST FOR THE GROWTH OF 4-YEAR-OLDS

	Fall	Spring	Final

MOTOR BEHAVIOR

Walks alone up and down stairs, one
  foot to a step
*"One-footed" skip
Climbs ladders and trees
Expert rider of tricycle
Can run on tiptoe
Hops on one foot

FINE MOTOR ADAPTIVE BEHAVIOR

*Copies cross
Matches four primary colors correctly
*Draws a man with head and legs, some-
  times trunk or features
Counts 3 objects correctly and answers
  how many

LANGUAGE BEHAVIOR

Speech shows only a few infantile substi-
  tutions, usually p/t/th/f/s and
  r/l/w/y groups
Gives connected account of recent
  events and experiences
Gives age
Eternally asking questions "Why?"
  "When?" "How?" and meaning of
  words
Listens to and tells long stories, some-
  times confusing fact and fantasy
Can tell names of siblings

*Regular Gesell test items.

PERSONAL-SOCIAL BEHAVIOR	Fall	Spring	Final
Dresses and undresses with only a little supervision			
General behavior self-willed and out of bounds			
Inclined to verbal impertinence when wishes are crossed			
Needs other children to play with and is alternately cooperative and aggressive with them as with adults			
Understands taking turns			
Shows concern for younger siblings and sympathy for playmates in distress			

TABLE 4: CHECK LIST FOR THE GROWTH OF 5-YEAR-OLDS

	Fall	Spring	Final
MOTOR BEHAVIOR			
Runs lightly on toes			
Dances to music			
*Skips using feet alternately			
Active and skillful in climbing, sliding, swinging, digging, and various "stunts"			
*Can stand on one foot 8–10 seconds			
Can hop 2–3 yards on each foot			
FINE MOTOR ADAPTIVE BEHAVIOR			
*Copies square			
*Copies triangle			
*Names four primary colors			
*Writes a few letters spontaneously			
*Draws a recognizable man with head, trunk, legs, arms, features			
Draws a simple house with door, win-			

*Regular Gesell test items.

dows, roof, and chimney

Counts fingers on one hand with index finger of other

LANGUAGE BEHAVIOR

Speech fluent and correct except for confusions of s/f/th

Loves stories and acts them out in detail later

Gives age and address

Defines concrete nouns by use

Asks meaning of abstract words

*Coins: names penny, nickel, dime

Knows ages of siblings

PERSONAL-SOCIAL BEHAVIOR

Undresses and dresses alone

General behavior more sensible, controlled, and independent

Serial domestic and dramatic play

Plans and builds constructively

Chooses own friends

Cooperative with companions and understands needs for rules and fair play

Appreciates meaning of clock time in relation to daily program

Protective toward younger children and pets

Comforts playmates in distress

TABLE 5: CHECK LIST FOR THE GROWTH OF 6-YEAR-OLDS

	Fall	Spring	Final

MOTOR BEHAVIOR

*Stands on each foot alternately with eyes closed

*Regular Gesell test items.

*Jumps from height of 12 inches—lands
on toes

<u>Fall   Spring   Final</u>

*Ball—advanced throwing

FINE MOTOR ADAPTIVE BEHAVIOR

*Copies diamond and divided rectangle
*Draws a man with neck, hands, cloth-
ing
*Adds and subtracts within 5
*Can print both names
*Can repeat 4 digits correctly

LANGUAGE BEHAVIOR

Understands abstract words, such as
"different"
Interprets and describes pictures, with
appropriate meaning and sequence
*Can name animals for 60°
*Knows month and perhaps also day of
birthday
*Gives correct number of fingers single
hand; and total both hands

PERSONAL-SOCIAL BEHAVIOR

*Ties shoe laces
*Differentiates A.M. and P.M.
*Knows right and left
*Recites numbers to 30

The teacher, of course, *will not use such a listing as items to
be taught,* but rather as examples of competency at different age
levels which will enable her to assess a child's strengths and
weaknesses in various areas.

This check list will enable the teacher to clarify her evaluation of each child in four fields of behavior, and will tell her
much more about a child than simply how far he has developed.
For example, a child who is above his age in language and

personal-social behavior but below his age in both motor and adaptive behavior is likely to be a child who has good ideas, which he can verbalize, but which he cannot carry out either with his hands or with his total body.

Conversely, the child with low, or almost no, language and poor personal-social abilities is bound to give a poor impression in a school situation. Yet the check list may show him to be at or above his age level in both gross and fine motor behavior and in adaptive behavior as well. Such a finding will help a teacher to appreciate this child for what he is worth and will encourage her to find ways in which he may express himself adaptively and motorwise without making too great demands on the language abilities which at this time he lacks.

But before a teacher can be effective within an evaluative conceptual framework, she must be sensitive to the special characteristics and the particular qualities of every child. There is a great deal of this behavior that cannot be graded or labeled in any precise way. Yet the teacher who knows young children, like the skilled clinician or pediatrician, is so perceptive that she can gain sensitive insights from what may seem routine behavior or play to the untrained observer.

She will want to gain, through her observations, information about a child's individuality, his reaction to people, his reaction to new or difficult situations, to transitions, to failure, to success. He may be very rigidly set in his ways; he may be very glib, talking about what he has done or plans to do, rather than doing it.

There is the child who is the good learner. He exhibits this characteristic not so much by warming up and improving as the examination goes along as by improving on retrials on the same test.

There is the bold, spontaneous child with little critical ability. He plunges into new tasks cheerfully, proceeds vigorously, and seems quite unaware of failure or poor performance. In contrast is the extreme perfectionist who has an excellent idea of his own limitations and resists trying anything which he thinks he can't do well. Such a child often has a fairly limited range of performance but performs very well within his range.

In contrast to this child who performs well within a fairly narrow range—who at four years of age may succeed in all the 4-year-old, all the 4½-year-old, and a few of the 5-year-old tests —is the child with a tremendous scatter of abilities. Such a child at four years of age may have successes up into the 6-year-old range but may have numerous failures at his own age or even below. Thus his successes may scatter from three-and-a-half right up to six years of age on a behavior test.

There is the child who is slow and cautious. At the opposite extreme is the child whose natural speed gets in his way, and who may thus be tense and energy-driven and may rush into a new situation and then later on break down, when he has had time to look around and evaluate. Such a child may be hard to hold to any second response or to repetition of any given test.

There is the creative child who gives his own little twist to any response; and the cut-and-dried child who performs well what is required of him, but with no extra flourishes. His performance is often speedy and precise, but with no elaboration. There is the child who uses language as a face saver—he not only talks a better test than he performs, but explains away little failures and inadequacies by explaining why he did it that way, or why his way is better than the examiner's way.

The focal child concentrates directly on the task at hand. He does not look around the room, seldom glances at his mother, and keeps not only his glances but his movements focalized within a small, central area. He usually gets right to work at any given task, without a lot of preliminary preparation or side excursions or remarks about other topics; works busily, steadily, and with concentration; and stops neatly when he has finished.

The peripheral child, on the other hand, seems temperamentally suited to perform almost any activity except the task at hand. He looks around, even moves around, contacts his mother, may try to distract the examiner. Even once he has begun the assigned task it is easy for him to get off the track. Such a child responds to an entire situation—often as far as eye can reach—not just to the task at hand.

There is the kind of child who needs to have his periphery filled in, as it were. Thus he does better in response to verbal test situations if he is allowed to use his hands in some simple manipulation of objects at the same time that he is talking.

And then there is the excessively oppositional child—the child who seems to feel almost a compulsion to behave in exactly the opposite fashion to that in which he is instructed.

There are children who require a good deal of praise and acceptance in order to turn out their best performance; others who go on their way more or less impervious to comments from the examiner. At earliest ages, praise does not have to be particularly discriminating. The kind of child who thrives on praise will accept almost anything positive and favorable that is said to him by an examiner. At older ages—especially at four and four-and-a-half—most children are more realistically self-critical, and thus praise has to be phrased carefully in order not to be unrealistic and therefore unacceptable from the child's point of view.

One good method of putting observations about any child's way of responding might be to classify each child in a group on the following rating scale, children being rated on a scale of one to four as follows:

TABLE 6: PRESCHOOL BEHAVIOR RATING SCALE*

INITIATIVE

1	4	
1. Motor Activity: Restricted movement; does not attempt climbing and/or other difficult motor activities.	Moves freely and easily through space; engages in vigorous motor activity; attempts difficult physical tasks.	1 2 3 4
2. Use of Conceptual Language: Limited use of conceptual language.	Makes comparisons; counts; uses concepts of size, shape, number, color (even though not necessarily correctly)	1 2 3 4
3. In Verbal Contacts: Limited use of fantasy; literal use of language; concreteness.	Expresses self imaginatively (plays adult and other fantasy roles).	1 2 3 4
4. Sex Differentiation: Does not differentiate between sex roles; behaves in many ways generally considered typical of opposite sex.	Recognizes "proper" or usual sex roles.	1 2 3 4
5. Bossiness: Is bossy in play, coerces others; punishes offenders; tattles to teacher.	Plays cooperatively with other children in play activities.	1 2 3 4
6. Leadership: Offers few ideas; lets things happen; fails to anticipate problems and/or consequences; is passive.	Volunteers for a task; shares plans and possessions; makes suggestions for activity; offers ideas.	1 2 3 4
7. Direction in Activities: Relies on adult direction; models activities in stereotyped fashion.	Extensively self-directed; decides for self what he wants to do and how to do it.	1 2 3 4

*Adapted from *Preschool Behavior Rating Scale,* developed by Mary B. Lane and staff of Nurseries in Cross-Cultural Education, San Francisco State College, San Francisco, California.

1   4

8. Sense of "Me-Mine" and "You-Yours": Does not identify own possessions; does not perceive that he has rights. | Differentiates between self and others by insisting on own rights; identifies own possessions.   1 2 3 4

9. Reaction to Novel Experiences: Sticks with the familiar; refuses to explore even when encouraged. | Searches out new materials and novel experiences; is particularly attracted by the novel; explores.   1 2 3 4

10. Response to Feelings of Others: Does not respond to others' wants or needs; is oblivious to desires or troubles of others. | Expresses concern when others are hurt or need something; attempts to console or help others; is aware of and responsive to feelings of others.   1 2 3 4

AUTONOMY

11. When His Play Is Interfered with by Other Children He: Gives in or withdraws; seeks help from teacher; runs away. | Sustains his activity in spite of physical aggression.   1 2 3 4

12. Agression in Play Situations: In play activities shows verbal or physical aggression toward other children. | Plays without hurtful aggression, with or beside other children.   1 2 3 4

13. Hoarding Materials: Accumulates and tries to hold onto things even though he does not use them; hoards. | Shares materials with others if he is not using them.   1 2 3 4

14. When Faced with Alternates in an Unstructured Situation He: Wanders aimlessly from one activity to another does not choose any activity; or just chooses the familiar. | Makes decisions easily and readily; chooses unfamiliar activities.   1 2 3 4

15. When He Completes a Task He: Has to be told he has done a good job. | Exhibits pride by taking time to observe his accomplishments, without seeking approval from others.   1 2 3 4

16. Introduction to New Materials or Situations: Refuses to explore even when teacher requests; depends on others for ideas for exploration. | Decides whether to participate or not; devises own methods and uses own ideas in exploration.   1 2 3 4

1   4

17. When He Desires to Do Something Very Difficult: He vacillates, then seeks help; gives up. — Takes a chance; insists on doing it himself; risks failure; continually tries.

1 2 3 4

18. Dependence on Adults: Depends on adult for directions for carrying out activity. — Proceeds on his own without dependence on adults.

1 2 3 4

19. When He Doesn't Get Own Way because of Necessary Adult Control He: Continues objection by whining, screaming, biting, kicking, sulking, throwing, etc. — Accepts control with temporary non-physical objections.

1 2 3 4

TRUST

20. Response in Structured Situation: Withdraws from participation and clings to adults. — Finds something to do.

1 2 3 4

21. Coping with Unexpected Situations: Cries, panics, withdraws, becomes immobile. — Explores alternative choices.

1 2 3 4

22.Response to Unfamiliar Materials: Hesitates, refuses contact, waits for teacher and/or others. — Readily explores.

1 2 3 4

23. Reaction to Situations which Call for Help: Cries, discontinues activity; gives up. — Seeks help from others when needed.

1 2 3 4

24. Movement from Familiar to New Activity: Stalls, delays, resists, refuses. — Moves easily into new activity.

1 2 3 4

25. Response to Separation from Familiar Adults: Cries, panics, continues to sob and grieve. — Leaves familiar adults without discomfort.

1 2 3 4

26. Response to Strangers: Withdraws, avoids, rejects, refuses to talk. — Moves toward strangers readily or takes them for granted.

1 2 3 4

27. Response to Change in Routine: Goes to pieces; regresses. — Accepts change readily.

1 2 3 4

1	4
28. Response to Disappoint-ments: Rejects diversions; cries; withdraws; continues to de-mand.	Recovers by seeking and/or ac-cepting other alternatives.
	1 2 3 4
29. Response to Hurts: Cries; withdraws; cannot be consoled.	Accepts comfort and aid; bounces back.
	1 2 3 4

The best method for a teacher to use in collecting samples of behavior is to identify one or two children each week as subjects for her special concern. She can pay special attention to these children in all their activities, and at the close of the school day, jot down objective data without interpretation. She can record what they have done, their interactions, their apparent feelings, their failures and successes, their style of play, and can write a brief factual report of what happened.

Although her attention will be focused particularly on one or two children, it may well be that the behavior of one or two others will merit recording. Five-by-eight filing cards are excellent for such notes. In the course of a semester there should be a card or cards for every child in the class. These cards will bear descriptions of significant episodes in the child's regular school day. Best results are achieved as the teacher reviews her card files periodically, with a view to learning whether a child needs more observation or whether his behavior suggests the need for some more specialized testing or structured observation.

In any event, through such recordings the teacher will eventually find herself in possession of specific data which will yield valuable information about any given child's behavior. She will have evidence suggesting patterns of dependency or leadership, conformity or creativity, hostility, insecurity, self-confidence, competence, apathy, tension, or vitality.

Planned and thorough scruntiny of every child gives some assurance that the quiet, less active child is not as likely to be unknown or misinterpreted as he might be without such special observation.

From time to time a teacher may feel that she needs more formalized or structured information about a child. A complete Developmental Evaluation[2] administered by a competent person may give the teacher data she needs in planning particular kinds of help to be given in the classroom.

2. Arnold Gesell, et al., *The First Five Years of Life* (New York: Harper & Row, 1940).

TWO

The Teacher

4

Personal Qualities of a Good Teacher

Nursery school teaching is not only a responsible but also a highly respected profession. It is not enough to have space in your house, a little time on your hands, and a general liking for children, to be considered a fully adequate nursery school teacher. It is now recognized that not only professional training but a real aptitude for this special branch of teaching is necessary if an individual is to find success in this pleasant but often difficult and certainly demanding profession. Nursery school teaching is not an organized form of unskilled baby sitting.

We shall discuss here some qualities which we consider basic for anyone who hopes to become successful in this field. We emphasize—good will is not enough. An intellectual interest in and curiosity about little children are not enough.

Physical characteristics. At any level of school teaching, a certain degree of physical stamina and generally good health are unquestionably necessary. Nursery school teaching makes more physical demands, òr perhaps more specific physical demands, than do most other levels of teaching.

First of all, a successful nursery school teacher needs to be a person not only of considerable physical energy but also of robust good health. Since there will probably be a full quota of sniffles going around the school during the winter, she should be one who is not readily susceptible to catching colds.

She not only needs a good deal of energy, but needs to be

sturdy and reasonably able to withstand or even enjoy both cold and rainy weather, since considerable time will inevitably be spent out of doors.

Nimbleness and agility are important so that the teacher can easily bend down to the child's level. Manual facility is also extremely important. Quickness of movement as well as quickness of mind is often necessary when a child suddenly is seen to be in a precarious physical position.

However, though a teacher must be able to move quickly when the occasion demands, the most successful teacher is often one who is naturally of a somewhat calm, slow-moving motor demeanor. Children seem to feel more soothed and relaxed in the presence of such an individual than in the presence of one who is tense and jumpy and who moves abruptly and overquickly.

An important physical ability for any teacher of any age children is the ability to appear neat and attractive and pleasant to look at. Children do not respond well to a teacher who is drab, listless, lifeless, or untidy. Dress should be comfortable and suited to the activities of the program.

However, here one of the many paradoxes of nursery school teaching presents itself. We have noted that a teacher will be most effective with young children if she is by nature rather slow and calm in movement, but that she will need to move quickly when the occasion demands. A further paradox is that whereas it is most important for a teacher to keep herself, and the physical surroundings of the nursery, neat and orderly, she must have the ability to remain undistressed by the frequent messes which will inevitably be produced as children play with paint, clay, sand, and water.

Important physical attributes in a teacher also include clear articulation, good peripheral vision, and acute hearing. A pleasing voice, but one expressing authority, is essential in talking to young children, but at the same time it is most important to avoid the syrupy manner of speaking sometimes adopted by people speaking to the very young.

Good peripheral vision coupled with alertness, which allows a teacher to seem to see around corners and if possible out of the back of her head, while she is at the same time giving full attention to what goes on in front of her, is an extremely useful attribute for a nursery school teacher. (Other useful peripheral awareness which can help forestall disaster includes awareness of temperature, of what all the children are doing as well as what each individual child is doing, and of any special crisis of any nature which may be arising.) There is a great, but natural, danger that in responding adequately to the situation immediately at hand, a teacher may overlook some important, and often dangerous, event that is going on in some other part of the room or playground.

Acute hearing can play a useful part in alerting a teacher to things going on in directions in which she is not looking and which even her good peripheral vision may not be covering.

As to the actual physical type of individual who may be expected to make the best teacher, no definite rules can be laid down—at least not at the present stage of our knowledge. However, it is probably safe to say that none of the extremes— extreme endomorphy, mesomorphy, ectomorphy[1] (or the extreme lack of any one of these components)—is desirable.

A certain amount of endomorphy is essential for warmth, for comfort, for the production of a generally relaxed and agreeable atmosphere. A certain amount of mesomorphy contributes to necessary physical stamina, helps in the physical handling of children, helps a teacher empathize with and understand the vigorously more active children. Ectomorphy contributes awareness.

A teacher may also profitably consider her own develop-

1. Described on pp. 28–29.

ment with regard to Erikson's psycho-social issues, described earlier. To the extent that she has unresolved problems with respect to feelings of security, decision making, enterprise, skill learning, identification, or capacity to love, she will suffer in productive relationships with children, their parents, and her colleagues. Her perception of the world will also have been influenced by the nature of her own upbringing. Potential prejudices or blind spots need to be scrutinized carefully, since attitudes are communicated in subtle ways in the entire teaching process.

Mental characteristics: One of the primary requisites of any effective nursery school teaching is a considerable knowledge of both the principles and the facts of child behavior. Nursery school situations as they arise need practical and immediate attention. But, in spite of this, they can usually be handled most effectively if the teacher in charge has, in addition to good practical techniques and a good "way" with children, a sound theoretical understanding of child behavior. A good teacher wishes to allow a child to be himself, but to do this she will need to know what "himself " is. A good teacher wishes, when she judges the time ripe, to help a child on to the next stage of behavior. To do this effectively she must know what the next stage is.

A thorough knowledge of the abilities and inabilities, interests and aptitudes which may be expected at any given stage of behavior helps a teacher to know how to set the stage in terms of physical equipment, as well as in arranging the day's program of activities.

An understanding of the psychology of individual differences helps a teacher to be aware of the needs of individual children. A theoretical understanding of these differences is an invaluable supplement to a natural "feeling" for what each child is like.

The ability to take or, when necessary, to delegate responsibility is another important, and again paradoxical, matter. Any good teacher, especially of course a head teacher, must be able to take responsibility. However, she should not feel that everything is on her shoulders. She must be able and willing to delegate responsibility to her assistants.

To be successful, a nursery school teacher must also have a good deal of common sense. She must be able to cope quickly and effectively with the many emergencies which will arise, as well as with everyday situations. She should have good judgment as to what is safe and what is not safe. She must have enough foresight to anticipate and prevent the more obvious difficulties. She needs sensitivity for good timing—and ability to recognize the psychological moment, even if this moment has not been scheduled!

A good teacher must live in a world which is larger than that enclosed by the nursery school walls. This is of course true of her own personal life, but it is also true so far as the children whom she is teaching are concerned. She needs to be informed about and interested in what goes on in the child's life outside the school—must think of him as existing in a larger sphere than just the nursery school. New and exciting, or just everyday, events at home influence the behavior of the nursery school child. Conversely, if the child's attendance at school tires him unduly, so that it has an adverse effect on his adjustment at home, as is sometimes the case, then this too becomes a problem which his teacher must consider.

A further requisite for successful teaching is an ability to arrange classroom space efficiently and attractively. Areas of interest need to be defined by suitable spatial arrangement, and by color and texture. Adequate surfaces on which to work, and ample storage or display of materials, should be accessible to children and related to the functional activities of the area. The teacher must provide messy and clean, noisy and quiet areas, small cozy places, and places for large muscle movement.

Thus a good teacher must in some measure be skilled in the arrangement of physical space and sensitive to beauty in interior decoration. Color, lighting, art display, mobiles, carpets, pillows, even a comfortable easy chair, bring warmth and charm to a room, and influence the behavior of children.

Any special talents or interests a teacher has—in music, art, carpentry, science, literature, drama—will enrich her classroom. All the basic arts and sciences have potential interest and value to the young child, providing the teacher knows how to present the discipline in a fashion the child can understand and enjoy.

Emotional Characteristics and Attitudes. It is of primary importance that a nursery school teacher be a reasonably well-adjusted, more or less fulfilled individual. She should have a life larger than the nursery school so that small happenings in school will not assume undue proportion. A teacher who is getting (and needing) too much emotional satisfaction from the children is likely to keep a child in a stage of clinging to her and depending on her which is not in keeping with the child's best interests.

A good teacher needs to have a good deal of self-confidence, but this self-confidence should be well founded and should not be built up simply from the fact that she has things well in hand because she always follows (and insists that others follow) a rigid and unyielding schedule. Flexibility is a prime requisite of successful teaching—flexibility and quickness in thought and action. It is important to be quick to pick up cues as they come along, to be ready to change plans to meet each new situation. These cues can come from the individual children, or from the nature and direction of the group activity at any given moment.

But along with flexibility, and equally important, goes its opposite, a real sense of orderliness and an ability to structure situations when necessary. Complete flexibility would lead to chaos in the nursery school. Flexibility is useful here in departures from the usual. A teacher who is temperamentally unable to set up or at least to carry out a reasonable routine or to command structure when necessary will have problems.

A good teacher must really like children. This is of course important at any level of teaching, but especially so here. If a nursery school teacher is merely "putting up with" children, she is almost certain to be a failure.

Especially important is a lively sense of humor. This is important not only because it adds to a teacher's effectiveness, but it is also essential for her own peace of mind. Though it is important to empathize with and respond to children warmly and humorously, it is even more important, perhaps, to be able to see the total situation and to view it with a leavening sense of humor.

It is useful to have not only specific creative or musical abilities, but also important to have a certain degree of dramatic ability. Self-consciousness is a great deterrent in nursery school teaching. An unself-conscious ability to dramatize is a great asset, and the teacher who is a bit of a "ham" may be among the most successful.

A certain degree of earthiness is essential for anyone who is teaching or taking care of little children. A nursery school teacher is going to need to take care of toileting, to blow noses, and to look after children when they become ill or are injured. She should not be squeamish about any of the less attractive aspects of those tasks. Nor, as we have suggested, should she be overly distressed by the mess which almost certainly follows creative activities with fingerpaint, clay, and sand. She should of course be able to restrict such messiness within reasonable limits, and be able to clean up after it so that the room will regain its original neatness and orderliness—but it is important for her not to be distressed while the mess is being made.

Being "good" with children is an essential (though not exclusive) requirement of being a successful nursery school teacher. However, it is also most important to be "good" with adults as well. This includes, of course, fellow teachers. But equally important, it includes the parents of the children. Perhaps more than at any other level of teaching, the nursery school teacher is in direct communication with the parent (especially with the mother), working with her to effect the most happy possible school experience for the individual child. Thus it is essential that a teacher be able, through her manner, to make parents feel that she is sharing knowledge and information with them and working out problems jointly with them, rather than that she is, from a position of superior wisdom, giving out authority, information, or criticism.

Special characteristics desirable for teaching younger, and older, children. Though an extremely flexible teacher should be able (and as a practical matter may be required) to teach both young and older preschool children, many find that even within this narrow age range they are better suited to the teaching of younger, or of older, children.

For the very youngest groups, the 2- and 3-year-olds, the most successful teacher is the one who is spontaneous and warm, expressive but not too verbal. It is important for the teacher of these youngest children to be able to pitch her language at the child's level without talking "down" to him. A somewhat slow-moving individual is best for these smallest children—but of course she must be able to move rapidly when the situation calls for it, and lethargy should not be confused with calmness.

Since there will be much repetition, both of word and of activity, at this youngest level, the best teacher will be one who is not bored by constant repetition.

Best with the slightly older groups, especially with the 4-year-olds, is a teacher who is somewhat forceful and dramatic. She must be forceful enough to get and hold the children's attention; dramatic enough to carry out activities in a way which will appeal to them. Rather than the capacity of experiencing repetition without being bored, this teacher needs especially to have a flair for creativity; has to be able to respond to new possibilities in the same materials, experiences, children.

In place of simple repetitive language kept to a minimum, older children prefer language which is used more maturely, in a colorful, stimulating, and expressive manner. Some degree of speed both of language and of general activity is not only permissible but somewhat necessary with older children. It is often important to think, to speak, to act very quickly with them. A good deal of energy and enthusiasm is also necessary in order that a teacher may empathize with and share the 4-year-old's enthusiasm and general excitement.

Quick thinking and quick action can often keep 4-year-old crises well in hand, but, with these children much more than with the younger ones, to prevent chaos and confusion, a good ability to plan and organize activities in advance is a vital factor in the successful functioning of a nursery school teacher.

Personality Characteristics Which Suggest Unsuitability for Nursery School Teaching. Certainly the most positive approach to finding out whether or not one would probably be a successful nursery school teacher would be to check over the foregoing list of characteristics necessary for success, and to see if the description fits. However, we should like to mention specifically a few of the personality or intellectual characteristics which seem to us most clearly to reduce the chances of success in this field.

First, of all, a strongly academic individual, more interested in children's behavior in theory than in the actual children, might do well to choose some other branch of child behavior. And a teacher too much interested in materials can get so lost in products that she forgets the process and neglects the children. A firm disciplinarian with strong and definite ideas about how children ought to behave might conceivably be more successful with older children.

Other unfavorable characteristics include the extremes of

the individual who is too ego-involved and the dreamy, unrealistic, uncreative, colorless personality. Children respond well to a teacher who is colorful and lively—but one who is too involved with herself will not be genuinely concerned about them.

A teacher who is impatient, short-tempered, or uneven and unpredictable emotionally will find that she does not have a good effect on the children's emotions or on the emotional tone of the playroom. Also, since little children are very quick to sense whether or not apparent interest in them and liking for them is real or assumed, those who lack a genuine warm interest in children will not be successful. Similarly, an insensitivity to children's feelings—such as might be expressed by talking about them to other teachers in their presence—is something which is difficult to overcome by conscious effort.

Anyone who has less than robust good health, or who has been unable to build up stamina after working with children, is almost certain to find the actual physical demands of nursery school teaching too great. And lastly, anyone fostering the delusion that nursery school teaching is an easy way to make a living is likely to find herself speedily disillusioned.

More men teachers. We should like to make a brief plea for more men teachers in our nursery schools. In the nursery school, as in the primary school, there is a real place for, and a real need for, men as teachers. Not so much men in preference to women, as men in addition to women.

To begin with, at any level of school teaching, it is generally agreed that it is desirable to have both men and women teachers. Some sociologists consider that in our city life today, with many fathers absent from their homes for such long hours, children tend to see only women at home and only women at school. Having men teachers in the school can to some degree make up for this absence of men in the child's daily life.

But, much more than that, there are many ways in which a man teacher, even of very young children, can be more effective than can a woman. Certain children of both sexes seem to respond best to men teachers. Also, men teachers can often assume successfully some roles which are not suitable for women. Especially with boisterous 4-year-olds, men teachers are ideal for conveying that note of unmistakable authority which is sometimes necessary for keeping order.

A man's voice helps convey authority to the very young child as to the older child. A man can give direct, sharp commands. "O.K. now, boys, cut it out!" may not be elegant speech, but it is usually effective. Or a man can convey a tone of "Just we boys" which is especially effective with the 4-year-old who is finding it necessary to express his masculinity by rebelling against any and all feminine commands.

There are many obvious advantages to men teachers. Most men are better at directing woodworking, heavy building, play in the "noisy room." Also, as opposed to the "Just we boys" attitude which he can build up with boys of the group, a man teacher is often much sought after by the girls, who may give him much the same kind of response they give to their fathers.

Perhaps most important of all, a man teacher or two offers an ideal antidote to the "sweetness and light" atmosphere which sometimes creeps into even the best nursery school. A man brings a new dimension into the group with his heartier tone and his new approach.

We believe, too, that a stint of nursery school teaching can be extremely beneficial to the man teacher himself—whether in preparing him for later teaching of older grades, for work in psychology or child behavior, or even for his own later life role as a father. May the day come when nursery school teaching becomes an accepted professional role for a man!

Although we have described general qualities that we consider desirable in a nursery school teacher, we realize that no one teacher will incorporate all these desirable qualities. Fortunately, there are usually several teachers working with each group of children, and children thus can have a relationship with a variety of personalities. Individual children, however, tend to identify primarily with some one teacher, who provides an important model in her mother-substitute role.

An excellent summary of essential characteristics in the personality of a teacher, which supplements our own, has been succinctly set forth in an excellent guide prepared by the Massachusetts Department of Health:

> The good teacher of young children is a person with a warm, genuine liking for children and an awareness of their emotional needs, apart from her own. She is sufficiently mature to be able to establish good relationships with adults and takes a professional responsibility for her work. She realizes that the nursery school experience is but one part of the child's life and, therefore, seeks to work constructively with his parents and other adults important to him. The good teacher has a comfortable attitude toward authority, deals with out-of-bounds behavior in a non-punitive way, but can set up appropriate limitations to a child's activity when these are needed. She is responsive and spontaneous but sufficiently calm and secure within herself to create a milieu of confidence and support within which the young child can grow.[2]

2. Massachusetts Department of Public Health, *Recommended Minimum and Preferred Standards for Agencies Giving Day Care to Children* (pamphlet), May 1952, Boston, Mass.

5

Preservice Training for Teachers

Since it is our belief that a very important part of the education of the child comes in the early years before he starts his so-called formal schooling, it is imperative that the training of nursery school teachers be considered with at least as much care and rigor as is exercised in determining educational standards for other teachers of children. Unfortunately, standards have not been consistently established or upheld in the United States. Too often programs for young children have been considered to be adequate when they met minimal standards of public health departments, with the educational background of the teacher, and the program she was prepared to offer, not being supervised at all.

In Chapter 4 we described what we considered to be desirable traits in the personality of a teacher. It is doubtful that any training program could produce such traits in personalities lacking them. However, in the education of teachers of young children it is primarily important that a person entering this field take seriously the task of understanding herself. Working with the dependencies or aggressions of young children, dealing with authority figures, or being in a position of authority oneself, for example, very often reveals childish or hostile traits in a teacher's own makeup.

For this reason it is most important that institutions training nursery school teachers have an effective counseling service, small classes, and skilled supervisors of student teachers in order to help the potential teacher discover the peculiar qualities of her own personality. In understanding herself, she will better learn to carry on her job of relating intimately to young children and their parents.

Such an understanding of oneself sometimes reveals a basic unsuitability for working with immature people, or at least for working with them in groups. It is partly for this reason that we recommend a brief practical trial period of teaching to precede any definitive decision to become a nursery school teacher. This practical trial will most economically precede or at least come at the beginning of any intensive period of course work, so that if it turns out that in actual practice an individual is going to be unsuited to or uninterested in nursery school teaching, too long a period of study will not have been wasted.

This practice period, which we recommend, may consist of a period of guided observation, followed by a reasonably long period of apprentice teaching. Such a practice period should reveal quite quickly (1) those individuals who cannot hold up physically to the demands of this kind of work; (2) those who thought they would like it but really do not like it in actual practice; (3) those who find it too menial and uninteresting; (4) those who like it but turn out not to be good at it.

When any of these factors is present, students who seem clearly unsuited can often be prevented from seriously committing themselves to this profession. Some may find that though they consider themselves interested in work with children, this particular type of work is unsuited to them. In such cases they may wish to continue study in the general field of child behavior, but may aim their studies toward eventual research, teaching of older children, clinical work, or therapeutic work.

Needless to say, any such practice period should be closely and skillfully supervised. Most students will not reach unaided their conclusion as to whether or not they should continue in the field of nursery school teaching. Ideal guidance not only should include an evaluation of the student as a teacher, but should include some evaluation of the student's personality.

Once the student has decided quite definitely to proceed with the academic training needed to become a nursery school teacher, we recommend that an educational program include the following.

A Basic Course in Child Development

This should cover all aspects of the development of children through the first six years, with attention to the crucial adjustments between child and environment. Such a course should acquaint teachers with the major theories in the field and should be accompanied by opportunities to observe young children individually and in groups.

Such a course should give emphasis to the intellectual development of young children. An effort to understand what it is that Piaget has to say should be made. However, intellectual functioning cannot profitably be studied apart from general aspects of personal-social development. Student teachers should be exposed to the various theories of personality development and how each deals with the importance of early developmental experiences, individual differences, stages of development.

Exposure to Different School Environments

A potential teacher should have an opportunity to observe and study various kinds of environments prepared for young children's learning. These might include structured models which prepare children in special academic skills and foster academic drill; so-called open schools where children initiate learning through their own activities; "child-development" models where children integrate skills through play in a progressive maturational process. An aim of such varied observation should be the clarification of her own goals as a teacher and the arrival at a decision as to which kind of program she would prefer to carry on as a teacher.

Some Familiarity with the Special Problems of the Exceptional Child

Every teacher should be acquainted with the special problems of children who deviate from normal patterns of development. Such exceptional problems include sensory defects, orthopedic handicaps, emotional and social problems, deviations in intellectual potential. One special kind of child of whom a nursery school teacher should be especially aware is the so-called learning disability child. The failure to be able to learn in the usual ways is usually not noted until a child is in kindergarten or first grade. However, a nursery school teacher should be aware of any difficulties or deviations in any child which might be expected to lead to later school problems.

Developmental Evaluation

We do not believe that assessment is the exclusive domain of the psychologist. Teachers need to be educated in a formalized attempt at understanding which utilizes specialized knowledge, tools, and techniques. A useful approach for teachers comes from a study of the Gesell Developmental Schedules, which enable a teacher not only to delineate patterns of behavior but to identify environmental factors that may be influencing behavior. Emphasis in such a course should be on the application of assessment information to the child's adjustment to school.

Curriculum and Student Teaching

In recent years there has been a tremendous proliferation of commercial learning materials available for use as teacher aids in working with young children. Teachers need to learn firsthand of their existence, and then to try them out and evaluate their usefulness. In a curriculum course students should utilize learning and child development theory in providing appropriate school experiences for young children. Emphasis should be given to language skills, reading and math readiness, sciences and social studies, music and art.

We recommend that a course in curriculum should accompany the time allotted to student teaching. The knowledge of what teaching aids are available, and the skills with which to use them, gives students the confidence and judgment needed to make decisions about what materials actually are appropriate to the needs and interests of the particular group of children they may be teaching.

We have described here only those considerations which we feel to be basic. Any college committed to a good program for potential teachers will offer more intensive and specialized studies in all areas, such as full courses in infancy, cross-cultural studies of children, the development of language, emotional problems in young children, assessment procedures for the multiple handicapped, research with young children, consultation strategies, psychobiological aspects of growth, to name a few.

A major by-product that should emerge from this preservice training is the development of what we call a philosophy of early childhood education. A student should start teaching with a fairly clear notion of where she stands on some of the theoretical questions basic to any practical working with children or with the parents of children.

Although the working out of such a philosophy has many

variations in practice, there are certain working hypotheses which seem essential for those who plan to help children.

In the first place, it is important that the intending teacher have an attitude toward people which emphasizes their successes, not their failures. The teacher should believe in the fully functioning self and believe that she can best help a child develop his potentialities when she praises him, not when she makes him feel unworthy. Whatever we do in teaching depends on what we think people are like: to this end, it is important that a teacher believe a child *can* (within his realistic limitations) rather than that a child *can't.*

She will also appreciate values, which will include *creativity, curiosity, resourcefulness, initiative,* and *tolerance,* and all her training will direct her to an understanding of how she can reinforce these values in her profession. For example, she will see that some attitudes and practices—a preoccupation with order or acceleration, authoritarianism, an intolerance of natural play, for example—are essentially noncreative and harm dignity and integrity.

She will learn to provide for children the conditions that nurture intuition and favor risk taking, avoiding "cookbook" approaches that provide inevitable reward of the right or predicted answer.

She will see the importance of a child's asking many questions, and putting material and thoughts into many new combinations as he also discovers the delight of doing things for himself. Children must have ideas presented in many different ways and at appropriate times, and thereby learn that tasks are in some ways similar, before they can come to abstract principles or understand basic structures. If a teacher gets something locked into a single system, there is a real danger of taking only one path to the exclusion of others, and thus cutting off a very important goal of education.

The present volume has not taken on the task of trying to encompass adequately all the aspects of teacher training. We are interested, rather, in suggesting its range and complexity and showing its general directions. Whatever means are used in providing theoretical or practical courses and experiences, certain purposes should be kept in mind.

An adequate program in teacher training will see to it that the prospective teacher be generally well informed about community life and about our civilization. She will know the young child, his limitations, his possibilities, the problems and course of his development. She must perfect her teaching skill through actual work with children, must understand parents and how to communicate with them, and be able to take her place as a useful member of a staff team.

Finally, to assure her continued professional growth, she must be trained both to know the history of early childhood education and to question traditional teaching techniques, and to look for better answers than may now be available.

In addition to course work, an intensive experience in student teaching is important. Ideally there should be two full years of such teaching, in four different age groups or situations: in nursery school, kindergarten, first grade, and in a clinic, hospital, day care center, or research laboratory. Such student teaching requires attentive and skillful supervision on the part of college personnel, supervising teachers, and teachers in the field who take on young apprentices. In many ways, student teaching is the heart of the preparation to teach.

One last generality might be mentioned in connection with the program we recommend. It seems to us that a training for nursery school teaching involves also knowledge about and some experiences with children in both kindergarten and first grade. Growth is irregular in the early years, and children who are chronologically of one age are often developmentally of another. Teachers must be well informed in all there is to know about children from infancy through six years of age. The school experiences of nursery school, kindergarten, and first grade are a unit, and within this unit the growth and behavior of children are extraordinary in their variety.

6

Staff Relationships

The number of different kinds of teachers varies from school to school. Some highly organized schools have a director or board of directors. Nearly all have a head teacher or teachers and a number of assistant teachers. Some have student teachers, parent teachers, or participants from the community.

Whatever the number of teachers, and whatever the number of roles, it is essential that the group develop some sort of circular model of interaction, so that decisions come from all the people involved. There should be no strictly linear, authoritarian model of decision making. The program must be shaped by all.

This means that any program for young children must provide a time when staff members get together to communicate with one another. This communication is an ongoing, time-consuming process. The teachers in any one group need a short meeting each day for planning and evaluating. Usually this comes at the close of a class session. Teachers must not simply dismiss children, quickly clean up a room, and rush away. Rather, when the room is in order and children are gone, teacher, assistant teacher, and student teachers need fifteen or twenty minutes to talk to each other about what has happened that day and what is planned for the next.

In addition, there needs to be a longer period of time, at least two hours each week, when the professional staff get together to discuss the program. This is a time when problems with children, problems in the adult world, or problems in the program can be dealt with. A spirit of mutual interaction and mutual respect must prevail. For every person a willingness to listen, to learn, and even to change is essential. Sometimes professional consultants can join the group.

Workshops in various areas of curriculum development offer opportunities to learn about materials, to invent new materials, or to see new meanings in the relationships of materials. Guests from the community, special lectures, or films relating to early childhood education can bring continued professional growth to the staff.

In addition, teachers should be enabled from time to time to be relieved of their own teaching duties so that they can look at the workings of their own group from the point of view of an observer. They should also have free time to observe other classes in the school or to visit programs in other schools.

A professional library should be available to teachers, and opportunities made available to attend professional meetings and to share experiences of these meetings with one another. All of this is in the nature of in-service training. As teachers work together they learn together, realizing that the education of teachers is an unending process. The preservice training described in Chapter 5 is just the beginning of what becomes a lifelong commitment to an educational process.

Observers in a smooth-running nursery school sometimes get the false impression that all teachers are working at about the same level, each doing simply whatever tasks come to hand, without much organization or advance planning. Nothing could be farther from the truth. Each individual must retain a reasonable amount of initiative and must be able to act of his own accord when necessary, particularly when there is nobody else on hand, or in an emergency. But major roles and responsibilities are not a matter of chance or expediency. Although there is overall cooperation, each person has a specific role to carry out.

We shall not, in the following outline of tasks, expect to cover all the activities and duties of each teacher. However, a division of labors somewhat as follows seems to provide an efficient program.

DUTIES OF HEAD TEACHER

The head teacher must, first of all, assume responsibility for the total situation. It is she who more or less sets the pace for and determines the climate of the school.

She makes such major decisions as which children to admit to school, which children may need "vacations," what to do in the case of major adjustment difficulties.

It is she who determines the general disciplinary policy as well as many of the practical details of maintaining discipline.

It is the head teacher who more or less determines whether or not the teaching experience is a growing and learning situation for all in the school or whether they are merely permitted to carry out her ideas.

She also determines whether or not, even in spite of the fact that there must be a hierarchy of responsibilities, there is also a democratic feeling among the teachers. The head teacher needs to be the leader, but ideally she should not stand out as the single figure of authority. Thus, in planning daily responsibilities, head teachers arrange that all teachers shall have opportunities in directing music time, story time, etc.

One of her main tasks is planning and supervising the work of her assistants. Much of this will be done in advance, but much also will need to be done on the spot. Thus, as well as having the behavior of the children in mind, she will have in mind the behavior of the other teachers. Head teachers too often forget that assistant and student teachers have individualities, just as do the children.

The head teacher plans the daily schedule, with cooperation from the other teachers. (In general she is responsible for any planning, though at times she may delegate this to others.) Not only is she responsible for the planning of the daily schedule, but also for carrying it out—for seeing that the various activities start and stop at the time, or approximately at the time, planned.

However, in most schools the head teacher is not simply an administrator. She should be able to teach, and in our opinion should do at least some of the teaching.

She should teach, but should not be tied down by the teaching. Ideally she should be mobile in order to go to any part of the group where her help is needed. And also she should ideally be free so that if a parent wishes to discuss some problem, if an important phone call comes, if people wish to talk with her about immediate research problems, if administrative matters come up, she can respond to any of these multiple demands.

It usually works out best if the head teacher plans her day's schedule so that she is normally left free both at the beginning and at the end of the morning, so that she is available for informal conversations with parents.

Not only are the children and the assistant teachers her responsibility, but the parents (so far as they have any demands) as well. In general it is wise for the head teacher to be the one to give guidance on any serious problems brought up by parents. Otherwise they are likely to get conflicting advice and conflicting opinions which may confuse them. This does not mean that assistant teachers should not be free to talk with parents. It merely means that complex and serious or difficult problems should be referred to the head teacher and that the head teacher should be informed of all communications with parents.

Thus the head teacher should have charge of parent guidance —not only that given in connection with the formal conferences, but also that given in informal consultations such as may take place during school hours.

The head teacher usually is the person who ultimately hires or helps hire the teachers, though all the staff should meet and evaluate new teachers. She is also responsible for the teaching of the assistants, and for implementing workshops and arranging for guest speakers (unless there is a director who has a leadership role in such duties as hiring and taking charge of teachers, dealing with parents, and carrying out administrative duties).

And finally, there are many miscellaneous duties which come under the care of the head teacher, such as planning and delegating all housekeeping activities and seeing that they are carried out. (She may have to do her share of these duties and will also have to see that any gaps are filled in.) She needs to supervise the ordinary buying of all equipment and supplies. She is also responsible, unless there is a director who takes this responsibility, to the fire warden and to the health officials in seeing that all of their rules and requirements are carried out.

DUTIES OF THE DIRECTOR OR BOARD OF DIRECTORS

As we have suggested, many schools do not have a director or board of directors. In their absence the head teacher will add their duties to her own. It is probably most customary, in the majority of schools, for the head teacher to do the directing. Listed here are the major responsibilities of the director, if the school has one.

These duties vary a good deal, depending on the policy of the school. In some schools the director likes to know each child and to follow closely the daily running of the school. Some directors are interested in doing or directing research. Some even like to take part in the teaching.

The director will hire the teachers, will teach the teachers, and will supervise, direct, or personally give any courses which are offered to the teachers. She will give leadership and facilitate communication and cooperation at all levels, so that the program is shaped by everyone.

She will ultimately set forth the guidelines which control the property, determine the general policies of the school, set tuition, carry out the many details of administration. But parents and teachers should help to formulate these guidelines.

DUTIES OF ASSISTANT TEACHERS

For each head teacher there will ideally be one or more full-time trained persons working closely with her. These are the assistant teachers. This task is actually somewhat difficult in that she needs to be extremely flexible. She must assist the head teacher when necessary, but she must also be able to take over full responsibility when necessary. Also, she must supervise the student teachers, participating in their learning.

She must be able to carry out any directions of the head teacher, but should also be original enough to maintain a general group policy more or less on her own when she is in charge. A good assistant teacher should not be just a carbon copy of the head teacher. She should be herself, able to bring her own special talents to the program.

Her main task is to be the person responsible for the group, either directly under the head teacher, or by herself when the head teacher is occupied elsewhere or otherwise. She is usually less mobile than the head teacher and usually remains right with her group.

An assistant teacher should be alert and responsible to things the head teacher may have missed. She should feel that it is *her* group even though she directs it under the supervision of the head teacher.

STUDENT TEACHERS

Many schools do not have student teachers. When they are present, their role and the amount of responsibility they take on depends partly on how much experience they have had previously, and partly on their individual abilities.

It is primarily important for the student teacher to think of herself as a learner. She has come to the school to learn, even though she will be learning by doing. She will inevitably be a participant, but she should at the same time be a good observer and a good listener.

Thus it will work out best if she is willing and able to go slowly at first. Initially it is important for her to be imaginative, creative, and even executive about small things, but preferably not about important things which effect the total running of the group. There is plenty of room for her to be spontaneous in her teaching, but ideally not with regard to the schedule or general planning.

Since no two students are alike, it is important that the head teacher or assistant teacher give each student an opportunity to experience success. Whatever her particular talents may be—with a group, with an individual child, or with a special area of the curriculum—she needs to feel good about herself before she can grow.

In the beginning a student is quite vulnerable to praise and criticism. Therefore those working with her need to be supportive of all that goes well, however trivial, so that she can grow in self-confidence. She should not be assigned to merely routine or menial jobs. She must be appreciated as an individual, her unique talents recognized, respected, and developed. Student teachers also need ample time to discuss the *reasons* for what goes on in a program, and to propose and refine their own reasons for behaving as they do.

It seems important that the student teacher have a supervisor *apart from* the head teacher or assistant teacher. She needs an outside person with whom to "level," a person who can more objectively assess and help with interactions, particularly on occasions when interpersonal conflicts arise. Sometimes a student teacher is not correctly placed in a situation that is best for her growth. Rather than leave her in a situation that is potentially destructive to her, bad for the head teacher, and ultimately bad for the children, the supervisor should arrange for her removal from that group or from any teaching experience.

Different student teachers have different amounts and periods of time when they can be available for teaching. It works out best, as a rule, if the student teacher can be at school for an entire session (rather than for just an hour at a time); and best if possible for her to be there for an extended and consecutive period of time, such as an entire semester.

PARENTS AS TEACHERS[1]

Having parents as teachers can be rewarding, since it provides a learning experience for them and, if they can come as learners, they do bring maturity to the experience. It does present difficulties, however. To some mothers, nursery school teaching is just a matter of custodial care—a glorified form of baby-sitting, and it may take a long time before they see it otherwise.

If you are going to have a basically untrained mother helper, you need very strong head teachers. Mothers who are raising children of their own often quite naturally have very definite ideas. Accepting the position of assistant teacher (or actually of student teacher in many instances) is difficult for many mothers.

As with assistant teachers, it usually works best to have mothers come in for a whole week at a time, rather than for a day or an hour at a time. Thus they become more like regular teachers, in the children's eyes and in their own. Also it is important, if possible, not to have a mother teach in her own child's group. It seems hard for the very young child to have to see his mother as a teacher as well as as a mother. With his own mother as teacher, the child is likely to carry over unfortunate and overdemanding home attitudes into school.

When mothers are going to act as teachers, they should ideally have some formal introduction to the situation, as for instance a conference with the head teacher, to go over some of the policies

1. In this brief discussion of parents as teachers, we are not considering those situations in which a mother has been hired as a full-time assistant teacher.

of the school. Also if possible they should have the opportunity to do some observing in advance of their own teaching.

Age makes a difference. A relatively young parent will probably find it easier to fit in than will an older one. A middle-aged parent who has already brought up several children might find it quite difficult to fit in as an assistant teacher, particularly if the head teacher is younger than she, and childless.

HOW MANY TEACHERS ARE DESIRABLE?

It is important to have enough teachers in any nursery school group; but too many can be as bad as too few. The question, therefore, is of course—how many is enough?

The number will depend on the size of the group, the age of the children, the number of rooms being used and their arrangement, and the quality of the adjustment of the individual children. More teachers are needed in instances where there are several difficult or atypical children in the group than when the majority of the children are normal and reasonably well adjusted.

As a very general rule we might suggest that there should be a minimum of one teacher to ten children, and more desirably one to four or five—at least for 2-, 3-, and 4-year-olds.

THREE

The School

7

Administration and Organization

PHILOSOPHY OF THE SCHOOL

It seems essential that the organization of a nursery school should represent a model rather than being merely eclectic, and that such a model involve a commitment to specific goals for early childhood education and the way they will be implemented. There are a number of models presently in existence: custodial schools, Montessori programs, industrial models favoring academic drill, child-development or "wait and see" maturational models, and "open classroom" models similar to the British infant school.

A model is important because it defines goals, and in essence defines program and teachers. In a sense it defines parents as well, since parents should select that model which seems best to them. Obviously it is desirable for parents to attempt to inform themselves about the educational implications of a program before they make their selection. Reading, discussion, and actual visiting of schools should be part of a parent's initial assessment.

The model will also define the nature of staff interactions, planning, training of staff, and the nature of any assessment program.

Once a program is defined, the director and staff need continuous planning to give assurance of a constant role of teacher as it relates to the child. Only thus, in a school where there are a number of teachers and frequent shifting of student teachers, can some measure of consistency be maintained.

In our opinion the most promising model is that provided by the open school in which children initiate learning through their own activities. The teacher, well-trained both in child development and in the nature of a young child's learning, is a catalyst in this setting. She sets the stage, prompts with questions or problems or materials, but does not take the job of learning away from the child. The teacher uses the child's interaction with equipment, materials, and his environment as the basis of her interdisciplinary instruction and keeps in mind long-term goals for the children.

Such a school, above all, encourages a child to choose from a number of options, to discover and develop his own interests, and to move at an individual rather than at a group pace.

PRACTICAL CONSIDERATIONS

Under ideal circumstances the education a child receives at nursery school may be, in some respects, the best he will receive in any formal way in all of his schooling. There seems more chance that his individual needs will be considered here, that the school program will be flexible, tentative, and modified to suit his individuality, and that there will be a staff adequate in size and ability to carry on education suited to his changing developmental needs.

Regardless of the basic philosophy of a nursery school, questions of building, finances, equipment, staff, curriculum, student body, and health regulations arise as common problems. Of basic importance are the different stages of growth of the children, the different abilities of each age group. The overall administration involves the theory of such differences as a primary basis for the groupings of children. Chronological age differences suggest three groups—at ages 2, 3, and 4—or groupings at 2½, 3, 3½, 4. Such groupings are not rigid classifications. While the ages of the majority of children in each group actually do fall within the age range set up, children with greater or less maturity may be placed in groups that do not match their chronological age. The so-called exceptional child might be in any group.

When a child's behavior suggests in any way his unsuitability for his chronological age group, intensive observation or a staff conference often suggests either his placement with children of another age, or some different type of handling. He might attend school more or less frequently, or might be given some other special treatment in the group to which he is assigned on the basis of chronological age.

Information given during the introductory interview, and the teacher's initial encounter with the child, are the usual criteria for the teacher's first tentative placement of the child. When the placement is for any reason questionable, the teacher can explain to the parents the school's system of grouping, and that changes often occur in the course of the year. Such communication with parents can afford an extremely valuable opportunity to present the idea that behavior does not always match chronological age, and that children may not, in the ordinary course of events, be ready for what is currently considered a first-grade experience exactly at the chronological age of six years.

Applications for enrollment are perforce handled in quite individualized ways. In schools where there are more applicants than places, the school must determine its policy about what factors will influence selection. A child's readiness, the parent's reasons for wanting him to be in school, the appropriateness of the school for the child, the age range, sex distribution, and overall balance of the group are matters which might influence enrollment.

When parents make inquiries about the school, it is helpful

for them to come to visit, if at all possible, while the school is in session. When they visit, they have an opportunity to learn about the school at first hand, and to observe the teachers and children. Parents at this time may ask to take whatever steps are necessary for making a formal application. This often involves filling out an introductory report form giving pertinent information about the child's developmental and health history, and making a small deposit of money.

Children may be considered for enrollment depending on their priority of application. When all places are filled, the names of additional applicants can be put on a waiting list. These children can be added to the group as vacancies occur or as groups are enlarged during the year. Sometimes schools like to reserve two or three places for the possible later enrollment of children who have special problems which might be helped through association with a normal group of children. Other schools may give priority in filling these two or three places to children of different nationalities, races, or religions. By spring, a well-functioning school usually has the enrollment for the following year in order, so that parents who are interested can be assured of a place for their child. Before the fall term, teachers generally get in touch with new parents to arrange an interview with mother and child before school begins.

The number of times and the hours children attend school each week is an arrangement that varies considerably depending on the philosophy of the school and the space available. Parents often select a school primarily on the basis of this arrangement. When all-day custodial service is not required because of a mother's working, it seems better to modify hours of attendance with regard to the age of the child.

Children of two have a satisfactory school experience if they come only twice a week for one and a half or two hours. Three-year-olds seem to thrive best on a three-morning-a-week, three-hour-a-morning schedule. Four-year-olds who do not nap are able to attend school five afternoons a week (or five mornings if space is available). We have found, however, that a 4-year-old usually does better with only three days a week of school. In fact, projecting into kindergarten, we wish that schools could more flexibly allow for an occasional Wednesday off for some children who would welcome a break in what seems to them a long week.

The size of a group usually varies depending on a child's age. If there is a 2-year-old group, it should be very small at first— starting with only four or five children, increasing perhaps to ten. The 3-year-old group might start with ten children and grow to fifteen; and the 4-year-old group might start at fifteen and grow to twenty. Midyear is a good time to consider taking in more children. An ideal teaching situation does not have more than five children for one teacher (usually four children to a teacher), and no group should exceed twenty-five children.

Sometimes shifting of children from one group to another makes for more vacancies in one group than in another. In the last quarter of the school year, in the spring, when children spend much time out of doors, the head teacher may decide to take in more children if the groups seem to warrant such additions. The spring is an especially good time to start 2-year-olds who may be coming to the youngest group the following fall, since their adjustment to an already organized group is easier than to one in which the majority of the children are new. Such a nucleus of "old-timers" makes adjustment problems somewhat easier in the fall.

In the spring it is wise to prepare a calendar for the next year, which can be given to parents who plan to enroll children in the school. Parents need to know in advance the dates of the opening and closing school sessions, winter and spring vacations, and special holidays. Many schools publish a newsletter once a month acquainting parents with the school's general policies and philosophy of education and giving information about such subjects as transportation of children, scholarships, conferences, finances, proper clothing for children, their food and rest. This bulletin also helps parents learn one another's names and the names of other children and of teachers.

Since administrative arrangements are, in a healthy, growing school, likely to be modified and improved as new personnel meet and exchange ideas, it is good at the outset for a school to prepare a loose-leaf booklet setting forth various policies in writing. These policies can be points of departure at staff meetings, where discussions can determine and refine what seems to work best in the dynamic relationships of parents, teachers, children, and community in the nursery school setting.

HEALTH

All nursery schools should arrange to have a pediatrician or other health person available during the school year for consultation regarding general health policies of the school. In addition, schools generally require a statement from a family physician to verify that each child is in good health and has had necessary immunization.

At the first meeting between parent and teacher there should always be a discussion of health regulations for the school. Teachers ask a parent to keep the child at home when he seems not to be feeling up to par, whatever the reason. The child should stay at home for at least three days after he gives evidence of a fresh cold, or has had an elevation of temperature, rash, upset stomach, sore or discharging eyes within the last twenty-four hours. Parents should notify the school of the child's exposure to any contagious disease and should keep him at home during the specified incubation period. If a child becomes ill at school, he should be isolated in a special room provided for this purpose, and his parents should be asked to come for him at once.

It seems especially important at the outset to enlist a parent's cooperation, since health regulations are managed largely by parents and teachers. It is worthwhile, therefore, to make a special point of urging parents to be observant, to watch out for any sign of colds or other illness *before* the child comes to school in the morning. Parents are more likely than teachers to be alert to any signs of impending illness: listlessness, overfatigue, irritability, or any acting in ways atypical to the child. It is well to urge, "When in doubt, keep the child at home."

Teachers, too, are advised to be alert to signs of illness, and always when a teacher greets each child as he comes in the morning, she should have his physical well-being in mind. If she notes any signs of trouble before the parent leaves, she should suggest that the mother take the child home. If there is any indication of more serious trouble after the parent leaves, and the parent cannot be contacted, either the child's pediatrician or one of the doctors available through the school's consultation service should be summoned.

It is not necessary to have a special nurse on the staff to examine the children each morning when there is good cooperation between parents and teachers. Nor is it necessary, in our opinion, to have a teacher look at the throats of children routinely as they enter school, since such a procedure might be frightening to many children. And in any case it seems that the average teacher cannot really see much from this sort of inspection. As to contagious diseases, it is wise for schools to check annually with pediatricians to find out what the current rules are. Schools for young children must be especially concerned to protect pregnant mothers from exposure to certain contagious diseases.

Generally, nursery schools are subject to health inspections from a member of the local board of health. These inspections may vary from one community to another and may vary with regard to the type of school. In any event the recommendations of the inspector help maintain safe, sanitary, and hygienic conditions.

In order to secure the approval of the health inspector, there must be adequate space (at least thirty-five square feet of free space for each child, indoors and out), there must be fire protection, and facilities for adequate heating, ventilation, lighting, cleanliness, sanitation, and first aid. The inspector determines whether toilets and washbasins are sanitary and sufficient in number; advises about cleanliness in serving food and in sleeping arrangements; and warns as to what may be hazards to safety. He usually questions about provisions for the medical examination of children and provides forms which family pediatricians are requested to fill in.

SAFETY REGULATIONS

Parents and teachers are constantly concerned, of course, about the matter of safety in the school. Safety is very much a matter of proper equipment and adequate supervision. The health inspector advises about general safety precautions, and the fire department will see to it through their inspectors that the building has adequate exits and fire walls and doors.

Equipment must be appropriate to the ages of the children using it, and must be sturdy and in good working order. Dangerous pieces of equipment such as swings and seesaws are not appropriate for young children. Fences and trees must be safe. Teachers must keep constant watch for nails that may stick out, splinters, rungs off ladders, loose portions of any piece of equipment. Chairs or benches that may slip should be protected with rubber caps; outdoor equipment that has become slippery with dampness should be dried before children use it. Broken glass, broken toys, holes in the ground, loose rocks that can be thrown must be taken care of. There should be access at all times to someone who can immediately take care of any potentially dangerous equipment.

Indoors a teacher must be especially careful that children do not put small pieces of equipment into their mouths or noses. Children must not run around with sticks, or with any sort of small equipment onto which they might fall. They should be discouraged from bringing such equipment as guns, knives, or ropes from home, for all of these are potentially dangerous. If they do bring such objects, these should be put away in a safe place while the children are at school.

Supervision indoors (especially in old buildings) involves stairs: a teacher should always precede children going down, follow them going up, have children go one at a time, and emphasize that there must be no pushing. Obviously some activities, such as outdoor climbing, require more supervision than do others.

This discussion of dangers may make the whole situation seem excessively dangerous. Actually, although teachers should be constantly aware, they should not be constantly apprehensive. A general observance of what is going on with all children and proper precautions with regard to equipment in general assure a minimum of accidents. Having basic rules which the children hear over and over again helps, too, and these rules should be strictly enforced. Such rules will vary from school to school. They may include such admonitions as "Don't lean out of the window," "Don't run down the slide," "Don't stand up on the slide," "Nobody throws stones."

In addition to all this, every school should carry some sort of accident insurance, and one or several of the teachers should have some training in first aid. A calm attitude, simple first aid equipment on hand, easy access to a doctor are all imperative. And when a child suffers *any* sort of accident, even though it may seem quite minor, the parent should be told about it before the child leaves school.

RECORDS—THEIR USE AND ABUSE

Record keeping can be either one of the most useful and helpful of a teacher's many activities, or at the other extreme can be one of the most useless, self-deceptive, and time consuming. Often a little thought given to the whole matter in advance can prevent literally hours of wasted time and effort.

KINDS OF RECORDS

Probably no two schools are exactly alike in the kinds of records which they customarily keep. However, here is a fairly basic list of the most commonly useful kinds of records.

1. An introductory report form filled out by the parents before the child enters school. This includes such routine information as name, address, telephone number, birth-health-developmental history of the child, number of siblings, race and religion of parents. This gives information useful in daily practice and for permanent records.

2. Report of initial interview with mother (which takes place on her first visit to the school). This includes information on the child's play interests, personality, general home adjustment, and also notes the teacher's observations about mother-child interaction.

3. Attendance records.

4. The teacher's report on the child's first day at school.

5. Records such as those described earlier which attempt some sort of systematic observation of each child in the class.

6. Fairly full, organized reports at intervals, perhaps once

or twice a year. A full report in January helps teachers to plan for the second semester. These more formal reports are based on the accumulation of other records.

7. Extra reports on special problems brought up by parents, or including any special information which parents may give.

8. Any kind of research records. These will of course vary depending on the research program which may be being carried out at the school.

9. Any records of health which may be required by the city or state. These records would include the name and telephone number of the child's pediatrician.

USE OF RECORDS

There are many ways in which well-kept records can be of considerable use in a nursery school. We do not have to try to convince anyone who has had even a little nursery school experience that a school can be run better with the help of a judicious amount of note taking and record keeping than without.

First of all, records are obviously useful for all sorts of routine reference purposes during any current school year. They are useful later in case a child's physician or subsequent teacher needs information about him. Also in cases in which a child returns to the same school for a second year, records of earlier progress and behavior can be useful for comparison.

For new and inexperienced teachers especially, the keeping of daily reports can furnish a good training device for sharpening perceptions. Such records are especially useful in the training of new teachers if they are checked over by one of the more experienced teachers. Such record keeping helps a teacher to see behavior in perspective. Sometimes it may seem to a teacher that a child is making little progress in some desired direction. A check of current behavior against earlier behavior may show that his progress is considerable (or vice versa). Well-kept and reasonably detailed records will enable a teacher to evaluate progress—her own as well as the child's.

Reasonably detailed records on individual children are useful in staff conferences when that particular child is being discussed. Records can also be useful in preparing a teacher for a parent conference; and, during such a conference, can supply pertinent details which can help clarify or illustrate important points about the child in question.

ABUSE OF RECORDS

Quite as important as the correct use of records is the avoidance of their misuse. Possibly in no area of education have so many teachers spent so many hours in the ultimately pointless amassing of illegible, useless records as in the nursery school field.

To avoid this easy error, any nursery school teacher who is keeping records should make a positive effort not to indulge in excessive note taking. She should be certain that any records she is keeping are kept for a purpose, and not simply for the sake of piling up records.

Record taking (and here we refer chiefly to the daily narrative records which most nursery school teachers do keep) should never take the place of good observation, thinking about, and analyzing behavior.

The sheer amassing of records in minute detail does not necessarily result in good research (when records are being kept for research purposes). Record taking for research should properly be selective and well thought out. A good deal of extremely careful thought and planning should precede the gathering of any research data. Research records are seldom any better than the thinking of the individual who makes them. Research directors have long since given up the futile hope that valuable research results will spring full blown from piles of daily records kept in great detail but with no special forethought.

Other special prohibitions which should be kept in mind include the following.

Records should not be too complex and cumbersome. Nor should they be illegible. If kept, they should be communicable from one generation to the next. (Certainly from one year to the next.) Sometimes making a digest or summary of daily records can pull them together and make them more useful to somebody else.

Any lack of respect for the confidential nature of nursery school records is an abuse. Parents should never see these records. Nor should they be discussed outside the school, socially or otherwise. It is a very easy and natural but unfortunate mistake for teachers to discuss school happenings outside of school, in the hearing of other people.

Material in records should as far as possible be reasonably objective and unbiased. Having head teachers examine the records, and having them reviewed and discussed in staff conferences, can help to keep them objective. This does not mean that they should contain no adverse comments, but such comments should be supported by specific data.

8

Purpose, Program, Questions

PURPOSE

A common and sometimes derogatory question often asked about nursery school is "Do the children just play?" Of course there is much more to nursery school than "just" playing, in the sense that the question is usually meant. But even just playing, in a well-planned and suitable situation, could justify the existence of a nursery school, since it is to a large extent through play that the young child learns about himself and his environment. In the nursery school this learning can be carried on in the best of ways and in a spirit of fun.

However, a well-planned nursery school offers much more to the child than "just" play. It gives him a chance to spend time in a physical environment which is scaled to and planned for him, and where there are a minimum of negative regulations about what he cannot touch and do. He can enjoy a wide variety of materials, not only in the numerous toys that are offered, but in music, books, and art. He can also play with a number of children near his own age, and he can increase his awareness of the world by the richness of things around him that he is helped to understand.

A child learns a great deal about personal relations in his associations with other children. One humorous statement as to the purpose of nursery schools describes them as "places where children hit one another over the head, under supervision."

Of course, there is inevitably plenty of open aggression among young children. Nursery school not only helps them get rid of aggression, but, when the aggression is excessive, it provides opportunity for adults to find out *why* such aggression exists. Problems involving excessive hostility, excessive energy, or frustration, which show themselves in aggression, can often be worked out. On the other hand, a weak or timid child may be encouraged to stand up for his rights by the teacher's saying to the aggressor, "You better be careful or he might hit you back." Such a statement frequently gives the weaker child the notion that he actually might!

In general, however, the teacher can show children *other* ways of solving problems than simply by means of aggression. Through judicious intervention, and through the use of language, children learn to respect one another's rights, ideas, and belongings, and to develop a sense of fair play in their dealings with one another. Nursery school provides guided socialization in giving children techniques for managing personal interactions. They learn the concept underlying good manners: consideration for the rights of the other person. Of course, development in good relationships is a long, slow process, and accomplishments will vary with different ages and individuals, but such learning can at least be begun.

Through playing with others a child is encouraged also in both spontaneous and in conforming play. When his spontaneous ideas are accepted and appreciated by others, as the basis of play, he is encouraged in his potentialities. Also, children who are nonconformists, but who have the opportunity to see others going smoothly and easily through routines, may in time accept group activities, too.

The child's experience is broadened in school by having to share the experiences of different kinds of children. He learns, too, to appreciate children with handicaps, and those of different racial backgrounds.

And in his relationships with the teachers, a child broadens his social horizon to include adults who understand and accept him in what may be to him unusual ways. Often such an association is the first a young child has with an adult apart from his parents; in it he can enjoy a friendship based on confidence that no matter what he does he will always be protected and that his behavior will be interpreted with reason, not prejudice.

A child not only has the opportunity to enjoy richer material and more complex social surroundings at school than he would have at home; he also has an opportunity here to develop his potential in a new way. Nursery school allows a child to function where he is developmentally, and at the same time stimulates him (but never *forces* him) toward the next stage of growth. And he is always encouraged in the development of basic values: a sense of curiosity, of resourcefulness, of achievement and responsibility, at whatever level.

Such growth takes place in an environment where a child has the help of teachers especially concerned with promoting growth in terms of his own personality. It is often much more difficult for a parent than for a teacher to accept a child's basic personality. Parents are frequently more directive, more concerned to make the child fit preconceived patterns, than is the teacher. So the child can have a sense of freedom at school that he often does not have at home. Freedom comes, too, in that for at least a few hours each day he is released from his incessant battle with his siblings. Tendencies to battle at school usually do not have such deep-seated emotional bases and are in any event lessened because of increased supervision and planning.

School gives the child a life of his own, and in so doing sometimes gives him a new perspective on his family and a new status therein. He gains a new importance in going to school, as do the older children, and in having experiences to tell to his parents. Going to school often breaks into a situation at home that has become child-centered. In going to school the young child may on the one hand increase his importance in a new way, and on the other hand may modify a too egocentric position. His making a satisfactory adjustment to school will give him a sense of independence, will get him used to the idea of getting away from his family. And an adjustment to school at the nursery school level may help the child who has trouble with such adjustment to have a less stormy time when he goes to kindergarten or first grade.

For the parents, too, a nursery school serves many purposes. Sometimes, without even the necessity of a teacher working with the parents, just the new experience of having the child go to school, with the lessening of home tensions which this brings, indirectly solves difficulties about feeding, sleeping, and elimination. In any case, nursery school helps considerably in giving the parent of the preschool child a breathing space. During these earliest years the parent-child relationship is often too intense and continuous. Home time can be happier if both parent and child have a little relief from one another. Siblings, too, benefit from the lessening of tension that can result from periods when the mother does not have too many children among whom she must divide her attention.

The nursery school is important for teachers at all levels and for the community in general. The school can serve as a training center for teachers and as a source of information for parents and teachers who want to know more about children. Medical students, nurses, social workers, psychotherapists, recreation leaders, religious leaders—anyone who wants to know more about what young children are like will profit from periods of observation in a nursery school. A well-run nursery school can also be used as a center of research, with observations directed not just to general learning, but with meaningful specific questions being asked and answered in the course of observation.

In the final analysis, the chief function of a nursery school is not to prepare children for the future. It is to help them learn to live and learn *now*. The school enables them to dare and care to make decisions, to organize experiences, to utilize knowledge, and to develop and extend their intellectual and emotional resources.

CURRICULUM

The curriculum[1] in a nursery school consists of those materials and experiences which promote constructive learning in children. The teacher must provide carefully planned and suitable tools for learning, with relevance to the child's intellectual, artistic, and social achievements and with regard to the ways in which children's lives can be nurtured and expanded.

Children learn in many ways. There are learning possibilities in every activity in a good program. Art, music, literature, science, social science, mathematics all provide disciplines that can be appropriately interpreted for young children, and all suggest specific materials that children can use to arrive at knowledge in these areas. Although we have mentioned the disciplines separately, in reality, they are woven together in such a way that each child and each group has a balanced overall experience, and the interrelationship of materials and knowledge is constantly prevalent. The teacher is the integrating element. She brings each activity to the children in ways that stress their relationships to one another and their relationship to earlier experiences.

Materials in a classroom are of most value when they can be used in a variety of ways and at many levels. Materials relate to a child's interest and should be readily available and manageable. Teachers see to it that children can experiment, can suc-

1. For detailed information about curriculum the reader is referred to *Helping Young Children Learn,* by Evelyn G. Pitcher et al., 2d ed. (Columbus, Ohio: Charles E. Merrill Publishing Co., 1974).

ceed, and can progress toward increasing complexity and competence in their encounters in the classroom.

Manipulative materials must be supplied in great diversity, with no "sets" for the entire class; and children must be allowed to work directly with them. The environment should provide materials developed by the teacher and children, and also common everyday materials such as rocks and sand, water, pets, plant life. "Found and scrounged" materials encourage teachers and children to see new uses in ordinary materials: egg and milk cartons, plastic boxes, styrofoam, floor tiles, wallpaper samples all have potential educational value. The range of materials and activities provided could include the following.

1. Art Experiences: Painting—tempera, watercolors, finger-paints, spray, string, easel, spatter. Drawing—pencil, crayon, Magic Marker, etc. Blackboard and chalk. Collage.

2. Crafts: Clay modeling, playdough, sculpture with soap or wood, papier-mâché, origami-paper sculpture. Printing—vegetable, letter, linoleum block, or wood block. Mobile construction.

3. Carpentry.

4. Imaginative play: Housekeeping corner. Small animals, planes, cars, garages, stove, puppets.

5. Music: Singing, rhythms, instrumental, listening to music.

6. Dance: Free expression, ballet, rock and roll, folk dance, body awareness.

7. Science: Scales, magnets, timer, clock, incubator, thermometer, magnifying glasses, test tubes, animal cave, aquarium, terrarium, materials for plant care, or for study of weather, ecology, machinery.

8. Play with Natural Materials: Water play, funnels, pans, dishes, watering cans. Sand play, indoors and outdoors.

9. Construction: Wooden blocks, boxes, packing crates,

Lincoln logs, Tinker toys, Lego blocks.

10. Fine Motor Manipulation: Small wheel toys, such as cars, trucks, tractors. Puzzles, flannel boards, pegboards. Also stacking and nesting and balancing toys.

11. Drama: Puppetry, dramatic games, acting activities.

12. Gross Motor Play: Indoors—hollow blocks, rocking horse, rocking boat, punching bag, climbing ladder, steps, jungle gym. Outdoors—jungle gym, wagons, cars, pedal toys, tricycles, balls, tires, large hollow pipes or barrels, slides.

13. Books: These should be supplied in diversity and profusion, including reference books, children's literature, and "books" written by the children themselves.

14. Homemaking Arts: Materials to be used in cooking, sewing, cleaning, gardening.

15. General Games: Circle games, team games, musical games, classification games. (Many of these actually do not require any very special materials.)

16. Letter and Number Learnings: Counting frames, tactile letter and numeral blocks, Cuisinaire rods, parquetry blocks.

17. Social and Language Development: Tape recorder, typewriter, Lotto game, phonograph, TV, radio, letter-writing and book-making materials.

18. Field Trips: Hospital, pet store, grocery store, construction site, subway, farm, factory, zoo.

19. Ethnic Studies: Holiday celebrations, traditions, simple exposure to foreign languages, books dealing with minorities.

The materials and activities listed are suggestive only. There is no standard list. Many more could and should be added. Teachers should be involved in selecting, ordering, and making materials. Play with materials, when guided by a sensitive teacher, provides a wealth of opportunities for learning. While busy hammering or sawing, blowing bubbles or pounding clay, building with blocks or knocking them down, feeding a rabbit or watching him hop, the child is learning about forces of gravity, balance, weight. He is learning meanings of words such as *fast, furry, heavy, soft.*

While reading and writing should not be taught in a formal sense, the young child is noticing shapes, sizes, colors, letters, and numbers. Thus introductory phases of reading, writing, and arithmetic are presented daily in a rich preschool program.

Activity is the medium of the young child's learning. He explores, he manipulates, he practices, he acts. Such activity and the materials with which he acts provide the curriculum in the nursery school. Children invest materials with multiple meanings, uses, and interpretations.

SCHEDULING

We have found that a program with a planned schedule, although a flexible one, seems best to meet the needs of the children in our groups. Although any group in general follows such a schedule, individual children frequently do not. However, there is always an effort to see to it that each child has the opportunity to enjoy as much of the program as possible during each school session.

Some children tend to get stuck in one activity during the period of free play, and it is helpful for teachers to introduce them to other activities from time to time. Children are encouraged not only to play but to talk, to reflect, and to laugh; to play and work in small and large groups; and to play and work alone. Younger and older children visit one another's groups. They especially enjoy this visiting for such experiences as music, when music is offered as a group activity. Also the usual program is put aside on special days in favor of such things as a parade, cooking, visiting a nearby garden or museum or firehouse.

Yet a schedule provides a general basic framework for the day at school: large areas of activity are planned and usually occur in sequence, although times for each activity vary considerably. One good overall plan involves outdoor play followed by indoor, and ending with outdoor. But even this plan may vary according to the weather, the needs of the group, or the mood of the group. Children in nursery school have little awareness of time, so that teachers determine whether outdoor play shall last for fifteen minutes or sixty, for example.

Children seem to vary in their need of structure or permissiveness in a program. A nursery school is uniquely able to adapt routines and expectations to the individualities of the members of each group. In the course of a year children may modify what initially may seem too great a reliance on structure, or too great an inability to follow a routine or adapt to a group. Such changes are most likely to occur when the child has opportunities for both "free" and "controlled" experiences so that he can find out the pleasures of both. In the nursery school program, opportunities for structure are particularly afforded during the group music or story period, when almost all the children together participate in music or listen to a story.

A sample allotment of time and activities for the 2- and 3-year-old groups is substantially the same, except that the 2-year-olds go home at 11:30 instead of 12:00 and consequently all activities are somewhat shorter. A typical schedule for the day for 2- and 3-year-olds might be as follows.

Outdoor play	½ hour
Indoor free play	1 hour or more
Music, singing, and rhythms	20 to 30 minutes
Milk and crackers	10 minutes
Stories	10 to 20 minutes
Outdoor play	Until they go home

When the children first arrive, parents bring them outside, except in the unusual instances when children prefer to start the morning indoors. The outdoor period at the beginning and end of the morning takes advantage of children's being in their warm garments at the beginning and close of the school session. Parents have a minimum of delay in picking them up when they are already dressed, and teachers have to undress and dress them only once.

With the younger children, it seems preferable to have a period of free play preceding the more formal music period, for the average young child is quite eager to explore and play as soon as he comes into school. Indeed, many cannot even wait to have their hats and coats off, but rush at once to their favorite activities. When music is introduced, it works best to put away as many toys as possible; big toys, such as rocking boats, horses, cars, must be moved away from temptation. Insofar as possible, children must be encouraged not to hold toys as they sit on the floor for the music period, for if they do, inevitably a contest arises as to who should hold each toy, and the music period can be distracted by such disputes.

Four-year-olds tend in general to stay with their interests longer than do Threes. Although the general allotment of time for various activities is substantially the same as for the younger groups, there is more likelihood of a variation in the program, since Fours may get carried away by a group project and teachers will not want to interrupt them. There is more place for special projects with the older children, too, such as long discussion periods at music time about something a child or teacher may bring in (a praying mantis, a picture of some Indians, for example). Or a larger number of the group may engage in a project such as the painting of a mural on a long stretch of brown wrapping paper on the floor. Fours have a great interest and considerable talent in activities that require fine motor skills, and elaborate projects with clay or poster paper may get under way.

Music period comes after the outdoor period, except on rainy days, when it follows free play. Those who do not care to have music can stay outside longer. Fours like to have such choices of activity. After music they need a brief "thinking" period to decide what they will do next; this prevents a wild scramble to a single activity and encourages a more thoughtful approach to an activity.

Fours can have a resting period, looking at books, after their free play. They sit on pillows, look at books, listen to music, or chat quietly with one another. Such a resting period is more successful with Fours than with the younger children, who are apt to grab books from one another and become raucous and playful. A number of the older children lie down and rest at this interval before milk-and-cracker time.

A good basic schedule for 4-year-olds involves the following general allotments of time.

Outdoor play	30 to 40 minutes
Music	10 to 30 minutes
Indoor free play	40 minutes or longer
Rest	15 minutes
Looking at books	
Listening to phonograph	
Talking, lying down	
Milk and crackers	5 to 15 minutes
Stories (children leave when	
they wish)	10 to 30 minutes
Outdoor play	Until they go home

QUESTIONS

There are four important questions relating to nursery school which are commonly asked. The first is *Should every child attend nursery school?*

Our answer to this question is "No." We feel that there are certain exceptional cases where it is better for a child to stay at home in these earliest years. Among these main exceptions we mention the extremely immature and dependent child who suffers more from leaving his mother than he gains in the school experience. Such children need more years at home, it seems, before they are ready for school.

Other children present a similar problem of nonreadiness, although not because of immaturity or dependence—perhaps rather simply because of basic personality factors. Such children take too much out of the teacher and parent in the process of getting to school and adjusting to it. Difficulties in such cases can become so exaggerated that it doesn't seem worth the complications for what the children get out of it. Sometimes such children merely need to win their right to stay at home if they want to—then they decide to attend!

We must also keep in mind that there are children who adjust well and enjoy school at one age, but who may do less well at another. Thus some adapt well at three, but at four either have a sufficiently rich life at home to satisfy their needs, or suddenly become dependent. If this is the case, there should be no reluctance on the part of parents to allow their children to discontinue school. After a brief vacation, many such children are eager to return.

Another exception is the child who has a very full life, with many playmates and good play opportunities, and who gets on well at home and in his neighborhood. When such a happy

existence would be unhappily interrupted, and if the inconveni-
ence of traveling to school or the expense of school might
present a problem, school might well be considered unneces-
sary. Such a child might well enjoy nursery school and profit
from it, but in his case school could not be considered a real
need.

Finally, if a child is highly susceptible physically to colds
and illnesses, or if he becomes so tense and tired at school that
he cannot nap at home, and is as a result very disagreeable,
attendance at nursery school might be unwise.

In general, however, we feel that most children do benefit
very considerably from nursery school. Probably in general
there are more Twos who really would not benefit from school
than Threes. At all ages there are those who will have trouble
in adjusting, but once they get over their initial adjustment
difficulties—and even in the process of working out such difficulties—nursery school has very much to offer in promoting
and enriching their growth.

A second question which frequently arises is *Won't the child
get tired of school if he starts so early?* Again, our answer is
"No." But of course much depends on the kind of nursery
school. Some schools have stereotyped, uncreative programs,
unchallenging to children after the first few weeks. The same
program may be offered over and over with an inflexible kind
of routine, with what seems a talented lack of ingenuity.

As a rule, however, school can offer something vastly different each year to each child. Almost any appropriate materials,
with skilled guidance, enable a child to experience the satisfactions of the age he is and stimulate him to growth toward the
age he is to become. Thus, even though a child seems to be
working with the same materials at different ages—blocks,
paint, clay, crayons, for example—he would use these materials
in different ways, satisfying different needs, depending on
whether he was two, three, or four years old. The materials

themselves become different tools as the child himself changes and their use is adapted to his growth. Teachers who are sensitive to growth do not attempt to confine experiences to rigid patterns. School is a constantly growing experience, each year different from the preceding year because each year the child himself is different.

So, unless the school is extremely impoverished and rigid, the child does not, as some people fear, have the same thing year after year till he gets to kindergarten or first grade. Nursery school attendance should not lead to boredom. Some especially uncreative children are bored no matter what is offered, and such children, of course, need special attention. But the average child in a good nursery school finds each year full of exciting explorations.

A further question asks, *Should nursery school be part of the public school system?* Certainly there are many hazards to its inclusion. Nursery school is expensive. It requires a good deal of space, a good deal of equipment, and a trained staff. It requires great flexibility, great understanding of children, great willingness not to have a too formal teaching situation.

Yet the nursery school can at its best provide the closest to an ideal educational situation that we have to offer the child, and insofar as this is true public schools would, if such inclusion were feasible, greatly benefit from what the nursery school has to offer.

A final question, which we have already discussed, is *Do children learn anything in nursery school or do they just play?* We have already answered this question in the pages just preceding. However, we might elaborate on our answer here, since this topic is currently so highly controversial in educational circles.

There are at the moment many strongly vocal adherents of the point of view that preschoolers should not be allowed to "waste" these precious early years in mere play, but rather should be given formal instruction in reading and arithmetic as early as three years of age. The assumption of these educators appears to be that the usual nursery school curriculum consists chiefly of messing about with paint and clay and, as noted, of "hitting each other over the head, under supervision."

These individuals forget that play *is* the child's work, and that as he plays in nursery school he lays the groundwork for the more specific and formal academic learning which will follow.

As the preschooler plays in nursery school he learns about people, both adults and children, and how to get along with them. He learns about space and time, about books and words, about numbers and letters and shapes and textures. He learns to express his own growing abilities in all areas at the level he himself has reached rather than in the way and at the level some formal system of education might require.

Schools for young children have long been aware of developmental progressions in learning. Children spontaneously use numbers at a very early age, and may have the first stimulus to counting in their own ten fingers. Young children see geometric forms in their buttons, in bars of soap, pieces of bread, crackers. They do not necessarily need exercises with wooden circles, squares, and triangles to teach them what forms are. They spontaneously practice and enjoy putting events in a series in the routines or rituals they set up for themselves, in the songs or rhymes they prefer, in the ways they arrange objects that come to their hands—blocks, raisins, beans, cereal. They do not need exercises with work books to teach such ordering. They practice writing on their own, given a crayon and paper, through scribbling, through making vertical and horizontal strokes and concentric circles. They naturally and properly experiment with upside-down forms, and left-to-right and right-to-left progressions, before they settle to our culturally established ways of producing written symbols.

Experiences with all these interests develop and are fostered by the teacher's attention and praise, by relations with other children, by opportunities to attach words or other symbols to experiences and to question their meanings and relationships. Schools for young children recognize that the child needs to have around him materials and people that provide many ways to help him express himself. He needs to hear many words, to associate them with objects, and to see words in print. He must have a wide acquaintance with many books that he enjoys. He needs such objects as blocks, sticks, beads, number frames to help give form to his number sense.

No child should be forced to use some single approach to a learning situation to the exclusion of other approaches, or be forced into any learning before he is ready. Basic in the philosophy of early childhood education is an appreciation of the undesirability of having only one system, or of having any learning started at an arbitrary time. It is important, for the development of all skills, to have a wide variety of materials and a teacher who knows how and when to utilize them. Children need to have ideas presented in many different ways and at appropriate times. They learn that tasks are in some ways similar before they can come to abstract principles or can understand basic structures.

Learning becomes meaningful as it is assimilated into a child's complete schematic framework. Too great attention to the learning of single tasks very often neglects the exploration of how a child comes to learning in primitive, spontaneous ways, how he has been changed in his learning, and how he can bring creative insights to his learning by approaching what he knows in different ways.

In short, though the nursery school as it is customarily conducted does not constitute a formal learning situation, in actual practice learning and play are often indistinguishable.

9

Physical Plant and Equipment[1]

Ideally, the nursery school building should be one which is used exclusively for the purposes of the school, so that it can remain set up and not be used by others. Since some nursery schools are used part of the time by church groups, or by clinics, or are part of a home or a larger school, so that the rooms must be used by other people when the members of the nursery school are not there, the equipment and space may have to be chosen with these other groups in mind.

Some nursery schools are especially built to be nursery schools. Others may have been made over from a building which formerly had other uses—an old house, a store front, a warehouse. A new school, built with the needs of the young child in mind, obviously has many advantages. It can be all on one floor, with ready access to the outdoors from the schoolrooms. It can be protected from traffic and other hazards and can have adequate space, heating, lighting, and ventilation.

There are a number of advantages to an old house that can be converted into a school. The homelike atmosphere of such a building, both outside and inside, is appealing to young chil-

1. The description of physical appointments of a nursery school given in this chapter is not meant to be comprehensive. Such information as is offered here is of a general nature. Readers who plan to organize a nursery school for the first time and who need specific information about buildings and materials will find more detailed information elsewhere, as in H. and E. Waechter, *Schools for the Very Young* (New York: F. W. Dodge, 1951).

dren in that there are often many rooms and hallways, allowing for a flexible handling of groups. Rooms for special activities are possible, such as a quiet room, a noisy room, a music room, a carpentry room.

Old houses also usually have odd-shaped rooms, rather than the standard rectangular rooms characteristic of most schools. L-shaped rooms, for example, offer a tremendous and desirable amount of visual and acoustical separation. The upstairs rooms in an old house can provide much-needed facilities for informal gatherings, places for parents and teachers to meet, a curriculum resource center for teacher and parent workshops, office space, or the usually much-needed space for storage.

Also teachers are not likely to worry, in an old house, that children may harm or damage the building, and the variety of space stimulates teachers to experiment with ideas as to how the existing rooms and home furnishings might be used.

The main drawback to such a physical plant is the difficulty of supervising so many different rooms. Of necessity, many teachers are required. Meeting health and fire regulations is more difficult, too, and there are hazards to safety in the steps, which must be very carefully supervised at all times. Old buildings are harder to keep clean. Teachers must work hard at painting and decorating to keep appearances in good form.

Whatever the physical plant, it seems wise at least to have a separate room for each different age group, and if possible, each group of children should have immediate access to its own play yard.

In recent years the study of arrangements of space for young children has become quite sophisticated. Rigid, barren classrooms with sets of materials and cumbersome stereotyped furnishings are unacceptable to modern educators. The new approach emphasizes a preference for movable furniture that takes up little space. Indeed the "furniture" in the most attractive classrooms can scarcely be considered furniture at all.

Teachers rely, instead, on tables of varying shapes and heights built from telephone spools or from fiberboard tubes topped with plywood or firm tri-wall materials.

Stools made from tubes can be individually printed and decorated by children and can also be used for personal storage. Slabs of wood are used for low tables. Low carpeted platforms and risers add cozy areas and provide additional seating. Multileveled structures are places for large and small groups. Couches, armchairs, pillows add homelike, intimate touches.

Walls are often covered with washable vinyl, which accepts staples and thumbtacks for making displays or hanging children's art work. A number of areas are carpeted, especially those designated for reading or for quiet play. The use of color delineates spaces, as do bookcases, plywood coated with chalkboard paint (so that dividers are also furniture).

Mobiles, sculptures, plants, art, bird cages, books, and displays of all sorts as well as careful consideration of lighting, color, and textures, bring various sensory satisfactions and stimulation to the children.

Classrooms can be organized into different activity areas, and such areas should be located in terms of their functional interrelationships (quiet, noisy, messy, clean) and should be scaled to accommodate up to four children comfortably. In addition, some areas should be expandable to accommodate larger groups. Materials should be stored and displayed so that children have easy access to them, and so that they can be restored to their places easily. Materials for the various aspects of the curriculum, described earlier, are thus attractively and conveniently arranged and placed in such a way as to maximize their learning potential.[2]

General planning for space must include toilet and washing

2. Further information about classroom space and furnishings will be found in *Schools for Early Childhood: A Report from Educational Facilities Laboratories,* Library of Congress Catalogue No. 78–139586, September 1950. Also in "Making Hard Rooms Soft Rooms," by Anita Olds, *Learning,* November 1972, pp. 36–42.

facilities, space for children's wraps, for storing little-used equipment, for setting out milk and crackers. The physical plant should also include an office or room where parents and teachers can go, apart from the children, to work or talk or telephone, a place where adults can leave their personal belongings, and where records and reports about the children and business records can be filed, whether these be upstairs or downstairs.

If it is at all possible, there should also be provision for one-way screens for parent observation and guidance and teacher training. These can easily be made by screening off with ordinary wire mesh a room in which no light comes from behind. The wire mesh should be painted with thin white paint on the side toward the children.[3]

The physical plant includes outdoor as well as indoor space. The best outdoor space would include seventy-five to one hundred square feet for each child on the playground. The outdoor area should ideally be adjacent to or at least fairly close to the indoor area. Safety must especially be kept in mind outdoors, since there is likelihood that the outdoors will offer more gross motor activity and equipment than the children have indoors. The play yard should be so constructed that children will be visible at all times; there should be no hidden corners where they can get out of sight. And the whole area might well be enclosed with some form of fencing, with strong gates secured by a catch on the outside.

Some sort of outdoor shed should be available for storing equipment. Such an enclosure might be large enough to provide a retreat in the winter for children who have become cold, yet are not ready to go indoors. Pets, too, can be sheltered in such a place.

It is most satisfying if the outdoor area provides growing

3. Arnold Gesell, et al., *The First Five Years of Life* (New York: Harper & Row, 1940), p. 356.

things. Children greatly enjoy flowers and shrubs, particularly those they can touch and pick. Trees are good, too, especially those with low, strong branches which can be climbed, such as fruit trees. The availability of dirt to dig, and grass to lie or roll on, autumn leaves to pile and toss makes the outdoors more enjoyable. There is need, too, of course, for a hard surface for riding tricycles and wagons, and maneuvering mechanical toys. Hard surface and dirt surface areas may be separated by means of fences. Younger and older groups may alternate in each area at the beginning and end of the morning, so that they have experiences with different outdoor spaces each day.

Sometimes it is helpful to have a "noisy" room—an indoor space near an outdoor area—equipped with mats, climbing apparatus, carpentry tools. Here two or three obstreperous children can be taken aside and allowed to expend excessive energy in legitimate ways.

Nursery school teachers can be inventive in using what is already part of the outdoors as equipment. We have already mentioned the value of trees, flowers, and leaves. Imaginative teachers can plan pieces of equipment to fit a certain terrain or can have local carpenters build such equipment as a bus or a cage house, whose barred walls can allow exciting zoo play of the animal-children. Even such things as a section of a tree trunk stripped of its bark and properly treated to withstand the outdoors can be used both for climbing or imaginatively as a bus or car. A dentist's chair or a discarded rowboat or any such object has its special possibilities.

Simple but very effective equipment may be suggested by packing boxes, about three feet high. Several of these boxes can be connected with six-foot-long plywood boards, about three-eighths of an inch thick. Such connections make wonderful bridges, and the resiliency of the boards makes them suitable for "jumping" boards.

Large outdoor equipment usually includes a slide, a jungle

gym, a sandbox with a good plywood cover. Smaller pieces of equipment can include one large and two smaller tricycles, two wagons, two cars, a steam roller, balls, and various kinds of digging equipment—trench shovels, pails, spoons, a tire for rolling, paint brushes and cans for outdoor "painting" with water, some sort of hose (unattached) to use with the cars.

Our particular concern is to avoid the use of stereotyped equipment. Imaginative teachers can train themselves to look at equipment from a child's point of view, to discover uses and possibilities in everyday objects which are sometimes more effective than expensive standardized equipment.

FOUR

The Child in School

10

Adjustment

GENERAL CONSIDERATIONS

Most children—and many adults—tend to find adding something new to their lives both stimulating and difficult. Adding something new means growing, and periods of growth are often painful as well as rewarding. We have described age periods when a child is thrusting forth in new directions, his periods of advancement in growth, as periods of "disequilibrium" which make him troublesome to himself and to others. The very young child is, of course, not sufficiently self-aware to know what is happening to him. He may feel unusually stimulated, tense, and excited. He may be frightened and anxious because of new feelings and experiences that threaten his relatively secure way of life.

From the very beginning of life the child must adjust to a variety of internal and external stimuli. A major and dramatic adjustment is demanded when he changes life in the uterus for life outside the mother's body. The mother helps in this adjustment by giving affection, food, and warmth. More changes come with creeping, with walking. Fresh areas of the environment are made accessible, and as the child moves out in his exploration of space, new demands are made on him with regard to what he may or may not touch, what is dangerous and what is safe, what may bring pleasure or displeasure to himself and to the next most important persons in the world to him—his parents. So even before the child begins nursery school, both he and his parents have already worked at problems of adjustment.

Although many parents may already be aware of the manner in which their children customarily handle new experiences, they may not realize that patterns of adjustment are likely to be repeated and are intimately involved in patterns of personality. Even the force with which children react to the stresses of biological growth is often predictable. Some children hit the "bad" stages of growth more violently than do others; for them the stages of 2½, 3½, 4½, for example, may be more tempestuous, or of longer duration, than for other children, who are able to assimilate forces of growth more smoothly.

Adjustment to new experiences in the environment also may follow a pattern. Some children have so many positive abilities that they have tools for successfully meeting new situations. And a past series of successful life experiences tends to build up a feeling of confidence in children, which is progressively helpful. Such children seem to like everyone and to think everyone likes them, so that they approach new experiences positively and successfully, and they often spontaneously help other children accept these situations.

Sometimes such children have been helped by the mother toward a positive approach. The self-confident, unfearful exploration of new horizons by the high-powered, mesomorphic child, however, seems to come quite independent of parental aid and quite unrelated to the success or failure of past experiences. He seems compelled by an inner drive to barge ahead into new experiences and seems relatively unaffected by the disaster or success of his actions. Sometimes it seems more a question of the world's adjusting to him, rather than his modifying his approach to adapt to new situations.

The adjustment which we wish to consider here is that of the child's first school experience, his coming to nursery school. There are relatively few children to whom this adjustment presents no problem. Indeed, initially, some simply cannot handle this new situation and have to give up, at least temporarily. They may be quite unready for a social experience outside the home even though their chronological age is the same as that of other nursery school children. Children need a full experience of being babies, completely dependent on a protective and loving adult, before they can be ready for an experience in a group of children. Sometimes the close arrival of another sibling has interfered with their full enjoyment of babyhood. Other children who consistently reject nursery school may have had an unusually happy experience at home and with children in the neighborhood which adequately satisfies their needs, so that nursery school is an unwelcome intrusion.

Others may give an initial impression of adjustment, then break down later. The parent and teacher must not make the mistake of believing that once a child has achieved an initial adjustment all his troubles are over. We are often particularly wary of a child who adjusts too quickly. He is often one who has been intent on "skimming the cream" from the situation, and he is very likely to have a setback later on. In any case, adjustment of some sort is a continuous process which the experienced teacher works at constantly.

Teacher and parent must not be dismayed if the course of the year brings repeated tears from a child, so long as there are happy and successful periods in addition to the troubled times. Children usually express their unhappiness in crying, and although the teacher must take the crying child from the group as soon as possible, since crying is often contagious and distressing to other children, any child's need to cry must be accepted even while the teacher comforts and attempts to distract him. A show of affection from the teacher may help children even when they violently seem to reject her advances. Verbalizations such as "Too bad" or "Let's see what we can find for you" or other soothing words may help; or the proffer of a lap, Kleenex, a hand. Taking a child out for a walk sometimes helps him get his sobs under control. A repetitive and silent pastime is good, too—dumping sand, pouring water. If, however, the child breaks down again when the teacher tries to take him back to the other children, she should probably summon his mother to take him home.

In some cases children are overfatigued by the strain of adjustment. Going to nursery school may cost them too much energy. Although they may seem to be all right while at school, the effort involved may make them overtired and tense at home, and it is questionable whether the adjustment is worth the price.

Although we have worked out what we consider to be the best way initially to present to the child the new experience of being with a group of children and separated from his mother, there is no overall long-range program which works for every child.

For those who do have difficulty, care on the part of the teacher and cooperation and understanding from the mother can often bring about an eventual good adjustment. Possible techniques are as numerous and varied as are the individualities of the children involved.

But it is not just separation from the mother that is involved in the child's going to nursery school. Most children have already adjusted to such separation in accepting a baby-sitter at home, when the mother has been away. At home the child is supported by familiar surroundings and toys. At school, however, he has lost everything, both parents and familiar environment, and must add to this the strange group of other children. The presence of so many other children, each primarily intent on furthering his own interests (frequently at the expense of others), is new.

Adjusting to the social inexperience of other children is

particularly difficult for the child who has enjoyed a somewhat protected adult society. The need to share possessions with others is often hard to accept. Many a 2-year-old, particularly, spends his first days at school in a futile effort to carry around and thus possess all the desirable toys he sees. He is often so handicapped by his possessions that he finds it impossible to play with them! Only gradually does he adjust to the idea that he does not need to clutch in order to enjoy, that there are "other" toys, and that there is such a thing as "taking turns." (A first-day 2-year-old wailed in grief at seeing other children at her table share the basket of graham crackers. Then she tried stuffing crackers into her mouth as fast as possible in order to control the situation, while tears streamed. Tension visibly relaxed as she saw there were still plenty of crackers. Fortunately the possessiveness of 2-year-olds is not directed always to the same objects!)

Also, the very multiplicity of new impressions is difficult to assimilate, especially in the highly aware and highly sensitive child. The space of the school must seem overwhelmingly large to a small child. A new child often wanders around in bewilderment, unable to orient himself in space, to find a teacher who means security or a mother who has disappeared from sight. Many a new child makes his way to all the doors, hopefully trying to open each and thus to find an answer to his dilemma. (It is important that a teacher see this need immediately and stay close to such a child to give him verbal and physical support.)

Children who have high auditory sensitivity may be overstimulated and frightened by the noise of the other children at school; they need to learn that all loud noises are not fearful, that children scream from delight as well as pain. Such learning, we may hastily add, does not best come by a head-on attack of this problem. The child who is sensitive to loud sounds needs first of all to be protected from excessive noise.

And there is a great deal of adjustment that comes through the acceptance of a close relationship with a teacher. This is an extremely important adjustment, closely related to the separation from the mother. The child grows in personal-social development as he learns that an adult other than his parents can be loving and attentive and understanding. The teacher becomes a mother substitute, yet fundamentally different from a mother in that her attention is available to all the children. Somehow the good teacher must manage to be personal in her affection, but impartial in her favors. The child who has a good experience with a teacher who really accepts him and understands him as he is develops a new perspective with regard to people.

This close relationship with another adult sometimes brings with it new and difficult conceptions as to the values in life. One excessively neat child from a very tidy home, horrified when she saw the children in the nursery school spilling sand on the floor, ran to her favorite teacher in alarm and pulled her to the spot so that something could be done to correct this misdemeanor. The teacher smiled, assured her that this was all right, and showed her how the sand could easily be swept up when the children were finished with their playing. The child, who was very fond of the teacher and respected her judgments, thereby moved into a new idea for social behavior.

When the teacher's notions of discipline are different from those to which a child is accustomed, this also can present a problem in adjustment. Some children have to test the limits of discipline at once to see what they can get away with; some find new approaches from adults quite threatening experiences. But when the child discovers the teacher as a friend, and often as an ideal, the ways of adapting to experience which the teacher represents reinforce or enlarge the teachings of his parents.

Usually, however, providing his mother remains at school, the child can accept any or all problems which arise and enjoys very much coming to nursery school. Just his mother's presence is enough to give him the security to take on new experiences. Consequently, all children should visit the nursery school with the mother the first time. With very young or immature children, the mother stays through the first sessions of school. The problem of adjustment basically becomes one of helping the child take on all the new learnings that nursery school provokes. First he may need the presence of his mother, gradually he needs only the support of his teacher, and increasingly he develops a self-confidence and security that come through problems met successfully and happily in interaction with the group.

That is, the techniques of effecting an adjustment to school involve a release from the mother and acceptance of the teacher and group of children at school. We shall describe some of the techniques that we have found helpful in adjusting the child to a release of his mother and acceptance of his group of peers.

SEPARATION FROM MOTHER

Introduction to School

"How do you go about adjusting a child to nursery school?" is one of the questions that inevitably arises at the opening of the school year, and the question usually means, "How do you handle the first major separation of mother and child?" Sometimes the problem is very easily handled, but often skilled techniques on the part of the teacher, and patient cooperation from the parent, are required. The age of the child, the personality of the child, and the personality of the parent frequently determine the course the adjustment will take.

Careful planning is necessary to assure the child of the most appropriate and congenial experiences on his first day at school. On applying for a place in the school, the parent will fill out an introductory report, which contains pertinent information about the child. This report tells the birth dates, nationality, education, and occupation of the parents; number and ages of siblings in the family; and the birth history, health history, and developmental history of the child. There is also space for reporting exceptional or significant facts in the family history, or the child's behavior characteristics. From such a report, the teacher may gain a general orientation to the child and his family, and be alerted to any exceptional deviations from a normal pattern of behavior or development. If this report reveals that the child has an unusual problem, the teacher may very well arrange for a psychological examination before the child comes to school. Or if this service is not available, she may wish to have an interview with the parents alone, to determine whether or not the child's problems can suitably be handled at nursery school.

In all cases, however, before the child comes to school with the group, it is wise for the parent, teacher, and child to have a preliminary meeting alone in the nursery school room itself. This meeting should take place near the time the child plans to enter the group, so that his memory of the experience can easily carry over to the first day of school. The teacher must see to it that the nursery school is attractively arranged for the visit: toys easily accessible on low shelves, the entire setting as bright and cheerful and well-planned as it will be throughout the school year.

After a pleasant and informal greeting to the child—some comment appropriate to his age about his clothes or about the toys at the school—the parent and teacher can sit together on small chairs in the nursery school room and encourage the child to examine the equipment. Often the child needs to hold his mother's hand as he walks around the room. Sometimes he prefers the security of his mother's lap and observes cautiously from this vantage. Or he may run gleefully from object to object, throwing things from the shelves, shouting with unrestrained delight. If the child is unusually shy, or excessively boisterous, the parent may become uneasy, but the teacher must urge her to allow the child to do as he pleases. Any pressure to conformity at this time may arouse a resistance that may later prove to be most difficult to overcome. Meanwhile, the teacher can observe the child and, depending on what the child is doing, have an informal interview with the parent.

Two things can be accomplished when the child thus visits the nursery school before he attends with the group. The child can meet the new environment in the way that is most congenial to him, and the teacher can observe how he adjusts to this fairly simple situation, and can thus make tentative plans for his next visit to school. If he is not urged either to start or stop activity, he will be more likely to be ready for his next big step—coming to school with the other children. His mother should accompany him on this visit, too, and again he should be allowed to meet the situation in his own way.

The conversation between the teacher and parent at their first interview must grow from the situation. The teacher wants to know as much as possible about the child, but if he stays close to his mother, or if he is self-conscious and attentive to the conversation of adults, the teacher must divert the comments to subjects of a general, informal nature. If the parent persists in a kind of remark that seems unsuitable in the child's presence, the teacher can tactfully suggest that this interview has been arranged only for the child to become acquainted with the head teacher and the school before the other children are there, and that very soon another interview will be arranged with the parent alone to talk about the child.

When a young child separates easily from his mother to explore the school, the teacher can ask general questions of the mother about the routines of eating, sleeping, and toilet training; about the nature of the child's play; or about any problems she may care to bring up. Such a conversation should not be carried on in the spirit of intensive investigation, but should serve to put the mother at ease in talking to the teacher, assure her of the teacher's interest in the child, and suggest the teacher as a source of help in the event the mother needs assistance in matters pertaining to the normal problems of children.

It is good for the child to see all the rooms in the nursery school on his first visit, and to look at the outside as well as the inside equipment, even if he must do this from his mother's arms. The teacher can describe the usual routine of the day to the mother, predicting what she thinks may be the child's reaction on his first day at school. She should encourage the mother to plan for only a brief session the first day and to expect to take the child home before he becomes fatigued, since first experiences are likely to be highly stimulating ones. In this preliminary meeting it is good if the child is interested in making something, as for instance in painting a picture at the easel, for this gives him a token to take home, a tangible link between his school and his home experience.

Since problems in adjustment vary with ages and personalities, techniques useful in expediting this adjustment vary accordingly. There are general procedures, however, for all children with regard to what the parent does in nursery school while she stays, and the manner in which she takes her leave.

Mothers often have to remain at school for more sessions with the 2-year-old than with older children, but normally the longest time a mother has to stay with any child is three weeks. Two or three sessions of a full morning in the nursery school are usually enough. Sometimes only one session is necessary, though a mother must be ready to return if the child suddenly needs her. Parents are encouraged to stay for one session at least, even when the child appears to be perfectly adjusted. Mothers who stay at nursery school are encouraged to bring knitting or reading, to be there mainly to afford a feeling of security to the child. They should try to be as "uninteresting" as possible and to do as little as they can with or for the child. From the beginning it is good to tell the parent to try to be "like the paper on the wall"; to sit in a corner in full view of the child, yet to be apparently too busy to help in the routines or to join in the play. Such a procedure on the part of the mother allows more opportunity for the teacher to get the child's attention and to make herself known to him as a special friend who can take care of his needs as well as join in his play.

As the child makes excursions away from the parent which take him farther and farther afield, and for increasingly long periods of time, the teacher can urge the mother to leave the nursery school playroom. Sometimes she merely moves out into the hall or to the teacher's office—to a place where the child can go at periodic intervals to check up on her whereabouts. Sometimes a child may want to carry all the toys from the playroom to the place where his mother is sitting. A teacher can handle this by saying that the child may carry off only one toy, that the other toys are "needed" in the big playroom, and that when he is "ready" to leave his mother he can come back to play with the other toys. (Words such as "need" and "ready" are extremely useful in dealing with children of nursery school age.) Usually the child's interest in a single toy will wane, and he can be persuaded to join the other children in the playroom.

After a mother has served her time in the playroom, then in the hallway, she can plan to leave entirely for a brief interval. It is well for her to tell the child where she is going and to assure him when she is coming back. Often she can leave one of her belongings with him as a token of her presence—her pocketbook or her scarf. A half-hour's absence is good to start with, and this should be arranged when the child is already happily occupied with some activity of his own choice. It is not good for the mother to be absent for the first time during activities that require group organization, such as music, stories, or crackers and milk. Such routines seem to be the most difficult ones for the child to accept, and it is a mistake to ask his acceptance of them while he is still coping with the problem of separation from his mother.

The mother may then leave for gradually increasing intervals depending on the success of her first excursions away from the child. While she is away, the teacher must carefully watch the child to pick up any signs of uneasiness. Here, as in many situations, it is well to anticipate a crisis, to provide a comforting lap before one is fearfully demanded, or to present a diverting situation before play deteriorates into loneliness. The mother should not go far away at first, and should leave a telephone number so that she can be summoned, if, in a teacher's opinion, her return might prevent an unhappy situation or if the child has already broken down.

The procedures for adjustment of the child to nursery school vary with his age. Many schools have groups of 2-, 3-, and 4-year-old children.[1] The 2-year-old child attends two mornings a week from 9:00 to 11:30; the 3- and 4-year-olds, three mornings a week from 9:00 to 12:00. These schedules are flexible, however; the development of the child and his particular needs indicate the group in which he belongs and the number of mornings he attends nursery school. Members of all the groups are usually taken in gradually at the outset; each group begins with a small number of children, although the beginning group is larger for each succeeding age. On the first day of school it is often wise to divide the children into two groups and to have only a short, one-hour session with each group. To the initial group of children are added other children as the situation allows.

The 2-year-old group, assuming that there is a 2-year-old

1. One system is to divide groups at half-year intervals, thus having 2½-year-old, 3-, 3½-, and 4-year-old groups.

group, is smaller than other groups at school, for the 2-year-old needs a great deal of individual attention. Particularly at the beginning of the school year, there must be enough teachers so that a teacher can take over the care of a child in much the way a mother does. Very often a 2-year-old adjusts to nursery school through his relationship with a single teacher. She must toilet him, sit near him when he has his crackers and milk, comfort him when he is frustrated, provide a lap when he feels insecure.

Most 2-year-olds demand a more "motherly" relationship with a teacher than do older children. When this sort of relationship is intense, a teacher has a special responsibility not only to provide the comfort a child needs, but to help him gradually find release from excessive dependency and attain happy play with other children and an easy relationship with other teachers. Children who have been unusually dependent on parents often transfer this relationship to a teacher. While the "mother" relationship of a teacher is a good one for purposes of adjustment, it must be considered a relationship that should be worked through, rather than one that should continue.

The teacher must know the simple, repetitive kind of play that is of particular delight to a 2-year-old. Often she must sit on the floor to show him how to play, doing the same thing over and over. When he joins in this play and finds it amusing and interesting, the 2-year-old is usually well on his way toward adjustment. Affection, humor, and the skillful presentation of simple amusements are excellent techniques for adjusting the 2-year-old to the nursery school.

The general techniques for adjusting the 3-year-old child are the same as those for the 2-year-old, except that all the periods of transition from mother to teacher, to other teachers, to friend, and then to group are much more quickly and easily managed. The teacher can often suggest play, or can initiate play by arranging equipment, or by offering a word of praise.

Her participation in play and physical care is not as great as with the 2-year-old. The happy adjustment of the 3-year-old very often depends on finding a friend. Intimate friendships flourish, and the teacher can encourage them by taking two children away by themselves to engage in a special project. Or she can secure the cooperation of mothers to bring two children together for play periods outside of nursery school, or to join in car pools so that they enjoy a special relationship with each other as they ride to and from school.

There are fewer adjustment problems with the 4-year-old child. (But when such a problem does occur at this age, it is liable to be severe and to take a long time to work through.) Four usually radiates good fellowship, and his high drive for social relations makes him a ready member of a group. When he comes with his parent to look at the school for the first time, he may be somewhat self-conscious. The teacher approaches him best in an indirect manner at first, casually walking around and telling him, along with other children, what to do with various pieces of equipment in the school. The 4-year-old is often ready to have his mother leave on the first day; indeed he sometimes orders her to do so.

Examples of Typical Adjustment Problems

Techniques for adjusting children to the nursery school must vary with personality. No overall program for adjustment can be described, because of the variety of personalities in any one group. The skilled teacher, through years of experience, becomes aware of certain patterns in children's personalities and remembers a number of particular devices which have, in the past, aided in adjusting such children to school. The problem of adjustment is often doubly complicated when a mother's personality also offers some patterns of resistance to an easy separation from her child. The following examples illustrate the complexity of the problem.

Jim, a 2-year-old with very little language, spent his first mornings in nursery school whining and crying. He hit his mother constantly and made excessive and unreasonable demands of her which she was unable to satisfy. When she picked him up, he wanted to get down. If she sat in one place, he pulled her to another. He dragged her to various piles of equipment, then screamed in rage because she apparently did not do with a toy what he wanted her to do. Jim was worse the second morning than the first, and his mother was embarrassed and confused. No teacher could reach him, for he hid his head in his mother's skirt and screamed as a teacher approached him.

A conference with the mother revealed that Jim had a very difficult relationship with her at home and that the difficulties were intensified, but basically the same, when she took him out in company. When Jim came the third morning and began to act in the same manner, a teacher picked him up quickly, told him to say good-bye to his mother, who was going to the store, and carried him quickly outside to the sandbox. Jim's outbreak of temper lasted only a couple of minutes. He quickly became interested in the sand toys. Within fifteen minutes the teacher was able to bring him back into the nursery school smiling happily, sufficiently relaxed to have a happy morning. Thereafter, at the teacher's suggestion, some person other than his mother, either his father or the mother of another child in the group, brought Jim to the nursery school for about a month, and his own mother called for him at noon. Jim had no trouble taking leave of the other people. The mother needed some help in improving her relations with her little boy at home, and after six weeks she herself was able to bring him without the pain of a turbulent scene at parting.

Henry, another 2-year-old, had a problem similar to Jim's. Unfortunately, in this case, there was no father or neighbor to help with the transportation. But arrangements were made so that Henry's older brother, who was eight years old, could come to play with him at school one or two mornings a week. Henry had no trouble on these mornings and entered with great enthusiasm into all the activities.

When his mother brought him for the fifth morning and he began to make a scene with her again, a teacher at once stepped in and took him in her arms and began rapid conversation about all the fun he had had on previous occasions. She waved good-bye to the mother and kept Henry rapidly moving from one activity to another, and soon he was playing without assistance. But Henry's parting scenes with his mother continued a long time. She needed considerable reassurance that he was indeed quite happy in a few minutes after her departure, so she was asked to observe his play from behind a one-way screen in the nursery, where she could watch him without being seen.

The teachers explained to Henry's mother that Henry's fuss at parting might continue for a number of reasons that should be of no deep concern to her. He was a child highly patterned in behavior, and with some children the pattern of resistance often persists even after the need for it is gone. Some children may continue dramatic parting scenes, even though they enjoy themselves after the separation, because the contest of wills with their parents is a source of pleasure to them. Often they enjoy the attention that their resistance brings. At other times crying may merely be the expression of the tension a child naturally feels at facing a new situation. As a rule calm and loving behavior consistently shown at parting, and a happy experience with teachers and children at the school, soon establish a new pattern at the time of separation from the mother.

In the case of the 2-year-olds Jim and Henry, an abrupt separation from the mother seemed to be indicated after they had been given the opportunity to spend several mornings in the nursery school with the help of the mother's presence. With these children sudden departure worked best. (Indeed these parents had already discovered that abrupt departure worked whenever they had to leave the child at home.) The longer the mother stayed, the worse the separation problems became. The mother's presence tended to intensify negative patterns of behavior.

In other cases, however, abrupt partings are completely inadvisable for both mother and child.

Mary (aged three-and-a-half years) was a child who had to go at her own pace and to make her own decisions. This had been a basic personality pattern from infancy, and her mother was wise enough to recognize it and respect it. A developmental examination helped the teachers to understand better this little girl's personality. She exhibited a very rigid, patterned kind of behavior, worked problems out surely but slowly within strict patterns of organization which she set up for herself.

Mary's mother had to sit in the hall for a long time, and Mary checked up on her with the same questions, in the same manner, for a number of days. Toward teachers' advances she turned an unreceptive, cold stare for the first week or so, then suddenly, and for no apparent reason, began responding to their attentions.

It became clear that Mary might adjust to school through a warm and intimate relation with a teacher who acted as a special friend and mother substitute to her. Mary verbalized this one day to the teacher, "I'm your little girl, and you're my little mummy." Indeed, she verbalized much of her progress to her mother, saying, "Today I'll cry a little while," or "Today I won't cry at all." She also told her mother when she felt she could try school alone.

But for a long time she needed the support of certain props to help her adjust to the routine. Each morning she had to ride a particular blue bike before her mother left; if another child was using the bike, her mother had to wait until it was free. Indoors she needed always to begin with painting, moving to clay, then to puzzles. Only half of her attention was occupied with these activities; she observed the other children as she quietly manipulated these materials. During music she needed to sit in a special rocking chair; for a long time she did not sing at all. But gradually the periods of watching became shorter, the rocking chair was abandoned. Mary was a happy member of the group, increasingly spontaneous in her play.

There are some children who cannot easily release their parents at school. If the parents waited for the "right" moment, involving a spontaneous decision from the child, they might wait indefinitely. Such parents need to be helped by the teacher to make their leave-taking quick and decisive. The teacher must take over and give a great deal of attention to the child at the time of parting, to counteract the tension and very often real apprehension that is overwhelming for the moment. With such children, the emotional upheaval usually does not last for long. They need support at the moment of stress, but frequently suffer more from anticipated troubles than from any real experiences.

Chip's mother was very much troubled by her son's worries about her leaving. "He talks and frets about it all the time at home," she said, "and he is afraid to get into the car with me, because he feels this is the beginning of the end." Once at school, 3-year-old Chip could not even release into play as long as his mother was around. He was so apprehensive about her threatened departure that he did not do much more than stand guard over her. The situation seemed to get no better with repetition; apprehension seemed rather to increase.

The teacher called up Chip's mother at home and suggested to her that at the next school session parting would have to be quick and decisive. She was on hand when Chip and his mother appeared; she explained to him in his mother's presence that his mother had to go away at once to do her errands, that she would return, and that the teacher would "take care of" him while she was gone. He of course cried, in a resigned and wistful fashion, and needed several kisses good-bye.

He was soon happily chatting with his teacher and playing with other children. In the course of the morning, he suddenly stopped his play, came to the teacher, and made crying and whining noises, extremely unconvincing manifestations of grief. "What are you doing?" the teacher asked.

"I'm crying," said Chip. Again the teacher comforted him, explained his mother's absence, and how he was being cared for. He quickly stopped his crying. Later in the morning he suddenly exchanged meaningful glances with the teacher and broke into a rather sheepish grin. "I'm not crying," he said.

"We must tell your mother when she comes that you didn't have to cry," said the teacher.

Now Chip remembers his role of grief only seldom, but from time to time comes to the teacher to remind her, "I don't cry any more." He has a great sense of pride in this accomplishment, and it is a real one.

As we have said before, when both mother and child are too dependent on one another, adjustment to nursery school is most difficult.

Irene (aged two-and-a-half years) also had a pattern of over-dependency that was reciprocated by her mother. The father explained the situation to the teacher, "The psychological umbilical cord has never been cut." Yet in this instance it seemed not dependency but the child's drive for power that was involved.

A developmental examination showed Irene to be both superior intellectually and socially mature. But her procedure in the examination revealed her tenacity in holding on to patterns. She held on to patterns at home too—only her mother could dress her, her mother had to sit by her bed till she went to sleep, only her mother could take her to the bathroom. Other patterns suggested her control of the environment too: a special cup for milk, a special fork, a special chair. Her mother was hampered by Irene's imperious demands on her time, for the child ruled that she would not play with her toys unless her mother played with her. She allowed such necessary defections as her mother's sweeping or preparing dinner. But as her mother worked she refused to play alone, sat and watched her, sucking her thumb, waiting till she was at her command again.

The first time the teacher attempted to keep Irene alone at nursery school, Irene gave a violent display of temper. She screamed, she hit, she threw away any object in which the teacher attempted to interest her. One thing attracted her attention; she liked to hold the guinea pig and to squeeze him until he squirmed and squeaked and ran away. Then she demanded his return and a repetition of the procedure.

Such a limited curriculum had to be discontinued and the mother reinstated in the school. The way has been long and tedious, progress painfully slow, for Irene has built up elaborate patterns, and the mother is elaborately enslaved. Again this is an example of how the difficulty is increased when two individuals are involved, for although the mother wishes to work through this problem, she is already deeply ensnared in it. She is afraid of her little girl and overpowered by her. And until she is ready to have a different relationship with her daughter at home, little can be done at school. Irene's behavior is an extreme example of 2½-year-old behaviors. Attendance at nursery school may be a complicating factor in such a child's life. Actually, continued attendance at nursery school might not be in Irene's best interests.

When both mother and child are not involved in adjustment problems, the way is easier. With Douglas, it was his mother, not he, who needed help. Her problem had to do with excessive fears as to health and safety, and a subsequent overprotection and need to be constantly near her little boy.

Douglas did not start school till late October, when he was three-and-a-half, because of the mother's fear of polio. When at length he started, she worried about the tricycles, the ladders, the open doors, the open windows. Although the teacher assured her that health and safety precautions were of paramount importance to the school, she seemed to need reassurance of special care for *her* son. One day when he came to school she reported he had just received a shot for an allergy. "Will you watch him?" she asked.

"Watch him?" the teacher asked, somewhat puzzled as to what she was to do.

"Yes, be careful. He may get dizzy and fall down!"

Douglas almost never falls, with or without shots, although he is quite active. He is a highly independent little child, unusually outgoing. Indeed, his extraordinary self-sufficiency in spite of the timidities that his mother is trying to instill in him suggests that all children may not be equally sensitive to such influences in their environment. For his highly fearful mother and overprotected environment have not at all served to set up patterns of caution in this little boy.

Although Douglas's mother stayed at school a number of days, he paid no attention to her, indeed successfully evaded the efforts she made to assist him. Only one major concession was made by the school to her need for extra protection. Douglas is brought to school a half-hour late each morning and taken home a half-hour early, so that he will not have to go out of doors as the other children do at those hours. Such a compromise seems to have provided a happy solution, and both mother and child are enjoying nursery school very much.

When parents themselves rebel against a child's tyranny and determine to be free, the way to adjustment is often a stormy one, but sometimes surprisingly short.

Such was the case with 3½-year-old *Johnnie.* He was a big boy, strong, boisterous, out of bounds and violent in most of his behavior. When his mother left, after a suitable period of observation and preparation, he flew into a rage, for he was accustomed to directing her activities. He attacked teachers and children with fists, and screamed "No" to any suggestion. Even when no suggestion had been made he would come up unprovoked, on his own, with a defiant "I won't eat milk and crackers." The teacher assured him he did not have to do anything. Sometimes he surreptitiously played with a toy, but on the side, out of the way of observation, for he was most careful at first to get no credit for compliance.

Two events seemed to help Johnnie in his tempestuous adjustment. First was the developmental examination, in which his behavior was the epitome of negativism. He either refused participation or participated in completely unacceptable ways. He threw the materials on the floor, scribbled on the table, banged the blocks, and shouted defiantly. The teacher-examiner calmly removed one material after another, allowed Johnnie to express the gamut of defiance. She did not pretend to approve of his defiance; she announced what were considered the limits of behavior and removed materials as Johnnie tested the limits. Yet she indicated, even as she controlled his behavior, that Johnnie was still acceptable to her as a child worthy of kind and considerate attention and interest.

Possibly this developmental examination, in which Johnnie

expressed extreme negativism and still was accepted, provided the needed opportunity for testing his acceptability and paved the way to compliance. Yet at school he seemed to have to save face by making a final demand. He insisted that his mother allow him to stand outside the door alone and watch her depart. He had to enter the nursery school on his own terms.

There was no sudden and dramatic end of a bid for power, however. Johnnie's pattern was too deep-seated for that. First he attempted to control the teacher who had given him the examination. He shouted commands at her, refused compliance with any of her specific demands. She learned to keep demands at a minimum, to approach him obliquely by talking to other children about what *they* could do. Then after Johnnie had performed she tried to remember to praise him for his very real accomplishments. Gradually creative activities replaced his interest in personal control. Another rugged part of the journey, however, has involved personal relations with other children, for, of course, Johnnie saw no way initially to approach them except in a dominating manner.

After three months he showed real progress and gave promise that by the end of the year he would have learned the difficult lesson that involved a readjustment of his total 3½-year-old personality.

Lisa, a 2-year-old child, was tall and well built, with light brown curly hair, dark brown eyes that looked habitually tired, with dark circles around them. Her expression seemed constantly watchful and attentive. She rarely gave the impression of being relaxed or at ease. Even her motions seemed tense.

Lisa clung close to her mother at first; her eyes surveyed every aspect of the room. She made almost no excursions away from her mother, but remained constantly watchful. As she watched she clutched a huge dirty blanket. This blanket she had to carry with her to each new situation.

Lisa's mother was able to leave after a couple of weeks, and Lisa was able to manage nursery school with special provisions. She could not join a large group in play, but seemed to like to watch the others as she rode the rocking horse or played with clay. In these situations she did not need her blanket. But when the whole group came together for music and stories, the experience seemed to be too much for her. She frequently burst into tears, needed a teacher's lap and her blanket.

A developmental examination finally gave a clue to Lisa's trouble. In the examination she showed that she was unusually aware of everything that went on around her. It seemed that as she watched she shared so intensely in the activities of the other children that it made her exhausted. Her physical mechanism was actually strained, and her limited emotional and social abilities fatigued by the demands her extraordinarily high visual awareness made on her.

The examination suggested the need for a simplifying of the nursery school day. The parents were advised to give high-calorie snacks (such as marshmallows) at periods of fatigue. More relaxing experiences were also encouraged with sand, clay, and water, which did not involve so much reaction to other people.

Lisa was soon able with such help to enjoy a full morning of nursery school without recourse to nervous tears. And increasingly the blanket, her needed implement for relaxation, has not been taken from the shelf in her cubbyhole.

Sometimes a child's adjustment to nursery school is threatened by a seemingly minor event. Since the child of nursery school age is usually too young to be articulate about his problems, a chain of unfortunate reactions may be set in motion by a small maladjustment which he cannot report and which goes unnoticed in the first days of school.

Often problems of this sort come to children who have apparently adjusted very well at the outset. The child seems to be busy, happy, and outgoing. The mother is very much pleased and leaves, and since the child is so well occupied and makes no fuss, he is liable to be neglected by a teacher whose attention is demanded by children who are more troublesome. Consequently, it is important in the first days of school so to control enrollment and supply of teachers that there can be a constant awareness of each child's reactions. A teacher must always be ready to step in when a child indicates even by such slight gestures as thumb in mouth, eye blinking, or unusual silence or thoughtfulness that something is amiss. If the teacher can step in and give love and protection *before* the child goes to pieces, his security may not be seriously threatened.

It was clear, for example, that 2-year-old *Danny* did not even notice that his mother was gone. He was constantly active, highly eager to explore everything at once. He did not even look up high enough to find out what the teachers' faces looked like, but kept up a running commentary as though he were talking to his mother. "Look at me, Mommie. See, honey!" he kept saying as he rapidly ran around. Then one day, when the joys of exploration began to fail, he began to look at the teachers. Suddenly his little face puckered and he was ready to cry, to howl for his "Mommie." But a teacher picked him up before the cry came, held him close like a "Mommie," gave him something to eat and drink, took him away from the group for special comfort, explained where his mother was, that she would soon be back, and until then asked if she could "take care of him." This worked.

Two-year-old *Stevie* had a problem similar to Danny's, in that he did not really realize what it meant to have his mother leave. She stayed near him for many sessions; he played happily but silently with cars and trains. Then one day she told him she had to leave but that she would bring him back some little hooks for the train that was broken. He waved good-bye.

Soon after she left, he suddenly got up from his play with a troubled expression on his face. Like a child walking in his sleep, he went to the next room. A teacher at once followed close behind. In the next room, he looked in a closet, looked in the bathroom, went to the back door which led to the outside. He was about to break into tears when the teacher went to him, picked him up, talked rapidly to him about how his mother had told her she said good-bye to Stevie and was going to the store to buy hooks for the little train. She then held him on her lap, kept reminding him of his mother's errand, and stayed close to him all the morning. He was soon rewarded by his mother's return with the hooks for the train, and another special gift, a book about trains. The mother took over the teacher's supporting role, and Stevie sat on her lap as the teacher read Stevie's new book to the group. The child went home happy, but sometimes such an experience is repeated several times.

Another child, 2-year-old *Carol,* continued to play happily after she said good-bye to her mother out of doors. But when she came indoors the change of scene prompted her to take new stock of her surroundings, and she suddenly felt a terrible loneliness. Again a teacher had quickly to step in and help her to manage the transition that was so difficult for her. Changes from outdoors to indoors, or from one activity to another, are frequently times when children become unhappy.

Another child, *Charlie,* aged two-and-a-half, was apt to fall into periods of silence and inactivity. A teacher had to watch for these, provide new toys, or shift him bodily to new interests. He was not naturally a spontaneous child, but if he had been neglected in these periods of inactivity, in all probability he would have been unhappy and at length resentful of school.

Still another child was particularly sensitive to noises and had to be taken from the group when the children became too raucous. He could not engage at first in the group music and rhythm session. Excessive sound was troubling and confusing to him. Still another child was upset by the behavior of the children in his car pool, and an alert teacher had to discover his troubled reactions in this situation.

In all of these instances it was important for adjustment that the teacher note early signs of trouble and make efforts to correct them as soon as possible.

It should be noted that the majority of these children described as having difficulty in adjustment are 2-year-olds. This difficulty in adjustment is the chief reason that many schools find it impractical to include 2-year-olds, having neither the experience nor a large enough staff to meet the demands of a slow adjustment. Some argue that Twos are too young for nursery school. We ourselves have found many children to be far more ready by two-and-a-half. (However, it must be admitted that these very children who have difficulty at two years might also have had difficulty as late as three years if they had entered school at this later date. But the length of their adjustment period might well have been shorter when they were older.)

A warning should be given here of the importance of differentiating between the child who can be helped to make an adjustment within a two- or three-week period, and the one who only becomes more anxious as time goes on. Thinking that considerable time was needed, we have in the past continued efforts at adjusting a child for a period as long as two or three months, only to find that the situation became worse rather than better as time went on. By the end of several months you may have a constantly unhappy child both at home and at school, and also a mother who feels both helpless and inadequate.

We now feel that it is wise to terminate these situations after an initial good trial period, emphasizing to both parent and child that he is not yet ready to come to school but that he will be in time. Often a child who has had this unhappy initial experience becomes ready in the spring and even asks to return to school. In the meantime the mother can be urged to plan social experiences for him with some other child, either in his own backyard or in a neutral place such as a park.

Techniques Useful in Effecting Separation from the Mother

The examples already given suggest that the separation from the mother must be carefully planned and that techniques for carrying through this separation may vary because of the age of the child, the personality of the child, and the personality of the parent.

Separation from the mother, it is clear, is one of the major problems of adjustment to nursery school. A review of the techniques which we have found valuable shows that they may be considered in six categories, as utilizing primarily (a) the mother, (b) the teacher, (c) other people, (d) objects, things, or activities, (e) routines, space and time orientation, and (f) the developmental examination.

a. *If the mother* herself is not too clinging and can accept the teacher's suggestions, her presence at nursery school for a time while the child makes his tentative explorations gives the child the feeling of security he needs to bolster his handling of all the new experiences. We have shown that although some children may be able to say good-bye to their mother, or may even order her to go, others may have to endure sharp pain at the moment of her leaving, because their own emotions at this departure are so intense. Such emotions are not always those of sorrow or insecurity. Sometimes they are expressions of rage from a child who is accustomed to dominate his mother, and such a child is sometimes helped if the adults can give him the last word and let him dominate in a token way.

For example, the child may have to sit on the doorstep and watch the car go, or he may have to order the mother to return after she is halfway to the door, for a second good-bye kiss. Still other children, while they are clearly ready for nursery school and ready for a separation from the mother, experience such feelings of unhappiness at saying good-bye that it is better at first if they are protected from the necessity of direct farewells. In situations of this sort, the mother can explain to the child while he is happily playing that "soon" she must go home for a while and prepare his lunch, or go marketing, or go to the dentist, and that the teacher will "take care of him" while she is gone.

It is usually good for the mother to make such statements in the presence of the teacher who is assigned especially to look out for the child. Then, if he begins at once to protest or complain, as he is liable to do, the teacher can distract him at once with conversation about something else, or she can divert him with some new or interesting toy. Once he is happily engaged again, his mother can slip away. As soon as the child notices she is gone, the teacher must be on hand to say calmly, and with a smile, "Yes, remember she told us she was going marketing, and that I was to take care of you till she comes back." Verbalizations about the routine help some children, too. "First we play, and then have milk and crackers, and then music, and after the story Mummy will come back to get you." Children themselves often talk about the schedule, seem to gain security from a knowledge of what's coming next and from knowing that the predictable sequence of events will at length bring mother and home.

The teacher must then stay close to the child and offer further reassurances and distractions as they seem to be necessary. It is well for the mother to stay away only a short time on these first excursions, or to be in a place where the teacher can readily summon her by telephone. Even if she is gone for only ten minutes, and the child has accepted this separation, progress has been made. When the mother returns, the teacher must be there to verbalize for him. "See, your mother came back, and I took care of you, and now we can tell your mother what you did while she was away."

Sometimes a child is helped by being given something of his mother's to keep: a scarf, pocketbook, postcard. Some children, especially 4-year-olds, can be reassured by phoning their mother in the morning. (Indeed, Fours often have to be adjusted through words and understanding. Humor, joking, making funny noises sometimes helps, too, in that it is distracting and relieves tension, but great caution must be exercised here in that some children resist humor when they feel frightened. In any case, humor should involve subtle communication so that the child is not overpowered, does not feel he is being made fun of.)

Younger children may merely need the simple verbal assurance that "Mummy's coming later" when they appear apprehensive or ask questions. And although you can talk about home and mother with some children in the first weeks of adjustment to this separation, with others it is the worst thing you can do. Four-year-olds are more likely to be able to handle this sort of verbalization than the Twos and Threes. With the younger child even an indirect reference to a mother in a story or song may bring tears to the eyes and set waves of homesickness in motion.

b. *The teacher* is working constantly with the mother in this adjustment, and usually there is a specific teacher who must work through adjustment problems with any specific child. It is helpful for the child to have some time alone with this teacher, whether she be the head teacher with whom he has had his first meeting, or one of the other teachers. If it is one of the other teachers, the mother may find that having this teacher at home one afternoon as a baby-sitter or as a guest at luncheon helps the child. He needs to get acquainted with her apart from the group, learn her name, and be assured of her acceptance and protection.

Usually the mother should not leave her child in the morning until this special teacher is free to look after the child's welfare. Difficulty sometimes arises, however, in that the child may become overly attached to this special teacher. Such attachment results in his not accepting a relationship with other teachers, or even with other children. This is particularly true with the highly verbal, adult-centered child, and when this problem occurs the teacher may have to use special techniques to effect a release of the child from too great dependence on her.

c. With some children, adjustment may be achieved with the help of *another child*. The normal sequence of adjustment, particularly with the older child, is first through a teacher and then through a friend. Indeed, even the use of the word "friend" helps with these children. "Come and see what your friend Billy is doing," the teacher can urge the child who is still hesitant about his role in the nursery school. Or "Your friend Billy is painting; perhaps you would like to paint too." Needless to say, it is always advisable to be assured that Billy will be somewhat cooperative in this arrangement.

Children who live in the same neighborhood, and whose parents can arrange for them to see one another outside of school hours, may thereby gain a "friend" who can be utilized for adjustment purposes. Parents usually welcome a list of the names and addresses of other children enrolled in the school, so that they can arrange for such visits. A child who has shared afternoon play or lunch with another child may find some measure of security in finding that same child at school.

Car pools may be a help, too. Joining a car pool allows the child who has not yet adjusted to separation from his mother to leave her in the less threatening atmosphere of home. Riding to school with other happy children may suggest to the child that school is fun. And the child may pick up a "friend" in the car with whom to play initially after he gets to school. There is, of course, potential danger in any car pool, especially if it is overcrowded and children of markedly different temperaments are put together. A quiet, gentle child may be terrified by a more raucous one, yet be unable to report his distress except by his expressed reluctance to get into the car. Car pools as well as school busses sometimes do a great deal of damage to the sensitive, unprotected child.

If not another child, some adult other than the mother may provide the transition necessary for adjustment. If the child cannot accept parting from the mother, he may still accept parting from the father, a maid, a neighbor. Even an older sibling may bring the child, and may even stay for a while. In some instances the presence of a younger sibling brings about an acceptance of school. The child in this instance may assume control of his brother or sister, show off the school to him, tell him what to do or not do, and through his superior knowledge and control achieve the feelings of security about his new experiences that he could not achieve on his own.

d. *Objects or activities* rather than people make the way easier for some. Some children have to keep on a special article of clothing associated with departure—a hat, jacket, mittens, or boots. Frequently in his first days at school a child, especially a 2-year-old, refuses to remove his jacket. He feels better if he can at least keep on his symbol of flight from the situation. It is wise for the teacher to respect his wish to have the acceptance of nursery school a tentative one. He will later signify his readiness to accept school by taking off his jacket, prepared to stay for the experiences of the morning.

Rituals are often important, such as riding a bike, saying good-bye in a certain way, having a piece of gum in a special room. Some children set up their own rituals; but sometimes the teacher or parent has to set up the ritual to help the child. Often this involves bringing something from home, which the child can carry around and show to the teacher or to other children, such as a paper bag or a suitcase filled with papers and pencils, a teddy bear, blanket, piece of orange or other remnant of breakfast.

In one instance, such an object brought from home helped by allowing the child self-righteously to express his feelings of aggression, and to assert his power. He would deliberately stand in the midst of children, holding a prized toy from home, or place it on the floor in full and tempting view of other children. Then, when the children would seize his toy, he would pounce upon them and vigorously protect his property and assert his rights. Only by such a curious maneuver did he finally release his period of "watchful waiting" and move into association with the group. Of course the teachers had to help him eventually to more socially acceptable ways of interaction with his schoolmates.

Animals—guinea pigs, rabbits, birds, turtles, fish, kittens— are also most helpful in the first days of school. A child seems to be able to forget himself in caring for a living creature smaller than he is. His tenderness and protective capacities can be enlisted by urging him to take care of the baby turtle, feed it, hold it, build it a house, read to it, let it sleep. In giving the care he himself seeks he gains in security and self-reliance.

Music or food is helpful very often. A record player or music box seems to soothe a child when he is distressed; listening to music calms his upset feelings. Crackers and milk, either at the beginning of the morning or any time that the child seems to be unhappy, are good properties to have in mind as great aids to security. Some parents object to sweets between meals, but when this is not the case a lollipop has often won over a recalcitrant youngster. Raisins or cookies or chocolate candy are always acceptable and comforting. And the teacher and parent need not fear that such props, once introduced, will have to be continued. Once the child is happy on his own in the school he will not need such tokens to distract him from feelings of unhappiness.

e. *Routines, space and time orientation.* The *kind* of group to which the child is initially presented may also be important. Some adjust best by being immersed in the group. Others adjust best by being separated from the group and do best with solitude at the outset, reading or enjoying music alone with a teacher, or with one other child. Some need to come to school first, ahead of the others. Some can start the morning best in the playground, but others do better to be indoors first. Those who are most at ease with materials, such as puzzles, crayons, painting, dolls, may do best to start inside. Those who prefer gross motor activites may do best outside. Some are helped by the enclosure of walls. Others are helped through the freedom of the outdoors. There are those who at first need quite a chance to watch. But these need eventual attention to keep them from getting stuck in nonactivity or in a single activity and thus being bored or filled with thoughts of home. They need gradually and repeatedly to be lured away from their solitary pursuits.

Some children need to be given a special job to do when they first arrive, especially a 4-year-old who is having trouble with adjustment. Children low in spontaneity need a special task when they wander around, unable for the moment to think of anything to do. Then they can help water the flowers, take care of the animals, set up the tables. There are those children who need to be needed. Four-year-olds especially often need to think they are needed. "Who would do such-and-such if you weren't here?" brings a smile of self-conscious pleasure and importance to their faces.

Some children need to be placed in a group of children whose chronological age is younger or older than their own. Some adjust best with the slow pacing and tendency to parallel play that is characteristic of the 2-year-old group. A highly social child needs the stimulus of group interaction and more dynamic play. Very often the high-powered child cannot sustain adjustment unless his attendance is shortened. He may need for a time only two hours a morning instead of three, or fewer days of school a week until he can manage school with less excitement and tension.

As this chapter suggests, adjusting a child to nursery school requires goodwill and patience. It also requires a refusal to be discouraged or defeated by the many small but important problems young children quite naturally and normally experience in leaving home and adapting to what for many is a first step into the big world away from home.

11

Techniques for Handling Children

GENERAL INTRODUCTION

It is difficult to discuss general techniques. As with all advice about children, there are rarely black and white answers, or clear-cut rules that mark the road to perfection. For example, it would be impractical to try to find one method of discipline which would work for all children. Some need firm treatment; some gentle. One method will work at some times but will fail at others. Human behavior is variable and paradoxical. The most effective approach to the subject of techniques is based on the knowledge that behavior changes with growth, and that the human being is constantly growing and changing.

This is particularly true with regard to children, and especially very young children. No period of growth is more rapid and dramatic than that of the first five years of life. So the nursery school teacher must first of all adapt her techniques to varying ages. A period of six months can bring about remarkable changes in the child, changes which demand quite different methods of direction.

Not only do workable techniques vary with age, but also with personality. Obviously the shy 2-year-old must be approached differently than the highly aggressive and outgoing 2-year-old. And the basic techniques useful with a 2-year-old must be amplified with the proper ways of dealing with the

180

highly verbal, the diffident, the friendly, the asocial, the robust, the frail.

Also, techniques vary with environment. The child in a new situation must be treated differently than the child in a situation that is familiar to him. The child in organized group play requires different handling than a child in solitary play parallel with that of a friend. A newcomer must be allowed considerable time for testing and exploring as he gets acquainted with rules and routines. No rules can be uniformly enforced.

Any teacher always has a group of "conformists" who enjoy routines either because of their personalities or because of their stage of development. Others care less to conform. If a child is permitted to go off alone with his book, to sit apart during music time—to do anything he pleases alone, so long as he does not molest the group—the teacher can count on the fact that a child's nature is basically social and can expect him eventually to do things *with* the group, rather than alone, providing that no unpleasant coercion or contest of wills is involved in the meantime. The young child cannot accept toileting or walking or talking till he is ready. His accepting a group involves even greater complications, and demands careful preparation for many children.

An important aspect of nursery school is that the environment can be arranged to fit the needs and abilities of the child. Accordingly, in the nursery school the environment is arranged to suit both age and personality. The environment should be manipulated to give the child a setting that allows him the satisfactions of being the age and person he is, and that provides him with the stimulus to move to the age and person he can become.

The nursery school, like successful play therapy, operates with the conviction that growth to age three takes place best when the satisfactions of age two have been happily and completely worked through. The 2-year-old is never urged to be a "big boy" when he needs the experiences of babyhood. But the environment of the nursery school is ready to challenge him to the next stage of growth, while still encouraging him in the expression of his 2-year-old ways.

Teaching in a nursery school requires highly specialized skills that can be acquired only through training. The nursery school teacher must have a rich background in theoretical knowledge of child development, plus an equally rich background in actually adapting her theories to practical situations. One is not more important than the other; and beyond both is something independent of all training and experience. The good teacher in nursery school, like the good teacher in any field, must have a native talent for working with people—a native understanding and sympathy with the thoughts, needs, and emotions of her pupils of whatever age.

The question of firmness or permissiveness inevitably arises in the use of techniques. Both teachers and parents have to learn to steer between extremes.

A misunderstanding both of the educational philosophy of John Dewey and of the psychoanalytic movement promoted a great surge of excessive permissiveness in both homes and schools during the last several decades. Dewey's idea that the child learned by doing and found satisfaction in his own creations frequently led to wild extremes of freedom in what the child was allowed to do both in school and at home. Freudian theory in a different way often caused havoc by raising the flag of guilt indiscriminately for sins of omission and of commission. Parents feared that if they were firm or punished their children, they might do irreparable harm to them, and often such parents practiced a kind of "compulsive permissiveness."

This confusion in the minds of conscientious parents is still widespread. Now, however, intelligent parents realize increasingly that they must trust to what they call their own common sense in making decisions about discipline. Thus they end up by judiciously balancing freedom and control for the child, depending on the three important variables: the age of the child, his personality, and the specific situation.

Teachers as well as parents learn from experience the things which they must be firm about, and communicate their self-assurance to the children. Children of any age like freedom, but they also like wise and firm boundaries. Sometimes inexperienced teachers find a group suddenly out of hand, and they wonder how it got that way. Often it is that they have communicated their own indecision by a quaver in their voice. Young children quickly notice such indecision and are almost invariably tempted to test its limits. A young teacher does well to work with experienced teachers for a while in order to build up her sense of what firmness is needed to maintain structure and order while encouraging the maximum freedom and expression of individuality.

There is a great deal of skill involved in bringing children with widely differing personalities to accept the order of a single group. Some children can be reached by straightforward directions, some need preparatory explanations. Thus they may have to accept the group on their own terms, and these terms may involve a long period of watching and nonparticipation. The child who becomes noisy and rowdy and disturbs the others needs to be taken to another room for individual play until he is ready in any real sense to join the group. Within two months after nursery school begins, the order of the group is usually so well established that the children enjoy the routines and even urge each other to conformity.

The discipline of individual children parallels group discipline, although it is not as difficult. Teachers succeed in discipline best when they do not regard it as punishment or simply as the use of prohibitions or negative commands. Discipline suggests leadership in cooperation as well as in the wise use of freedom.

No child was ever made insecure by the knowledge that a stove is hot and that he must not touch it. Most children are able to accept reasonable boundaries. A small child likes to become familiar with his boundaries and limits. Frequently parents who change their places of residence a great deal when children are very young have difficulty with discipline because no consistent rules can be established about how to approach the environment. A child likes familiar things and routines. The child is born into a world of infinite complexity and gets security by having his freedom within definite limits which parent and teacher must set for him. This is true both at school and at home. A baby is happier in a playpen than he would be alone in a large vacant lot.

The techniques which we shall discuss in this chapter suggest specific ways we have found helpful in dealing with the child in the nursery school. First we shall discuss two basic techniques of general importance: the technique of awareness and the technique of using appropriate language. Then we shall consider techniques for helping children get along with other children, techniques for managing the various routines in nursery school, and techniques for effecting transitions from one routine to another. Since the techniques involved in toileting, eating, dressing, participation in music and stories vary so much from age to age, these will be described in a separate chapter.

THE TECHNIQUE OF BEING AWARE

The technique of being aware is especially important in dealing with the child of nursery school age. The good teacher must have what we call "peripheral" vision, as contrasted with a highly "focal" or concentrated way of looking at things. Somehow she must learn to be attentive not only to individual children, but to every child in the room. She will try never to stand or sit with her back to any part of the room. Her position will always be so strategic that she can comfort Mary, help Paul with his puzzle, yet keep attentive watch on a block-building situation in a far corner, and caution a nearby teacher to move to the high ladder at the far end of a room where an active 3-year-old is beginning to mount.

She moves about in the room from less complicated to more complicated situations. She never leaves the room without telling another teacher of her whereabouts, and assuring herself that the children have constant supervision; yet she never assumes that a part of the room is "covered" simply because another teacher is there. So long as she is in a room the *entire* supervision of the room is her responsibility.

As a crutch to her awareness, she can count the children frequently. She should know how many children are present each morning, how many are playing in the room she is supervising. This kind of check-up acts as protection for the child who is inclined to wander and for the child who may withdraw unhappily from play to solitary brooding.

As far as possible, the teacher will have been alert to possible physical dangers in the environment and will have tried to eliminate these before the children come to school. Though unanticipated dangers inevitably emerge, the alert teacher will arrange equipment so that such dangers are kept at a minimum. High toys must be moved away from windows; a piano may be pushed in front of a door that provides easy access to a hallway; high locks must be put on doors that cannot be watched all the time.

The teacher must also be attentive to the orderliness of the room. During morning play she keeps the room picked up. As children move from one kind of play to another, she removes the clutter from the floor. Rolling toys especially should be removed from the floor when they have been abandoned, for they are hazards to safety. And when there is too much clutter on the floor, children get restless and scrambly.

At the close of each morning's session toys must be picked up and arranged in inviting display on shelves that are easily accessible. The doll corner must be made neat; paint and clay must be found fresh and attractive each day. Often the children will join the teachers in picking up, especially if this is done in a spirit of fun.

Although children are specially adept at making a shambles of a room, their best play is initially stimulated by an arrangement that is orderly and attractive. Attractiveness includes bright, fresh colors; primary colors are especially appealing. The furniture and general appearance of the room must not be shabby or dull.

A teacher's awareness of the environment includes a sensitivity to temperature changes. She must open and close windows, adjust the heating mechanism, put on or take off children's sweaters as the temperature demands. When teachers are unaware, little children may play all morning in a warm room in sweaters and rubbers until they become wet and clammy with the extra heat.

Also, the teacher should remember what each child has worn to school, so that sweaters or scarves are not forgotten or misplaced in the rush of dressing to leave. She will remember any favorite toy or possession a child has brought to school and will see that he remembers to take it home. Always the morning's planning includes an awareness of time and its proper allotment so that it is not necessary to rush children through any of the routines.

A teacher's awareness considers the future as well as the present, the emotional as well as the physical needs of children. She will make a note of how long some kinds of play are likely to last. When a certain child enters the group, she will know at once that the play will deteriorate. So far as possible she will

anticipate trouble, and before a crisis occurs will provide diver-
sion, redirect play.

But this will not be her inevitable procedure. Occasionally
one should allow hostilities open expression and permit destruction after unsuccessful efforts at creativity, though this is
not commonly advisable in normal play. For rules governing
children's behavior must always envisage unusual as well as
usual situations, situations often created by children's emotional needs.

The teacher must be especially aware of the child who may
get rooted in one spot. She must give a smile, take a toy near
him, and begin playing with it. She may pick the younger child
up without comment and talk to him of a new kind of play.
Usually a quiet, relaxing setting is helpful: water play, clay,
records or a story, some crackers and milk with the teacher's
comforting support to help the child regain his equanimity.

The child who becomes overstimulated may also need help,
for overstimulation is contagious in a group and if allowed to
run its course may lead to chaos in the nursery school. A
teacher must take away the leader in such a group, not in a
spirit of punishment but of continuing fun. Sometimes she can
lead him to a quiet interest. Often, however, he does not need
quiet but a complete outlet for his excessive energy. In schools
with an abundance of room and teaching help, a special room
may be available. At the nursery school in the Gesell Institute
there is a "noisy room" equipped with a carpentry set, mats for
tumbling, materials for sand and water play, large plywood
boards and blocks for construction. The hyperactive children in
a group may be taken to this room for unusually energetic
projects.

The teacher must make provision for the child who needs
preparation for routines, who makes transitions from one activity to another with difficulty. Such a child may need a word
of preparation, as "Next we are going to have milk and crack-

ers," or "When you finish playing with the doll, we are going to put all the toys away." But with other children, words of preparation only arouse negativism. In these cases it is best to move into new routines with no comment. A teacher can communicate a feeling of inevitable authority without saying a word. Other children, who may both resist preparation and defy authority, can be managed through distraction. With such a child a teacher may walk up, take his hand, talk about something else, and lead him to toileting or whatever the activity may be. The child will usually respond in a positive way before he knows what has happened.

VERBAL TECHNIQUES

Verbal Techniques in General

It is as important for a teacher to know how to talk as to know what to say. Our firm belief is that a teacher should be as natural as possible with children, and this implies talking to them in the same voice she uses with adults. It is an occupational hazard with nursery school teachers that they often develop an unusual intonation, a too high inflection of the voice with too much repetition of statement and too much of a suggestion of questioning or tentativeness in their voices.

At its worst this hazard develops to a babyish simper, and it can be an excruciating experience to hear a group of teachers talking to children in this highly artificial manner. It is a great advantage if a teacher is gifted with a gentle voice yet one that can be raised to firm and clear articulation when the necessity for discipline or direction arises. A harsh, loud voice is inappropriate for a teacher.

The ability to modulate tone, to achieve different effects through loudness and softness, is highly valuable. An extremely gentle statement, or even whispering, can command the attention of a highly raucous group and can communicate relaxation and gentleness. Similarly, a firm tone of voice communicates the need for order as much as words do; a teacher can let children know by her tone when she has taken a last stand and expects obedience. A rich variation in tone is one of the best assurances of a successful story period; the dramatic expression of words acts as a spellbinder for even the youngest children and is effective in commanding attention even when the sequence of thought escapes them.

If a teacher also has a good singing voice, her vocal equipment is complete. Singing is one of the most highly enjoyed of children's activities, and they learn their songs by imitation of the teacher's singing. It is a mistake, however, to overuse this technique of singing. Some teachers have a song for every activity. But the judicious use of singing is a technique that can calm or change some activities which seem to be getting out of hand.

General advice about *what* to say must stress not saying too much. It is better to talk too little rather than too much, if extremes are inevitable. A child soon ignores the constant chatterer, for it is too troublesome and uninteresting to be attentive to all she says. Too much talk usually includes too many inappropriate words; it is difficult to select only the words children will understand if conversation flows too freely.

The second bit of advice about what to say is that teachers should be specific rather than general in their choice of words. Children between the ages of two and four have little capacity to understand abstract words. They react better to several variations of a specific suggestion. For example, instead of saying, "You could put the toys away," or "You could do it better," the statement "You could put the cars on the red shelf" brings concrete reality to the child's attention. Sometimes the direction needs the accompaniment of example. The teacher can take a car, put it on the shelf, and say, "Here is a car on the red shelf. *You* put a car on the red shelf."

Finally, a teacher's statements should be, as far as possible, positive rather than negative or tentative. She must have a tone of expectancy that a thing will be done, and of course must carefully select those activities where there is a reasonable assurance that they can be carried through. It is inadvisable to make a suggestion to a child in the form of a question, because this tentative position usually suggests "No" for an answer. "Do you want to put the car on the red shelf ?" nine times out of ten will, as indeed it literally should, bring a negative response. If a teacher is merely exploring the possibility of engaging a child's interest in an activity, the words "maybe" or "when you're ready" are valuable protective measures. "When you're ready, you could put the car on the red shelf " allows the child *not* to be ready, with the teacher's full acquiescence.

Other words often have magical effects. "It's time to put the car on the shelf " or "You need to put the car on the shelf " carries amazing authority to a child. Older children sometimes respond well to counting: "When I count five, you could put the car on the shelf." Failure of this technique is obvious and deflating, however, and certainly requires careful selection of the child on whom it is used. Its value comes in putting the matter up to the child. The autonomy for action or decision, through simple verbal techniques, can be subtly shifted from adult to child and can encourage his feelings of both independence and cooperation.

Not every child is ready to cooperate in putting the toy away or in going to the toilet, or in any number of things. When all the usual approaches fail, the teacher just puts the toy on the shelf herself or lets the child wet his pants. Some children require months to be ready to cooperate. The one thing which is ill advised is to create a situation of tension between teacher and child. Careful watching of the child and of his growing maturity will after a while give the teacher an opportunity to get the cooperation which the child himself, basically, wants to give. This freedom from tension is the most important single aspect of the nursery school. A teacher can keep her equanimity for a three-hour session in a way a mother, who has the child twenty-four hours a day, finds difficult to achieve.

A teacher must always show interest in a child, and this can be managed with a smile or some comment about his activity or person. The teacher needs to have a stock of small talk for children. She need never fear that what she has to say in matters of this sort will be boring or too repetitious. Children provide most attentive and appreciative audiences when an adult gives them her interested attention.

A comment about a child's shoes is appropriate for all the ages in nursery school, the comments becoming less personal but more elaborate for the older ages. The shoes of a 2-year-old are usually his favorite article of clothing, and merely to remark that they are red, brown, black, or "nice and new" will bring an appreciative response. The 4-year-old may like to talk about "other" shoes he has, or cowboy shoes he will get, or that his shoes are *"big,* because he is four years old." Four-year-olds often enjoy discussions of unusual aspects of clothing, such as the color and materials of the inside of their pockets. Comments about how they got to school or what they will do when they get home are good when children are well adjusted, for they provide a welcome link between past and future and between the worlds of home and school.

Comments about what a child is doing encourage his activity; such comments make him feel appreciated. It is good also to praise the activity in progress and the activity that has been completed; motivation for desirable action can be managed in great measure through positive, casual comments of this sort. Motivations to friendship can be given simply by the use of the word "friend" with the 3- and 4-year-old child. "Your friend

Jim is digging in the sand. You could dig there, too" may be the start of a great friendship if the teacher persistently works on the theme and provides special occasions for the "friends" to be together.

It is particularly important that the teacher have a stock of small talk for milk-and-cracker time, when the children are relaxed and quiet and usually ready for conversation. A favorite topic is what has been eaten for breakfast. Everyone can make a contribution and can enjoy the pleasure of being understood. Conversation can also be stimulated by changing pictures appropriate for childish interests in the room where the children have their midmorning snack. "See the butterfly," "See the cow," "See the boat" often encourage quite valuable conversation about personal experiences with these objects. The weather, favorite television or radio programs, Christmas, birthdays, baby brothers and sisters, their own houses are also subjects that provide a sure and invaluable supply of small talk with little children.

This time of day is a good one for rehearsing children's names, to help the youngsters get acquainted. "Mary's eating her cracker," or "Johnny has a new red shirt," or merely an enumeration of each child's name helps the children to know one another.

Finally, the teacher should know what to say to a child who asks too many questions. The highly verbal child who has spent a great deal of time with adults, particularly the child who is poor at using his hands, may follow the teacher around with a constant barrage of questions. She should give honest, factual answers to his questions, but needs to set limits to how much time she will devote to this sort of thing. Turning the questions back to him often changes the pattern. "You tell me" or "What do *you* think?" makes the occupation not quite so pleasurable to the child. Finally a firm statement that she has answered all the questions she can, and that it is time for the child to do something else, is a conclusion that the too talkative child must learn to accept.

Humor is one of the best verbal techniques to use with children. It is important to be aware of what is humorous to a child and to show an appreciation of his own humor. This humor is usually simple. The 2- and 3-year-old child, for instance, always thinks it is funny when his shoes come off with his boots, and loves a good laugh over this surprising, ridiculous situation.

The young child laughs at simple repetitive games like "Peek-a-boo," or at the repetition of foolish sounds like "Bang" when a car comes down the slide. Animal noises in a fairly exaggerated tone are usually considered extremely funny, and a quick kiss on the ear or a hug brings an appreciative giggle from most children, as well as giving them the assurance that they are loved away from home in a way they are loved at home, and this adds to a warm, affectionate feeling of well-being and security.

Most children love the humor of exaggeration or complete inappropriateness of logic. It is funny to call things by the wrong colors: "Do you have on a red undershirt and pants?" "I bet your tummy's purple!"

"Did you ride your rhinoceros to school?" is considered the height of a humorous remark by a 4-year-old. The appeal of such fine books as *Horton Hatches the Egg* and *McGelligot's Pool,* by Dr. Seuss, lies largely in this sort of highly exaggerated, ludicrous statement.

The 4-year-old child especially likes the humor of words. He loves to experiment with sounds, make up silly words. Edward Lear's *Nonsense A.B.C.* with such verses as

> A was once an apple pie
> Tidy widy

Nice insidy

Apple pie

brings convulsive merriment to the 4-year-old.

But 4-year-old humor, like most 4-year-old activities, can quickly get out of bounds. What starts out as a merry play with words can degenerate to silly name calling: "You old stupid head," "You silly fatso." The teacher must firmly squelch a tendency in a group that goes beyond the bounds of good taste and order and leads to open hostility.

Humor is a good device to snap children out of a trying situation. Humor can postpone the necessity for an unpleasant decision. It is a great face saver since it is difficult to be aggrieved and amused at the same time. However, the teacher must be cautious with oversensitive children lest they feel she is laughing *at* and not *with* them. Only an understanding of a child's personality and adroit manipulation of an impersonal sort of humor keeps the teacher from offending children with her laughter.

A review of verbal techniques suitable for each age will illustrate ways in which the teacher's approach may vary with the age of the child.

Verbal Techniques at Different Ages

2 Years

Verbal techniques are now beginning to be more important than physical, whereas at eighteen months the opposite was true. It is important to keep language simple, concrete, and repetitive. There is no need to fear boring the 2-year-old with repetition. The world is all so new to him that repetition helps him to feel comfortable. It is, however, best to keep language at a minimum. Adults who talk too much to the 2-year-old inevitably use words he does not understand. Such verbosity from adults may set up patterns of not paying attention in the child.

Often it is necessary to follow or to support verbalization with action. Thus, rather than simply saying, "Go wash your hands," a teacher leads a child to the washbasin as she utters this direction. Similarly it is better to say the more specific "Put the blocks on the shelf " than simply "Put the blocks away." Also it is useful to supplement the suggestion with demonstration.

In some instances words, even though not fully understood, can become signal or conditioning words. For example, "It's his turn," even though the child doesn't understand fully, seems to provide a formula that often works even at two. The words help the child to wait, temporarily to give up. But the teacher should not use these words unless she is prepared to see to it that the child who has given up gets some substitute satisfaction, or *his* turn later. Also, such words as "again" and "another," although they are abstract, convey, with demonstration, the notion to a child that there are more experiences or more possessions available to him.

The teacher can try to get the child himself to use verbal rather than physical approaches in a dispute by saying, "Tell him what you want; don't hit him," and then seeing to it that this is in some way carried out, even if she has to supply the words. Children of this age respond very well to verbally expressed affection, combined with physical manifestations of affection.

2 ½ Years

Questions such as "Where does your coat go?" can be good motivators. But it is important to avoid questions which can be answered by "No," such as "Do you want to_____?" or "Would you like to_____?" In general, it is good to avoid giving choices, for children find, as soon as they have made a choice in one direction, that the other is highly desirable.

However, sometimes giving choices about things that do not matter may act as a motivator. For example, putting milk into both a blue and a red cup, and asking, "Do you want the blue one or the red one?" may first bring the selection of blue, then the selection of red, but in any case milk will not have been the issue in question!

Face-saving directions are useful, such as, "You could_____," or "How about_____?" It is wise not to meet the child head on with a too direct command, unless this is absolutely necessary. Verbalization about some neutral topic can be used as a distraction when children become especially negative or insist, "Me do it myself." The teacher can talk about something else, while actually doing something for them (such as putting on a snowsuit with which they have had great difficulty). Or a running commentary which does not cue them to a negative response, such as "I wonder if you could go down that big slide; I wonder if it's too high for you," may motivate them to a desired activity.

This last verbalization also appeals to the child's love of praise and pride in accomplishment. Such appeals seem foolproof at most ages and work especially well with the 2½-year-old when they are directed to his being big, strong, or very attractive. For example, the remark "You have such a pretty dress, I hope you won't get it dirty" may be a special motivation to cleanliness. Verbal expressions of affection as well as of praise are highly effective.

It is important to speak slowly and carefully and to emphasize certain words. Getting just the right word or phrase is important. When the child is older, there is more choice as to what words are effective; at this age just the right word is essential. There is still considerable need for the specific. "Dangerous" is not an effective word. It is better to say, "If you do such-and-such, such-and-such will happen."

3 Years

Language now takes on a whole new texture and dimension. It is no longer necessary to repeat so much, or to say just the right thing. Spontaneous, two-way conversations are now coming in. A remark from a teacher often sets a child off on a series of associative responses.

Play and routines usually go so smoothly at three that a

teacher is not aware of verbal techniques. However, specific concrete suggestions still work better than general ones. It works best to put things positively rather than negatively: "We put the books on the shelf," rather than "We don't throw the books"; or "We put the blocks down quietly so that they don't break." It is still best to avoid "Do you want to?" for necessary routines or other important issues. And certain words can be extremely successful as motivators—"big," "new," "surprise," "different." Verbal praise and expression of affection are still most effective.

Face saving is less necessary than at two-and-a-half, but still such tentative phrases as "You could help," or "Maybe," or "How about?" are useful. Most Threes can listen when reasoned with and may give in and change their minds. Giving a command in a whisper is now often extremely effective, both in getting attention and in inducing compliance.

3½ Years

Going to extremes, such as speaking very loudly or very softly, works well with children of this age. They themselves, too, like either to shout or to whisper. Indeed, since most behavior tends to be exaggerated at this age, the teacher must be careful not to let extreme behavior get out of hand. The *timing* of techniques is therefore important to prevent excessive exuberance or negativism.

The element of surprise can be a timely distractor or motivator. "Do you know what?" is usually a question that interrupts a child's actions or thoughts and makes him receptive to the idea of some pleasant information. The idea of something new and exciting can be emphasized by the use of such words as "surprise," "new," and "different." Also a child can be distracted from undesirable behavior by some question such as "Did you ever go to the zoo?" Verbal praise and expressions of affection continue to be useful and important: "I like you," "You're my friend." One cannot, apparently, overuse this technique.

Spontaneous verbalization is likely to embellish and accompany a child's play with other children, and the teacher, listening to this conversation, can utilize it to further her own techniques. Good behavior, more imaginative play, can often be furthered by repeating one child's conversation to another, or by pointing out some attractive activity of one child to another.

Play with imaginary companions may be at its height, with much verbalization from the child to his companion. But the child may be highly embarrassed if a teacher makes any comment about this. He usually regards his imaginary companion as a special, private friend, and it is infrequent to have references to such a companion made at nursery school, where other companions are available.

However, children of this age often call themselves by some name other than their own, and a teacher can sometimes motivate them to desired behavior by using this other name: "And now Mickey Mouse does so and so," or "Now Kitten can do so and so." A teacher's verbalization can also be helpful in bringing an excluded child into play: "But he's the milkman," or "You could invite her to be your guest," or "She could be the grandmother."

4 Years

Praise and compliment, for appearance or activity, continues to be one of the most effective techniques for making things go smoothly. The remark "That's the handsomest shirt I ever saw" is certain to bring appreciative response in a child. In praising activities and abilities, however, it is important to use new and interesting adjectives and not to praise something which the child, now much more self-critical, knows to be poor. Instead of saying an artistic creation is good, for instance, it is better (when it is clearly *not* a talented production), to remark, "That's an *interesting* painting," or "That's pretty good, especially since it's the first time you've ever drawn a horse."

Frequently verbalization about expected good behavior from the child produces this expected behavior. Also, it is possible to help children use this very technique with other children. The teacher may say, "I bet he really appreciates the way you helped him," and this statement may not only surprise and please both participants, but may really help them to cooperative endeavors.

Teachers can interpret other people's feelings or give reasons why they do certain things. And the teacher can help children realize the effectiveness of verbal techniques: "I think if you ask him nicely, he'll give you that toy." Although the teacher still needs to help the excluded child by suggesting roles he might fill in play, it is possible with the Fours to make a direct suggestion that another child be included in play. The 4-year-old is more ready to be aware of another child's potentialities in play, and can respond to such a simple suggestion as "You can ask Bernie to come and play with you" without the necessity of the teacher's providing a special niche for Bernie.

At this age the concept of "It's the rule" (that no one brings mice or guns to school, or goes out of the yard) will often be accepted without question. However, it is important not to over-use this expression in small, temporary situations, such as "It's the rule that you have to give him that toy." The expression "It is (isn't) fair" is often effective even though a child may not fully understand it. Special, silly words, whose meaning the children have come to accept, are often more effective than a plain statement. Thus "Don't push" is far less effective than "Don't be a goober" (pusher).

Although a positive suggestion is still most effective, Fours can respond well to the negative of "Never, never, never" or "We don't throw stones, because people can be hurt." The teacher must determine when it will be more effective to discipline a child verbally before the group, and when she will take him aside and have a serious talk. When children are reprimanded before the group, they are apt to become silly. A private talk often works best.

Fours especially love exaggeration and verbal silliness, and a teacher's verbal participation in these interests, or her appreciation of their interest in the gory, bloody, and violent, can direct her techniques when she wants to be certain of getting attention.

TECHNIQUES FOR HELPING CHILDREN GET ALONG WITH OTHER CHILDREN

Once the child has accepted a separation from his mother as inevitable, or even desirable, nursery school stimulates his growth in all his potentials—in gross and fine motor areas, in language, in adaptive use of hand and eye, and in personal-social adjustment. In the first three areas, there is little necessity for special techniques on the part of the teacher to smooth the way. The child chiefly needs suitable materials at hand to stimulate his growing mind and muscles. The demands of growth and his own lively curiosity keep him in constant exploration of his environment.

The unusual opportunity afforded by nursery school, however, is that under ideal conditions it stimulates growth in social areas at a very early age. Children face the problem of adjusting to other children, not in the streets or with an unsupervised neighborhood group, but in a group suitably matched in age, and with the constant protection and supervision of an understanding adult. Here children grow in their conceptions of what other people are like, of what is pleasing, what is practical, what is expedient with their peers. And they learn what is fun—the joy of an experience shared with another child, or with a group.

To help the child in his relationships with other children, the teacher must be keenly aware of the nature of social potentialities of children of various ages and must adapt her techniques accordingly.

With the 2-year-old, for example, the teacher must realize that play will be chiefly solitary; children will spend a lot of time watching other children or engaging in parallel play. Children will engage in a good deal of physical exploration of each other—

especially aggressive approaches. Hitting at this age does not necessarily mean dislike—it may be the only form of social contact that the child knows. A child may begin by stroking another child's hair because he likes the way it looks, then he may pull it to see how it feels. A teacher must realize that she is going to have to teach 2-year-olds the absolute fundamentals of getting along with other children. Often it seems that the 2-year-old might enjoy school more if the others were not there, and the teacher's main problem may be to get them to tolerate one another. Also, children of two years dislike and have little ability to give up possessions or to share them.

Since the 2-year-old is so primitive in his ability to play with other children, it may be well to start a child in school in a small room with just one or two other children. There should be duplicate toys, to avoid quarrels over possessions. When the inevitable struggle over control begins, it is well to have an identical toy to hand to the second child. The teacher can stimulate parallel play by her verbalization. "He's making a cake for you. You could make a cake, too" is a suitable remark for two 2-year-olds pounding their respective cakes at the clay table.

Social relationships can be interpreted in positive ways: "How nice that he made you a cake," or "He likes to do the puzzle with you," or "He wants you to ride him on the train." Hitting and other physical approaches should be turned into something positive, if possible. Instead of hitting another child, the molester may be encouraged just to touch or stroke the other child. Or he may be given something to hand to the other child. The child should be helped to excuse accidents and aggressions by the teacher's saying, "He didn't mean to" when another child knocks over a building or snatches away a toy. The teacher must try to set the matter right, to show other ways of social interaction.

By the time a child is two-and-a-half, there will be much more social interaction than at two, but usually such interaction tends to be negative and destructive. There is a great deal of grabbing, hitting, and the manifestation of extreme possessiveness. Children seem not only unwilling to share the toy they are playing with, but want to control those toys which they have played with, or might plan to play with. Consequently, a great deal of physical separation and protection is needed. The teachers must try to anticipate and to protect children from too many situations where they will need to be negative, aggressive, and possessive.

For example, when children get into trouble it is wise to take them away from the situation at once. (Often picking them up and carrying them to a part of the school where they are alone with the teacher is best.) Usually the removal of one child is sufficiently unusual to stop the trouble, and the teacher can talk to the child, explain what the difficulty was, then take him back to the situation so that she can show him another, more effective approach. Several quick moves are often necessary: a quick one of separation and then one of placating and then perhaps one of reinstating.

Sometimes, instead of moving the child of two-and-a-half from a situation which is fast becoming a shambles, discipline by use of talk is quite effective. Whereas with the 2-year-old it is important to keep words short and sentences short, six months later a long flow of words directed to a child may calm him even when he doesn't understand too much of what is being said. The teacher can then take advantage of the momentary calm, separate the aggressors, restore the shattered situation, or introduce a new interest.

There are several standard bits of advice that the child of two-and-a-half does understand and that the teacher can use as verbal techniques. She can verbally suggest the use of substitutes, when one child is grabbing toys from another. "What else could he use? What can we get for him?" With such queries the child changes rapidly from the attacker to a solicitous helper, eager to get some *other* toys for the aggrieved child, and usually, with the teacher's help, both children are at length satisfied.

It is sometimes amusing to note that after a period of this sort of indoctrination a child may do this sort of substituting on his own—he protects a toy he is playing with, but goes off to get another to proffer to the aggressive child. Or he may even be the aggressor, and try to give another toy instead of the prize he wishes to carry away. It becomes clear that the children have not worked out all the fine points of barter, but they at least can come to have the idea that barter, rather than forceful attack, is the preferred method to get possession.

The teacher can also be helpful in quarrels over possessions by using the magic word "needs," which the 2½-year-old seems to accept: "But Johnny *needs* it," is often considered to be an adequate explanation. The teacher can also talk about taking turns, even though she will have to use strong supervision to make the idea of taking turns work in practice.

Positive maneuvers can also be utilized. The teacher can encourage natural expression of affection between children. "Peter likes you," she can say to the child sitting beside Peter. Repeating children's names to each other, commenting on their clothes, their activities, what they do at home brings them to one another's attention in ways that are not competitive. It is easy, too, to encourage humorous interaction among children of two-and-a-half. This is particularly useful out of doors, where they can be shown the amusement of making silly faces or silly sounds or engaging in silly actions, such as all stamping their feet. This sort of interaction is best out of doors, because the child of two-and-a-half can be carried away with foolishness and is more likely to go out of bounds in his enthusiasm indoors than out.

Indoors the teacher can make an effort to see that the shy children play together and the noisy ones together, so that the shy children are not overpowered. Such an arrangement should not be considered a permanent one, however, for noisy children overstimulate each other very often, and the shy ones often precisely need the sort of expression that the highly extroverted ones can encourage them to give. But in the early stages of adjustment, it is well to match like temperaments.

Adjustment of child to child is also helped if the environment is so set up that it suggests imaginative play. The teacher really needs to participate in play and show children of two-and-a-half what to do, or tell them what to do. They will cooperate but they have so little experience with playing with one another that they cannot initiate play or carry it on very far without the teacher's immediate help and participation. She can sit in the doll corner, for example, and while she dresses a baby she will ask one child to cook the supper, another to set the table, another to put the baby to bed or iron the clothes. Sometimes several try to carry out the same activity at once, and then the teacher must make a judicious settlement of such contests in the manner that has been suggested. But she can keep the play moving a long time by her presence and verbalizations about play. She can help block build-ing too by sitting on the floor, occasionally placing a block, mostly supplying encouragement and verbalization about the blocks al-ready placed. "Will a car fit on this road?" she can ask about a vertical alignment of blocks, and thus set up a highway. "Who lives in this house?" she can ask about a pile of blocks, and then welcome the stuffed animals, dolls, or cooking utensils that may be added to the structure, and demonstrate how these might fit in.

By the time a child is three, the teacher's role in adjusting children to play is less active. She can enrich and elaborate play by standing near and offering creative ideas. But she does not need to help and demonstrate as she did with the younger child. Such questions as "Who'll be the doctor?" or "Now I wonder who's going to cook the dinner?" can be enough to start an elaborate sickroom drama or marketing spree.

Teachers can now talk really effectively about "friends" and a great deal can be done with this concept. If there is sufficient mention that a person is a friend, that person tends to become a friend. (However, twosomes tend to predominate in play, not threesomes.) A child can be persuaded to imitate the positive thing a "friend" is doing. Some can learn to come to school without crying, be toilet-trained, play happily, just because the friend does these things. Sometimes just a few words, directing attention to another child, may be all that is needed to get a child to go and play happily with that other one. "Oh, look at Muffy!" may prompt a good half-hour of happy play between two children.

Cooperation, sharing, taking turns all seem at this age to come more naturally and with less help from the teacher. There is less but still some need for the use of special phrases such as "He needs it," or "When he's finished." They may need and accept a little help about taking turns; "Ask him when he is going to be through with it" is a phrase that is often helpful.

Verbal techniques can usually solve quarrels right on the spot, without separating the children, with the teacher's saying, "Now tell me what happened." When there is trouble, children may accept suggestions, as "I don't think that was a good idea" or "Let's think of a better idea." Teachers can now allow a certain amount of quarreling, shouting, rowdy play—watching to see that it doesn't go too far. This kind of play often helps children to like each other. After they have knocked over a pile of blocks, they sometimes squeal in delight and enjoy a time of "swimming" among the blocks on the floor, tumbling and falling on them. The teacher can step in and start a new structure, or get their help in picking them up before exuberance gets out of bounds and some-one gets hurt.

Thus the teacher's role in adjusting 3-year-olds to each other is more to encourage or start friendships, or give ideas for elaborating play, than actually to discipline or give children techniques for getting on with each other.

Such techniques also carry on at three-and-a-half. There is, at three-and-a-half, more of a tendency for a group to become over-excited and rowdy, however, because of the increased tension of the child of that age. Planned activity such as pasting, crayoning, painting, rather than free play, helps alleviate many tensions. Or a teacher can help calm a group by whispering to them, thus getting their cooperation in being quiet. The child of three-and-a-half often destroys his adjustment with his peers by wearing himself out with his tensions.

At this age, groups of more than two begin playing together, and group play requires more imagination. But there is also a marked tendency toward exclusion of certain children, and a teacher's efforts must be directed to encouraging group play and trying to prevent the exclusion of particular children. Sometimes the teacher herself can come into the group bringing an excluded child, without saying much. The extra child may be accepted along with the teacher, who might suggest some role for the excluded child to play: "He's the milkman bringing the milk," or "He's the mailman," or "He's the puppy playing on the floor."

With 4-year-olds, teacher techniques can be applied before the day starts, in planning the day's program. Most 4-year-olds like group work and planned activities and can best adjust to other children when the play is flexibly organized. The teacher needs to plan in advance centers of play for small groups—doll corner, block corner—and plan that highly noisy or aggressive play will not interfere with quiet play. For the 4-year-old has a notion of what is proper, is not likely to tolerate cars in the doll corner, for example, as the 3-year-old would be more likely to do. Four-year-olds like projects: making murals, pasting, coloring. The standards of accomplishment, of course, should not be beyond their age, but they like sitting down together at a table (providing they are permitted to leave when they wish) to engage in such projects.

However, although the teacher of the 4-year-old recognizes that most children of this age are gregarious and ready for group activities, she must realize that some will be lonely. She must find a friend for those who need one and, as earlier, make use of the word "friend" and plan things that two can do together. It is good to have on hand the kinds of equipment that take two to play— the rocking boat, a game of Lotto. Pointing out similarities can stimulate friendship and liking, too: "You have the same color hair" or "You have the same kind of shoelaces." The 4-year-old likes to do special jobs, and friendship can be stimulated by having two children carry a board or clean up the guinea pig cage or set out milk and crackers. Play with dough and clay where not too much conversation is needed can help the solitary 4-year-olds get acquainted with one another.

The solitary child at four may be excluded by groups, even more than at three-and-a-half, since differences are not only noticed but often verbally remarked upon. Again, teachers can help the excluded child by giving that child a special role to play. Also, if a child is not accepted well by the others, the teacher can admire some activity or performance of that child, so that others may admire it and him.

The teacher stimulates play at four largely with equipment. Furnishing costumes and props suggests wonderfully imaginative play. Equipment must be changed around and increased throughout the year. The teacher does well to hold back certain kinds of equipment, adding it during the year as a means of stimulating new play. The active, exuberant 4-year-old often goes out of bounds in his play, and the teacher must have techniques to calm a group so that the quieter children are not overwhelmed and so that the rambunctious ones do not destroy possibilities of play by their destructive foolishness. Music, beating time, organizing a small rhythm band can help calm down a bad morning. A quiet time sitting on pillows (Fours need often to be "contained" in this way by having a special place to sit) and listening to music or a story takes care of play that has deteriorated to destructiveness. Supervised carpentry or play in a "noisy room" (a place apart from the group where they can let off steam for a while in legitimate ways) can help children get rid of aggressions or an overabundance of energy.

If there is trouble in the group, the teacher may by the next day change the physical setup so as to avoid the difficulty. Right at the moment of trouble some project, such as "moving," changing the equipment around, may help. Now more than before, children can work out their own disagreements. If the teacher has to intervene, sometimes just standing near is enough. Sometimes reasoning will do the trick. Sometimes physical intervention—carrying a child away from the group—is needed. Humor can often save a situation, if the teacher understands and hits upon something that will be funny to 4-year-olds. Ridiculous and complicated words to describe the state of affairs may make quarreling children begin to laugh and to imitate or elaborate on the foolish words. To end a quarrel, often no more may be needed than to make the statement, "It's a rule that————." Fours seem to be quiet impressed by the magic of the word "rule," perhaps because it seems a depersonalized concept. The teacher can also use such a physical prop as her watch to depersonalize her decision about taking turns. "I'll look at my watch and let you know when it's your turn" seems to be an excellent formula to manage the problem of taking turns.

Such are some of the techniques for helping children to play with one another. With many children, separation from the mother is managed fairly speedily. But the matter of association with members of a group is a dynamic situation in which the child constantly needs guidance as he grows and changes.

12

Techniques for Routines and for Effecting Transitions

TECHNIQUES FOR ROUTINES

The routines of eating, sleeping, and toilet training represent the first demands of society on the young child. The parent has already made demands in these areas before the child comes to nursery school. However, problems in these routines at home do not necessarily mean similar problems at school. Very often a child will use the toilet at school and thus begin his toilet training, which may have been unsuccessful at home. Or he may drink milk for the first time at school. Even sleep problems have been known to be alleviated by a child's attendance at nursery school. His new interests and new way of life sometimes set up different and improved patterns with regard to sleep at home.

At the Gesell Nursery School we do not have a formal resting period during the morning. We do alternate quiet times with active times, and so plan the morning that children are ready for sedentary activities such as music, story, milk and crackers after they have worked off energy in more active physical ways. The child who does not wish to take part in these quiet activities is not forced to do so, but he is not allowed at these times to behave in a way that will disturb the rest of the group.

He may go off and play in the doll corner alone, play with sand, look at books, or listen to music in another room with the supervision of a teacher. But he may not gallop around the same room with the others, make loud noises, or otherwise disrupt a group that is quiet.

Some nursery schools do not believe that there should be scheduled routines; such schools often adopt the more permissive attitude toward discipline. And while extremely free, non-scheduled schools can be very spontaneous and creative, often such an atmosphere provokes lazy, uninspired teaching.

The chief danger in routines, it seems, is that they may become too rigid. If a teacher finds herself depending too much on very rigid routines and schedules, she might question her fitness for teaching young children. There should be considerable flexibility. Routines should have a sequence, but not a set number of minutes for each thing. Also there must always be great respect for individual differences. As we have already suggested, some children may be allowed to occupy themselves in other ways meaningful to them, rather than take part in all routines. Such freedom, of course, demands enough teachers so that if a child cannot fit into the routines, a teacher can be with him if he has to be somewhere else.

One of the great arguments in favor of routines seems to be that most children enjoy them. For many they not only give boundaries, but provide a positive experience. Omitting or changing routines distresses many children. Without them, each child might set up his own, which might not mesh with any kind of possible group activity. We feel that nursery school increases in value as it makes the children enjoy group experiences. A routine, not too rigidly imposed, seems to give security to children who might otherwise be anxious. It seems to give them anchor points, helps them to understand, gives them something to know and cling to insofar as it gives some predictability to the events of the day.

Children often worry vaguely about what is coming next, and routines give them clues. They like to talk about what comes next—"After milk and crackers we have stories, and then we go outside." Such a sequence is convenient for a teacher in directing children, and in reassuring them of the inevitable occurrence of some highly desirable activity. The frequent tendency of the child at home to set up his own rituals when he has to deal with the experience of separation in sleep, for example, shows that routines are reassuring. A child tends to deal with the stages of tension in his own growth, particularly at the ages of two-and-a-half and three-and-a-half, by creating new rituals for himself.

Events which are apt to occur regularly for every child at school are toileting, music, milk and crackers, listening to a story, and dressing. Music, milk and crackers, and stories are group activities, in that most of the children participate at the same time and respect whatever social limitations may be involved for the general welfare of everyone in such participation.

We shall describe specific techniques for managing each of these routines, with special regard to the different ages of children in order to illustrate ways in which general techniques may vary with age.

Toileting

General Comments

There is more variation in the routine of toileting than in any of the other routines. In general, 2-year-olds are taken to the toilet soon after they come in from their outdoor play. This is not handled by bringing all children to the toilet; many are not ready for the experience and may resist. Verbal suggestions prompt many 3-year-olds to go; some may need to be taken during the period of free play. Fours, also, need suggestion sometimes, for they are so busy and happy in their play that they do not like to interrupt it. But the whole procedure should be made as casual as possible and should consider each child's individual needs.

It is important to have no pressure, no unpleasant experiences in connection with this routine. This seems to be a function about which a child particularly wishes to exercise his autonomy, and it is usually better to have "accidents" than to tangle with a child's feelings of independence.

It is well to have a regular time for toileting, usually midway through the morning (although some children must go earlier). In midmorning, the young children can be taken one at a time. The teacher can say to the older ones, "Would anyone like to go to the toilet now?" The regular time gives some assurance that all children at least have a chance, or reminder, for toileting.

Hand washing is not insisted on after toileting at any age; it is only suggested that the 4-year-olds wash their hands. At the younger ages, the toileting procedure is usually complicated and time-consuming enough without adding hand washing. Younger children also dislike being taken away from the wash basin once they begin the happy project of elaborate hand washing.

2 Years

In general, the 2-year-old is unaware of the whole problem, comes to school in diapers and rubber pants, and doesn't want to have any attention paid to this matter at all. If he has a bowel movement, however, this is usually apparent and should be attended to.

The teacher must look for readiness, and readiness might even be encouraged. For example, the child who has become aware of his toileting functions can sometimes profitably be taken to the bathroom on some pretext or other (to wash his doll in the basin, or to give his Teddy a drink), and thus he can see the others who are using the toilets. Taking a child who is not yet trained to the bathroom along with one who is, is sometimes helpful. The teacher should make no advances to the child who is not ready, but should give her attention to the child who is, and might praise his performance.

When the child shows interest in the toilet, it is better to have him come to school in training pants rather than diapers. Training pants are easily changed and allow the child to notice the puddle he makes. Sometimes a child who has had an accident will allow the teacher to change his pants in the bathroom—he may even sit on the toilet while this is being done. So long as there is no unpleasantness involved in this procedure, it may be a good idea in associating the bathroom with the puddle that has just occurred.

Some children have already started toilet training at home and need help in carrying it on at school. Boys sometimes need help in aiming. Some boys prefer to sit down on the toilet for urinating. Some children demand privacy—but this is more common at three than at two. Some children at two, three, or four have great reluctance to use the school toilet and say they want to wait and use the one at home. Sometimes these children wait till their mother comes at the end of the morning and use the school toilet then.

2½ Years

Only a minority have accidents at this age. About half the group ask for toileting when they need it, so there is not the same problem as earlier. Those who just don't care if they are wet, however, have such a long way to go that it is a mistake to make very much of the matter.

The child's general pattern of negativism may operate with regard to toileting, even though he is already "trained." If he resists, it is possible to try picking him up and talking about something else as he is carried into the bathroom. But if real resistance persists, it is wise to abandon this procedure too. Any forcing might lead to bad results at home and might harm his adjustment to nursery school. Most children at two-and-a-half years are too alert for tricks that worked with the 2-year-old, such as holding their hand, or taking their doll into the bathroom.

3 Years

There are still quite a few who object at this age to toileting at school, particularly during the first few weeks. This should be respected. Most, however, are toilet-trained. They will tell when they're going, and will ask, if they need any help. They are apt to need help in pulling up pants. Most tell spontaneously or agree when reminded. Routine toileting is necessary only for the younger ones in the group. The teacher often asks about toileting just before putting snowpants on for going outside. But the majority ask when they need, or go by themselves.

The teacher may offer to go to the toileting room with those who need to be asked. A few at this age insist that they want to go at home. Or a few have to bring their own potty, and this need should be respected.

A 3-year-old who has an accident may be much embarrassed by it. The teacher must give as much reassurance as possible and minimize the problem. If girls try to urinate standing up, the teacher can assure them that little girls do it the other way.

3½ Years

This age involves the same techniques as at three, although the child now has increased independence. A child of this age is apt to express his typically increased tension by urinating frequently.

4 Years

Toileting for the most part is now very casual except with immature children. Very few problems exist at this age, though some child may have an individual problem. The first day at school, the teacher shows the toilets to the children and tells them that they can use them at any time, and that they can go by themselves or that if they want a teacher to go with them she will.

Then the teacher may need to remind some who are too busy to bother.

Most still consider toileting a social situation. A few, however, are beginning to need privacy and this should be respected. There may be a little difficulty because of the extremes of curiosity and need for privacy which different children show at this age. One who needs privacy might need to be protected from one who shows extreme curiosity and silliness about this function.

Thus children may go whenever they wish, but just before rest time all go to the bathroom to wash hands and can go to the toilet at this time if they wish. A final reminder is given before heavy outdoor clothing is put on at the end of the morning.

Milk and Crackers

General Comments

At milk-and-cracker time most of the children sit in chairs at a table and share graham crackers from a common basket, pour milk from a common pitcher. Some children who are not ready to join the group, especially at the younger ages, have their crackers and milk apart, standing up. Most children join in general conversation at the tables, pass the crackers to one another, and often pour one another's milk.

This routine should occur at some scheduled time. It is best, in general, near the middle of the morning. Food at this time restores energy and provides a good social experience. It seems best to have it follow another routine of the group, such as music or story time, so that it is easier to get the children to the tables as a group. If it follows free play, participation might be more scattered. Planned activity before and after milk and crackers seems to make all the group activities easier, since transitions can be facilitated.

The teacher must allow leeway about manners, but should encourage politeness by example, at least to the extent of "Thank you" and "Please" and generally pleasant conversation. It is wise to keep a sponge on the table, to wipe up spilled milk easily, with no show of irritation at this inevitable happening. Teachers should pass the crackers quickly so that the children won't stand and reach for them and thus spill their milk.

Some parents worry lest children will eat too many crackers and thus "spoil their lunch." We feel, on the contrary, that in the unusual excitement of the school experience, food as nourishing as milk and graham crackers gives a much-needed support. It does not seem necessary closely to limit the number of crackers they can have, since this is a good food served at an appropriate time of the day. When the basket of crackers is finished and some of the speedy eaters with insatiable appetites ask for more, the teacher can satisfy them by saying, "That's all," and showing them the empty basket.

If the teacher can add an occasional lollipop or lifesaver to the habitual milk and crackers, especially at festive times, this is much appreciated.

2 Years

Two-year-olds need to have the lunch period rather early to keep up their energy. Some even have to have extra food before the regular milk-and-cracker time and must be fed earlier and apart from the group.

From the very beginning, some will sit down at the table, and this number increases as the year goes on. A would-be wanderer can sometimes be persuaded to join the group by sitting on a teacher's lap—or on his mother's, at the beginning. For some, it is difficult to join the group. Children who don't want to sit down can be given a cracker, or their milk and crackers can be put nearby, so that they can eat apart if they wish.

Children like to try pouring their own milk and should be encouraged to do so, while the teacher keeps a hand ready to steady and direct those who have difficulty. Conversation will be at a minimum; the teacher will have to initiate and for the most part carry on simple conversation.

2 ½ Years

Even nonconformists at this age seem to accept and enjoy their milk and crackers. They like to eat. Most enjoy the occasion boisterously. They often bang their feet on the floor, squeal, dunk crackers. All this is permitted up to a point. Rather than forbid, a teacher can get their attention by telling an interesting story, by whispering, by showing another way to eat crackers. "One cracker at a time; there are enough crackers for everybody" is a statement that is usually repeated over and over again.

When they leave the table, which some do sooner than others, they must have a specific place to go, and a teacher must await them there. Teachers can direct activity, if story time comes next, with such sentences as "When you've finished you could go and look at a book," or "I wonder what story we will read today—do you think you could find a book about a fire engine?"

3 To 3 ½ Years

Children like to sit by special friends. They like milk-and-cracker time, but they are apt to be boisterous and silly, wiggle, spill milk, shout, bite graham crackers into the shape of guns and then shoot with them. Sometimes the teacher must take a boisterous child away from the group to calm him down. In general, however, the group can be controlled by distraction. Very simple conversation will do this, such as "Do you know what?" "I know a secret," "Do you know what kind of book we're going to read next?"

Any sentences using the words "surprise," "secret," "different" are effective, as is calling attention to some child's clothing, or something on the wall. Whispering can calm them down, too, or getting them to whisper. But a teacher must not be too intent on keeping the situation in antiseptic calm. The children are pleased if their enthusiasm and boisterousness are appreciated, and if the teacher can join it too to some extent.

They can obey simple rules, such as not having the cup too full or not pouring milk from their cup back into the pitcher. Milk will, of course, be spilled. The teacher must not be angry, surprised, or annoyed but should merely say, "Oh, you spilled your milk!" and wipe it up.

4 Years

Fours enjoy milk and crackers, and conversation is really good. One thread of conversation can last for a whole period. They save places for friends. This is allowable, but if there is too much trouble the teacher may have to decide arbitrarily or plan for turns. Girls like to linger and chat; boys are more restless.

Now they can abide by the rule "One cracker at a time," but the total number of crackers to a child is not usually limited. Most can wipe their mouths and throw cup and napkin away. There is some teasing about this, and they may put their cup in the teacher's so that she has to throw both away!

Dressing

General Comments

Since the children keep on their outdoor clothing and play outside at the beginning of the morning, dressing comes only at the end of the morning when the child prepares to go outside. This is a routine, in that dressing occurs at a regular time and all children participate. Participation is not necessarily all at the *same* time, however, since some children prefer to hear more stories than others, and the story period may precede the child's going out of doors. In this routine it is good to have a large enough staff to make the activity move quickly, and to plan so that children who are not being dressed are happily occupied and contained in one room, so that most teachers can help the children who need assistance. When half the group is dressed, a large enough staff permits two teachers to take this group out first.

It is good to dress the most aggressive and boisterous first and have these among the first to go out. Only a few of the group are boisterous and difficult about dressing; the rest are usually docile.

Clothes are labeled and placed in individual cubbies. Children and teachers soon learn to identify which clothes belong to which child.

2 To 3 Years

The procedure may vary from child to child and day to day, and children at this age are better at taking off than putting on clothes. But the teachers have to do most of the dressing. Usually there is too little time to make much of a game of dressing or to wait for self-help. However, lavish praise is bestowed on any who help dress themselves at all.

It is best to keep the younger children in one room while they are being dressed. Teachers bring the clothes to the room where children have had their story. Children are given more books to look at, and there is more music from the phonograph to divert those who are waiting. The effort is to keep them from wandering, since the teachers have to give most of their attention to putting on the clothes.

4 Years

All children can now help to a certain degree, and some can dress themselves entirely. If the teacher can put the snowpants on the floor, correctly oriented, this may be all the help the children need. Praise for the one who is independent often gets the others to imitate with "I can do it too. Watch me."

Four-year-olds often need a lot of space when they are getting dressed. It often works to put clothes in piles around the playroom and to encourage children to dress by their own pile. In any case, they need to have enough space so they won't get into fights, and so that their snowpants can be stretched out on the floor. They may need special help with drawstrings, zippers, rubbers, or gloves.

Music Time

General Comments

Almost all children like music. They like to participate in music directly—by singing (even if they are not producing the "correct" tune), and by responding with body movements to sound. A teacher can stimulate a child's interest by singing tunes for him, and with him, by beating the rhythm, by clapping, beating a pan, swinging a ball, slapping the floor with hands. The child often likes best to respond with his entire person to especially rhythmical music.

Favorite songs for singing are the nursery songs and simple folk songs. Also popular are songs with dramatic interest, or songs reflecting children's everyday life, such as seasonal happenings, or common events at home or school. Ballads, work songs, chants, spirituals adapt themselves easily to a child's singing interest. And possible kinds of rhythmic response are more numerous than the average adult can imagine: children not only love to clap, gallop, hammer, jump, march, roll, stretch, swing, walk, but delight in both singing and rhythms in spontaneous creative improvisations.

At music time all the children gather around the piano, sit on the floor (or lie on the floor) and listen to the music, or participate in the music by singing the various songs and engaging in the finger play that often accompanies the songs. All the children together participate in the rhythm bands or rhythmic activities that follow the singing time. The nature of the songs and length of participation, of course, vary with the ages of the children in the group, but even 2-year-olds seem to enjoy such an experience.

Music for the group seems best when it comes at a regular time, so that all other toys can be put away and the opportunity for distraction be lessened. All teachers should free themselves to participate in music, and thus help the boisterous and timid to accept the routine. Singing and participation from the teachers show the children what to do.

It is helpful to have a piano, or some musical instrument such as the autoharp or guitar. Such instruments help children discover the tunes and rhythms of music. Materials for rhythm bands—drums, bells, xylophones, musical triangles—may be introduced as early as two-and-a-half with considerable success, for part of the period.

Music time can provide varied experiences. Children begin by sitting on the floor in front of the piano, and singing a few songs; sometimes they select the songs, sometimes the teacher does so. Quiet songs seem to provide the most satisfactory beginning, since children have just come from active free play periods. Finger plays and songs demanding dramatic actions encourage the children to participate in other ways. Bodily responses to rhythm music—flying like a bird, pretending to be an airplane, etc.—afford other kinds of action. Dramatic response becomes increasingly more complicated as the child gets older.

Some children may have to stay apart from the group and listen from a nearby room. Some children enjoy only music that lends itself to bodily activity. Such children can help the teacher get milk and crackers ready in another room, or can look at a book, or listen to records, until the teacher thinks they can profitably join the group in rhythms. Some have to sit on special chairs to help them restrain their tendency to molest other, quiet children. Some simply cannot resist running around the room and screaming. When this is distracting or encourages mass participation in a similar kind of behavior, the boisterous child must be taken away to some other kind of activity.

One teacher should have the responsibility for planning and directing music each day, to ensure interest. But as in other planning, flexibility is important so that the children can express spontaneous creations, or so that the teacher can shorten or lengthen her program as the situation demands. Usually children can sustain an interest in music for about a half-hour, providing the program is sufficiently varied, and suited to their ages.

2 To 2½ Years

Children can be brought most easily to music by the singing of songs they have already heard at home. In general, the Mother

Goose Nursery Songs are best for this purpose. "Twinkle, Twinkle, Little Star" and "Humpty Dumpty" seem to be universal favorites from first to last. Simple finger plays, such as "Two Little Dickie Birds" or "Cobbler, Cobbler, Mend My Shoe" or "Open, Shut Them," are also popular.

Two-year-olds do not seem to mind singing the same songs at each successive music time. New songs must be introduced very gradually, and must be very simple. "Chug-Chug-Chug, I'm a Little Tug" seems to represent the level of accomplishment which can be expected. With new songs the teacher often needs such props as a picture showing what the song is about, or an object such as a car, a doll, a teddy, a farm animal, to whom the children are to sing their song. She needs to say the words of the song first (and many other times) to help the children learn the words as well as the music.

Dramatic response to music involves simple bodily actions—running, jumping, crawling—where each child is on his own. As the year goes on, simple combinations of children, such as the lineup for a train or several circles for "Ring Around the Rosey," are possible. Rhythm bands are worth working with, although they seem chaotic at the beginning, since children are liable to become more interested in controlling their neighbor's instrument than in using their own.

Quiet singing usually precedes active participation. With young children it seems best not to alternate the two, since it is very difficult to bring them back to quiet singing once they move around the room.

3 To 3½ Years

At the beginning of the year, children of this age experience music in much the same way they did at two and two-and-a-half. But before the year is far along they demand more complicated songs, songs with more dramatic flair. Children of three-and-a-half like exaggerated noise or quiet or humor in a song. Television favorites are apt to make a bid for popularity.

Children, too, are much attracted by a "theme" for the music period, such as a visit to a toy shop, and singing about all the things they see in the toy shop; or going with a teddy bear on a picnic and singing about all the things they do. Showing pictures or producing props to make such themes more graphic assures more universal interest at music time.

Children are rather self-conscious at first about offering their own words to a tune, or their own dramatic motions, but beginnings can be made which come to flower at four. Rhythm bands, with children as "directors," are much better than formerly.

4 Years

This is a particularly rewarding time to listen to and to discuss children's ideas (they are now more articulate than before) and to encourage their efforts to express themselves in music. Children love to make music themselves, and music time can often be initiated when they are still at free play and start chanting a tune. Other children may pick this up quite spontaneously; the teacher may move in with encouragement to keep it going, and may help with dramatic props. This "made up song" can be repeated and added to again and again.

It is often amazing where a simple idea may lead. For example, children may make a boat and want to sing a boat song. A teacher can explore what boats children know about (and they know a surprising amount), what they feel about boats, and can ask them to make the noises or motions of rowboat, sailboat, motor, speed, fire, excursion, ferry, police, swan boat—or ocean liner, tug, destroyer. A discussion of boats may lead to the naming and dramatization of other things in the water—fish, bell buoys, rocks, waves, gulls. Thus music and rhythms may come from a discussion of related things that move; or the process may be reversed and children may do what the music suggests.

Fours are very much interested in discussing and manipulating materials and relating these to music—scarves, ropes, plastic balls, for example. They ask, "Is it light, is it heavy, does it bounce, does it break?" Then they match musical sounds and movements to the materials.

Children are now able to have a longer, richer listening experience with music than before. Sometimes they respond actively, sometimes passively, to classical music. It is interesting at times to see the different kinds of responses of Fours in matching colors to music records, sometimes at the easel or with crayons, but especially with finger painting.

Fours are also very attentive to parents or friends who come to school and play an instrument—guitar, flute, drum, violin. The younger child is often not content unless he can handle the instrument himself. Fours, however, can be a most appreciative audience.

Story Time

General Comments

For stories, the children gather on the floor in a special room apart from the general playroom, where there are no toys to distract them. (No toys are allowed at any of these group activities, for the presence of a toy in a child's hand inevitably leads to snatching by some other child and subsequent interruption of group activity. Children learn to put such toys on a shelf till "later.")

Quiet music from a phonograph may set the tone of this period. As children come in, each receives a book to look at. Children are more selective about what book they choose to "read" on their own, as they get older. They are also more likely to sit in special places, usually on a cushion on the floor, and to sit longer than does the younger child. Some do not look at books, but lie on their pillows and listen to the music. Others talk with their friends about the pictures on the walls. Others gaze at the fish in the large aquarium, in what seems like hypnotized fascination. No loud talking or rough play is permitted in this room; a child who cannot be quiet is taken somewhere else.

Two-year-olds can listen to stories for about twenty minutes; 3-year-olds for about half an hour. Some 4-year-olds can sit and listen as long as stories are being read. With 4-year-olds the situation can be so managed that children who want to leave early can do so without disrupting the group. With the younger children, a more sheeplike tendency operates—when several children leave the room, most of the others follow.

The management of the routines of music and stories requires planning and skill from teachers. In general, we must emphasize that to carry out these activities successfully a teacher must have fairly regular and familiar procedures, as well as considerable art in communicating stories and music to children. This art involves little tricks to get their attention and usually calls for some dramatic ability and a voice that is clear and pleasant and can adapt itself to a variety of tones. It also means that the teacher who takes on the tasks of directing music or reading stories must be very sensitive to the general age characteristics, and to the individualities, of children in her group.

Some young and high-powered children cannot participate in music unless they sit on a chair or on a teacher's lap. Their overwhelming tendency to touch and explore supersedes their interest in music, unless they have such boundaries to their activities. Other children need to be brought into the group with frequent comments directed to them personally, such as "Here's a song that Bobby sings especially well" or "Here's a story about going to a store—did you ever go to a store like this one, Kim?"

Some children have to be a prop man in music—for instance, holding up objects that the other children are singing about—a cow, star, pumpkin, etc. Some have to sit beside the teacher at the piano to help her play—this is usually less discordant if they sit so that they bang the higher range of the scale. Such banging can be managed only if a number of children do not want to do it at once. Frequently only one needs to do this, and he often displays a very good sense of rhythm in his accompaniment.

It is helpful to have as many teachers as possible participate in music and stories. Not only are a number of laps needed, especially for the younger children, but the children are more likely to take part if they have the example of the teachers to stimulate them. The teachers must sing, do the finger plays, crawl around the floor like a bear, jump like a rabbit, fly like a bird— do whatever the children do, and encourage the children, too, to spontaneous response to music and stories, by their interest and praise when such spontaneity occurs, or by asking children to "tell some more about the song" or "show what else we can do."

The reading of a story to the group comes at a regular time and in a special room. This room should be apart from the main playroom, if possible, and should be a small room with a rug on the floor and with enough pillows available so that each child can sit or lie on a pillow on the floor if he wishes. It is important that the children remain seated when the story is being read, since other children cannot see the pictures in the book which the teacher reads when a wanderer obstructs the view.

There should be a good supply of books for each child to look at on his own when he first comes into the room. He may select a book from the low bookshelves in the room, or from a large basket where many of the books are kept, or he may accept one that a teacher gives him. When he first comes to the room, he may, if he wishes, lie down and listen to the victrola music. He cannot bring his crackers or any toys into the story room, and a teacher should be on hand to supervise and arrange the children in proper places as they come into the room.

When the teacher begins to read to the group, she holds her book up so that all can see and speaks loudly and clearly enough so that all can hear. It is important that she begin with an interest- ing book, hold up an interesting picture, and talk in general about what she is going to read. All other books must be put away, or children must sit on the book they have been regarding and thus have it ready for future attention when the story to the group is finished.

Flannel boards are also very good in affording variety. In addition, the teacher can sometimes tell children stories without using a book or pictures. Children are usually startled initially when there is no picture to look at, but if the teacher is a skilled storyteller, they enjoy and benefit from an experience robbed of the usual visual props, which are increasingly in demand.

It is helpful, in providing books for the children, to consider the kinds of books most appropriate for the different ages. For although there are many individual differences in children that are influential in fostering their degree of interest in books, such as their attention span, their use of language, and their comprehension of language, the age of the child suggests in general both his potentialities and limitations for enjoying books.

Often children ask for stories in the middle of their free play time, but although the teacher may look briefly and comment on the story they select, she asks them to save it till story time. Usually there are not enough teachers to allow attention to be diverted to reading during the period of free play, and some children need a more varied day than such overattention to books would provide.

2 To 2½ Years

At first children mill around the room and many teachers' and mothers' laps are needed to suggest to the children that they can enjoy a book without having immediate contact with it. Or children can be set down over and over with the explanation, "So you can see the pictures better." After about six weeks of school most children learn what they have to do in order to enjoy the story. Some very high-powered ones, or children with minimal language, cannot stay in the room for longer than is involved in listening to one story. Twenty minutes is usually long enough for story time.

Of primary importance for the average 2-year-old is simplicity —large, clear pictures with few details, a situation of minimum complexity, simple language with no abstract words or ideas. Also, Two likes to have one idea repeated over and over. Indeed, his interest in repetition suggests what is perhaps the most important criterion for the success of a book intended for a child of two.

The 2-year-old's limited experiences center chiefly in the here and now. Thus he enjoys books which depict the sort of sights he commonly sees and the sort of day he commonly experiences. He likes to hear about getting up, getting dressed, eating breakfast, taking a walk, playing with a wagon, and going to bed in his crib.

Two-year-olds often wander about, look at books only briefly, talk aloud even while the story is being read. Also these younger children listen to fewer stories. As the teacher reads to the group, she encourages those who want to continue looking at the book they have been given when they first came in, to sit on this book. When they can thus control the book they have, they seem to be more relaxed about listening as the teacher reads.

Younger children sometimes need to walk up and touch the book, put their faces as near as possible to the page. They need repeated urgings to sit down so that children behind them can see. Children particularly prone to wander can often be settled by providing them with a special chair to sit on near the teacher.

3 To 3 ½ Years

Children of three usually enjoy books very much, and most can listen for a half-hour. They become completely carried away by the events in the story.

Although the 3-year-old can enjoy those books which have been described as suitable for two, he is usually ready for somewhat more complicated fare. He continues to like simplicity of story and picture and reference to experiences with which he is likely to be familiar. But the range of his experiences is now greater, and such seasonal happenings as building a snowman, going to a birthday party, may not have been part of the 2-year-old's conscious world. Three's expanding interest includes other people he is likely to see or hear about. He likes books about road menders, carpenters, painters, postmen, taxi men.

The world of fantasy becomes more distinctly appealing as the child moves on toward four. With three-and-a-half, the age when imaginary companions are at their height, it is little wonder that the stories of anthropomorphized animals are very popular. *Curious George*, by H. A. Rey, deserves special mention because it is such a favorite with Threes and Fours. This book and others in the same series about this agile little monkey have an appeal that seems to come from that quality which makes cartoons so enjoyable to children—a combination of the fantastic, the human, the humorous, and the daring in a fast-moving, highly dramatic story.

And although the horror of some of the Grimms' fairy tales has shocked a few sensitive children and many sensitive parents, most 3-year-olds show great enjoyment of the old favorites— "Little Red Riding Hood," "Three Bears," "The Fox and the Little Red Hen." It seems that the average 3- and 4-year-old child can handle these themes with equanimity. He enjoys aggression and wickedness and imminent disaster with bears, wolves, and foxes as villains. He seems to enjoy the threat to security, but he seems to remain personally secure and unthreatened in his belief that evil will get its due reward.

4 Years

The 4-year-old enjoys a long period looking at books, and a long period listening. Indeed, some children at four will listen as long as a teacher will read. It is not unusual for children to sit in rapt attention while five or six books are read for a period as long as forty-five minutes. Usually, however, a half-hour is a long enough time for the story period.

Since four is an "out-of-bounds" age, it is not too surprising to find that the 4-year-old has a voracious appetite for the dramatic and that no situation seems fantastic enough to overtax the constantly inventive imagination of the fantastic, fanciful Four. Four-year-olds also like books that experiment with words as well as with ideas. They like words flowing in alliterative abundance, words in magical chants, words with extremes of sound effects. They seem to be unusually able to enjoy humor, both of word and of situation.

Complexity of event and possible horror of situation seem to add value to many of the 4-year-old's favorite tales. Executioners and miraculous rescues from destruction have much the same sort of appeal that the Grimms' fairy tales afford. However, caution must be exercised to protect those children who cannot tolerate a fearful or tension-provoking story.

The 4-year-old also likes complexity of illustration. He enjoys an abundance and diversity of tiny details. Whereas the 2-year-old demanded a single picture to the page, the 4-year-old delights in searching out numerous minutiae in illustrations to stimulate and satisfy his constantly expanding interest and imagination.

TECHNIQUES FOR EFFECTING TRANSITIONS

Any discussion of nursery school techniques must include a consideration of techniques for effecting transitions. Often the child who has had trouble in coming to nursery school in the first place will also have trouble in shifting from one activity to another even after he has adjusted to school. Such children seem to be enamored of the *status quo* and need special help to make any kind of change attractive. Just as there were many individual differences with regard to adjustment, there are numerous differences in the way children handle transitions. The techniques we propose here, however, are general and do not consider individual problems.

2 Years

Arrival. Personal contact with a teacher helps. A teacher must be on hand to help in the very real problem of detaching the child from the parent. The 2-year-old seems in general to need to go from person to person; he does not like to be led to a room and left on his own. The teacher may need to pick him up or hold his hand or talk to him. Some Twos need only distraction. Others need some simple formula each time, such as "Shall we go and see the bunny?" or "I could find a good puzzle for you." They like to have their name mentioned, with a greeting such as "Good morning, Nicholas. I'm happy to see you."

Going outside. The assurance of a teacher's attention is important. Twos like to have their attention directed to something specific outside, such as "Let's go out and see the slide."

Taking off outdoor clothes. It seems easiest for an adult to sit on a low chair and, holding the child on her lap, take his clothes off. This is seldom complicated, for the child offers little resistance.

Leaving free play for music. It is easier to make this transition if children and teachers change the environment by picking up all the toys that children have been playing with, and putting them on the shelves. All the large toys, such as rocking horses, trucks, ladders, should be moved to another room. Such cleaning up gives the signal for the transition, allows the children to participate in it, and removes distracting objects so that they can better give their attention to a routine.

Going to milk and crackers. Children like to tiptoe, skip, creep, or use some such special type of locomotion, to some special tune at the piano.

Leaving. Since most children are ready to leave for home when the time comes, there is little difficulty with this transition.

Summary. From any one activity or place to another, picking children up and carrying them, or taking their hands and leading them seems to be an effective technique. Luring with a favorite toy also works. Personal contact, setting up the physical situation, repetition are the main devices effective at this age. Often it is not necessary to say anything. Words do not play a major role at this age.

2½ Years

Arrival. Children are apt to make trouble about leaving their mothers and are liable to hit mother or hit teacher. A variety of adjustment techniques may need to be called on here. Or children build up their own transitions, as by kissing parent good-bye.

Going outside. They often say that they don't want to go outside. But after their outdoor clothes are off, they may insist that they do. It is not unusual, after they have been out about five minutes, for them to want to come in. The teacher must work at distracting them to keep them satisfied, as long as possible, where they are.

Taking off outdoor clothes. Most run around and some do not want their clothes taken off. The teacher must hold and distract the reluctant ones, and take clothes off while they are unaware of what is happening. They don't hang things up without personal supervision. A picture for each cubby helps give a clue where each child's clothes go.

Leaving free play for music. The same techniques as at two are effective, but more verbal techniques which suggest the positive. It is unwise for a teacher to expect much help from the children in picking up the toys.

Going to milk and crackers. A number refuse to walk, skip, tiptoe, or creep and must have their crackers and milk brought to them wherever they decide to station themselves.

Leaving. Children are now likely to make a fuss about leaving. The mother is liable to be embarrassed if the child runs away or hides or has one more turn or otherwise doesn't comply with her request to leave. She then often talks too much or uses poor techniques in her embarrassment, and eventually may try to drag away a screaming child. If such trouble develops, the teacher may help the mother by suggesting that she bring a "surprise" to lure the child away. A package, which the child can unwrap as he leaves, containing raisins, cereal, or a little sandwich, sometimes is enough to make departure pleasant. Or the teacher could help by asking the child, "Will you show me your car? What color is your car? Let's see if I can find your car." Or she can lure him along by suggesting, "Let's go indoors and get your painting (or a graham cracker) before you go." The teacher can help the child save face—he needs just a little help. Or she can ask the mother to sit in the car and then can say to the child, "Let's try to find your mother. We'll go a different way. Let's surprise her."

Summary. At this age children are likely to resist almost any transition, and the teacher must be prepared to cope with resistance. Physical and verbal techniques combined are needed. One must be ready for a slow release even after interest has waned. It is important not to hurry children too much. This is both a perseverative and a dawdling age. If rituals have been set up by the child, try to use them instead of fighting against them.

3 Years

Arrival. Threes are usually eager to come to school, and many get out of the car by themselves and precede their parents into the school. They like to be greeted, but often have time for no more than a cheerful "Hi" in return.

Going outside. The majority are eager to go outside and like outdoor activities.

Taking off outdoor clothes. When they come in, they are all so eager to get to playing that all clamor to be undressed at once. The teacher can unsnap a few snaps and unzip a few zippers to get them started, and then tell them to try the rest themselves. She can also suggest that they help one another in specific instances. Their attempts to do so are usually futile, but they often enjoy these efforts and are thus kept happily occupied until it is their turn to be helped by a teacher. Some children cannot wait at all, however, and rush to the playroom with all their warm clothes on, apparently unaware that they are so heavily clad. Few have any interest in hanging their clothes in their cubbies; they are too interested in starting to play.

Leaving free play for music. It is still necessary to clear toys away in order to help children get their attention directed to music and to keep them from being distracted. Many will cooperate in this project. When the teacher begins playing the piano, they all come and sit down in front of it, on the floor. Children want to bring toys from their earlier play, but if they are not separated from these at once, an inevitable quarrel over the possession of the toys will interfere with the music. High-spirited friends may sit beside one another and become progressively more boisterous unless they are separated.

Going to milk and crackers. Verbal suggestion and special music are usually enough to bring them to this welcome event.

Leaving. Usually they are happy to leave and there is little difficulty about this. Some need to perform one more trick or have one more turn at something.

Summary. Once children of this age have learned the routines, they usually like to follow them and thus go from one thing to another without difficulty. Often the merest verbal suggestion is enough. They like the routine, have it in mind, follow it, talk about it. "First we have this and then we do this," they may say spontaneously. Words are usually enough to motivate them, but they themselves, with their gross motor drive better in hand, may like to run, jump, or hop into the bathroom or elsewhere.

3½ Years

Children of this age present problems in all transitions very similar to those common at two-and-a-half. These problems are more difficult to solve, however, since there is more guile on the part of the child, and consequently more subtlety and skill are needed from the teacher. Children demonstrate extremes of opposition loudly. Often they are tearful and wailing. Sometimes a teacher can take them by surprise and override their objections by such a word as "Scat!" when they are balking.

Or the teacher must be alert to outwit them in more sophisticated ways. They need new approaches. The fact that something worked once does not mean that it will work a second time. A teacher can try verbal humor or discussions of things that have gone on. Children are often distracted by a discussion of something they have read in a story as the teacher asks, "Do you remember this or that?" They are also extremely vulnerable to compliments about their appearance and good behavior, even when they are behaving their worst. Sometimes a teacher may need to go back to physical handling.

4 Years

Arrival. Since children are more sophisticated at this age, it is important that the child be greeted on arrival in a manner that takes his individuality into consideration. Generalized greetings are not good now. Most like a warm, personal greeting, and some comment about what they are wearing, who brought them to school, and what they're going to do. They enjoy having some specific job to do at once, such as helping with the pets or helping prepare some materials. Children who have some trouble entering the group may be helped by being allowed to bring something from home that they plan to show or share with the group. At the younger ages such tokens often cause trouble, because the child must work so hard protecting them from his predatory peers, but 4-year-olds respect property brought from home. They can be helped in releasing parents with verbal suggestion, such as "We'll say good-bye and then look out the window and wave."

Going outside. Children now are so identified with the group that if the group goes outside, most want to go too. When there is any resistance, the teacher can introduce humor, such as an exaggerated way of walking, funny talking, or chanting. Counting the steps or singing a song using all the children's names helps too. With some, just taking a hand and talking on the way out provides sufficient distraction.

Taking off outdoor clothes. If an interesting activity is coming along immediately, the children will race to be among the first to get their clothes off and get to the activity. If they have trouble, the teacher can help. If they balk, she should ignore the resistance, talk about something else, and resume help at an appropriate time. She may expedite matters by such a ruse as "I'm so eager to see what color pants you have on today."

Leaving free play for music. In the schedule in our school, with Fours, it has seemed best to have music directly after the children come indoors after their play outside. In this way just those children who choose to come to music come in; a small group sometimes stays outside. Finger play and action songs will settle a group down when they first come in to music. Transition from music to free play is benefited by some help from the teachers. The teacher plays "thinking" music, and children remain quiet on the floor until they think what activity they are going to take up. This prevents a general scramble to the same activity, or aimless wandering.

Going to milk and crackers. Teachers and children help pick up the toys and set up milk and crackers. A rest time follows, in the same room where the story will be read. Planning ahead helps this transition as the teacher says, "You better go in and rest now, because after rest time we're going to do so-and-so." The promise of a new book or a special book can facilitate going to the story room.

Leaving. Generally they are glad to see their parent. Delays are mostly to show something they can do. Those who are reluctant to leave sometimes fall prey to an appeal to their spirit of competition, as the teacher says, "See if you can beat me to the top of the hill" or "I'll race you to the gate."

Summary. Transitions are in general easy for 4-year-olds because they like the schedule and like to participate in what the whole group does. Balking tends to be an individual problem and can be handled individually. A well-planned schedule fits what the children would naturally like to do, with rest after active times, and active and interesting periods following rest. It is necessary to plan so that the whole group won't move all at once, causing confusion. It is helpful to send children from group activities one at a time by some device such as "When you feel a tickle on the end of your nose, you go," or "The boy with the blue pants can go now." Movement can also be planned through friends—they want to be selected to do certain things with certain friends.

13

The Child with Special Needs

Early in the history of the nursery school movement, many schools followed a policy of having what they considered a "regular" group of supposedly normal children in everyday, or every-other-day, attendance. Into this group they introduced, from time to time, a certain number of "problem" children— as many as they felt the group could absorb without interfering with its own effectiveness. The idea was good but did not always work out too well.

The reason seemed to be this. Early in this century, relatively little was known about the developing stages of child behavior. Many of the so-called problem children referred to a nursery school were referred because of what we now consider the normal obstinacy of the typical 2½-year-old; the uncertainty and insecurity of the typical Three-and-a-Half; the boisterous out-of-bounds behavior characteristic of the quite normal Four. Inevitably, as such children remained in school for a few months, since stages of equilibrium and disequilibrium in the preschool years often alternate at more or less six-month intervals, they moved on into smoother behavior. And many of the supposedly normal children moved on into stages of disequilibrium and exhibited behavior which did cause problems.

Thus many schools gave up the distinction between problem and normal children, and so far as facilities permitted, accepted children (except those who were extremely deviant) as they applied. Nursery schools made every effort to meet the individual problems of every child—whether his special needs resulted from age or individuality factors—but such problems were not made a basis for discrimination or labeling.

However, then as now, it was recognized that there are some special kinds of children whose behavior characteristics lie outside normal limits. Teachers asked themselves, as we still do, to what extent can a regular nursery school include the retarded child, the gifted child, the deaf, blind, or crippled child, the autistic child, the child who speaks a different language. New kinds of problems are recognized today—hyperkinesis, minimal brain dysfunction, learning disability.

To what extent can any or all of these be included in a regular nursery school? To what extent can we expect to help them? To what extent *should* we attempt to meet the special needs of such children when and if they conflict with the smooth running of the group?

There are many atypical children who can unquestionably benefit considerably from at least a limited amount of nursery school attendance. However, any such attendance should be carefully planned to meet the special needs of each individual child. Nursery schools should not, in an excess of kindness or zeal, adopt a blanket policy of throwing open their doors to any and all handicapped children. There are many who will not benefit from nursery school attendance.

Whatever the special problem of the child in question, it may not be so much his kind of problem or even the seriousness of the problem (though that must always be considered) as his ability to adapt to and to benefit from school attendance that will determine whether or not nursery school would be desirable.

Some children even with rather severe handicaps seem so confident and friendly, so adaptable, that everybody gets on with them, even to the extent that their handicaps may go more or less unnoticed. Others with relatively minor handicaps seem to be so aware of these handicaps and so bothered by them that they have a hard time gaining acceptance from other children and fitting into the group.

It must also be remembered that in all special cases, acceptance is a two-way thing. Not only must the child accept the group, but teacher and group must feel comfortable with the child. The extent to which the other children accept a child depends a great deal on his own personality and approach. The extent to which the *teacher* accepts the child may depend to quite an extent on her. Certainly any teacher must make every reasonable attempt to overcome any prejudice she may have against certain handicaps. But a teacher can be a very good teacher in general and still not be especially effective with certain kinds of children. This handicap on the part of the teacher must be accepted and respected until or unless she herself can overcome it.

Those who screen applicants for nursery school should have knowledge and techniques which enable them to recognize children who might not be expected to benefit from the usual nursery school and who need a special kind of school or special care. In such cases the school should see to it that the parent is referred to the appropriate agency or physician or other child specialist who can care for the child's need if such provision has not already been made by the parent. Or sometimes it is effective for such a child to have limited participation in a nursery school as a supplement to a clinic's or doctor's care.

Schools which undertake to include exceptional children need to do careful planning. The school must be sure that the children who are accepted will benefit from the experience. To this end there must be appropriate diagnostic testing, and reasonable assurance from a referral agency or physician that in their opinion the school will be potentially good for the child.

Special children frequently need special transportation or limited hours of attendance. Sometimes special physical accommodations or special curriculum materials need to be supplied. In some instances a teacher's time needs to be sufficiently freed so that the child will be assured of her more or less constant surveillance. Tutorial sessions from teachers in the school are sometimes in order, or arrangements made so that the child can work with a special consultant from outside the usual school staff. There must be adequate expectation to work with the families of these children.

Except for children with severe handicapping conditions, most young handicapped children can be served effectively in programs for presumably normal children. In such programs children have a maximum opportunity to be treated and educated *as children.* Too often special education programs see the disability or handicap first and lose sight of the many aspects of normal functioning in a child. The fact that a child is deaf or blind does not mean that he may not be well endowed in physical and motor skills, for example, and these should be developed as fully as possible, along with any special efforts that may be made to allow the child compensatory education because of his special disability. All aspects of development—motor, adaptive, language, personal-social—must be recognized and developed to their maximum.

Although many nursery schools can do an excellent job of filling the needs of the child with special problems, so far as his overall development is concerned we must underline our belief that the school takes on a major educational responsibility in endeavoring to help such children. The school needs constant awareness of the areas where a child requires special help and tutorial, psychiatric, physical, or medical sessions to supplement the regular school program.

We also emphasize again that there are many instances in which the child himself might benefit, but in which the cost to the school and to the other children might be excessive. Any benefit to an individual child must in such instances always be weighed against the effect which his presence may have on the total group. We shall discuss a few of the kinds of special children who might well fit into the program of the ordinary nursery school.

The retarded child. The kind of atypical child who most often attends school is the child who is mentally retarded. As with other difficulties and differences, a great deal here depends both on the degree of retardation and on the personality and drive of the child in question. A placid, slow-moving defective child who is reasonably good-natured and amenable can often fit very satisfactorily into the average nursery school group at his own developmental level. An aggressive, unruly child might not be able to make a good adjustment even though his developmental level might be closer to normal. The personal habits and social behavior of such a child must also be evaluated. A child with too little control might actually constitute a safety hazard to himself and to others.

In many instances of retarded children, attendance might help the parents, but it might not be too helpful to the child himself. The prognosis and future plans for the child also make a difference. If the child's level is very low and if he probably is soon to be institutionalized, nursery school might not be worthwhile. But if it is planned that he will continue to live at home, the school experience might help a good deal in giving him a chance to experience a normal social situation.

At any rate, attendance should always be on an experimental basis. It must prove not to take too much out of the group. Unless the child in question seems to be showing some (even though slow) improvement, it may not be judged worthwhile to continue.

In cases where nursery school is being considered for a retarded child, a preliminary developmental examination could be most helpful both to his parents and to the teachers in determining whether or not school attendance should be tried.

When nursery school attendance does turn out to be successful with retarded children, as is often the case, it can socialize them, relax them, help show whether or not they may later fit into regular kindergarten when they are older. School can often help to establish some of the basic personal habits which the home may not have succeeded in establishing. Also, even when school may not change the child too much, frequently it turns out to be worthwhile because of the benefit a parent derives from the opportunity of receiving help and advice about the child from a skilled teacher.

The slower-developing child, as well as the retarded child, can often benefit by nursery school attendance. This can be especially true in the case of an immature 5-year-old who seems ready for some school experience but is not fully ready for kindergarten. Often such a child adjusts very nicely to, and enjoys and benefits from, a 4-year-old nursery group experience.

In fact, now that more and more parents and schools are going along with our own feeling that it should be a child's behavior age, rather than his chronological age, which determines the time of school entrance, many 5-year-olds are not being entered in kindergarten. This means that many nursery schools are now offering a 5-year-old group or prekindergarten group for 5-year-olds who may not be fully ready for the demands of kindergarten.

The blind child. Another problem with which the nursery school is frequently confronted is whether or not it can successfully include a blind or partially sighted child in one of its regular groups.

In the case of completely blind children, or those who have only light and dark perception, a nursery school planned especially for such children, with special equipment and program, is ideal. Sighted children may or may not be included in this special group, as the policy of the school dictates. If such a nursery for blind children is not available, it is usually worth trying to have a child attend a regular nursery school. Such attendance would, however, have to be on an extremely individualized basis. Such a child should be permitted only as much school experience as will benefit him and will not tire, upset, or confuse him.

It is no small undertaking for a school to try to include such a child, who will need special and constant attention from a teacher or from his parent. Any attendance should definitely be on a trial basis. The school must ask itself two questions: Does this experience benefit the child, and is it or is it not too hard on the group? Attendance at first should be extremely limited to be certain that it is not overfatiguing.

There are of course many simple precautions which must be taken when a blind child is attending school. His first visit should be alone without other children being there, so that he can get used to basic landmarks. Furniture should not be moved too often or too much during regular sessions when he is present, as moved landmarks confuse him and could constitute an emotional hazard. Someone, teacher or parent, should be constantly aware of his activities.

With all the possible complications involved, sometimes it turns out to be impractical to have the blind child in a regular group. When this is the case, the experiment should be readily relinquished without anyone feeling that either the school or the child has failed. Such an easy termination is facilitated if the attendance is considered from the very first to be on merely a trial basis.

The deaf child. Deafness is one of the easiest handicaps for the nursery school to work with and can be one of the most rewarding. Actually it is not so much the degree of deafness which may determine fitness for school as the child's intelligence and general personality makeup. A well-constituted deaf child can successfully accomplish a good deal in nursery school, whereas an extremely atypical deaf child often does not fit in.

School attendance, if it turns out to be practical, can be very important for the deaf child. We prefer that he attend a regular nursery school rather than just a special school for the deaf. A regular school gives him a chance to see normal children playing, to learn from them, to imitate them. In such a setting he can become accustomed to responding quite normally, as normal children do, to other normal children.

The parents of a partially deaf child can help the school to know what words he can say and can respond to, and often his adjustment seems quite within normal bounds. However, here as with other handicaps, though the school should adapt to such a child when necessary, the main question is, Can he fit into a usual group without too much special attention and without seriously disrupting the adjustment of the group?

Deaf children often become real favorites in a nursery school. There is much that a teacher can do to help the other children respond to a deaf child effectively. Thus she can tell them, "Look right at him when you talk to him." Having a child like this in a group can be a very rewarding experience both for the teacher and for the other children, who often can actually see his improvement. Deafness in early childhood may be initially only in the high-frequency range. A good nursery school experience is especially rewarding for a child with this kind of deafness.

The crippled child. There is a serious question, with any crippled child, as to whether or not nursery school attendance is desirable. Each case should be decided on its own merits. Before the school experience is decided upon, there should be an initial check with the child's doctor, his physical therapist, or his psychologist. If the child is admitted to the group, there should be continuing contact with these specialists.

The length and frequency of his visits to school should be carefully regulated by what will be beneficial to him. If school seems to be really helping him, he should be allowed to continue. But the desirability of continued attendance should be constantly reviewed.

As to the response of the other children to such a child—it should theoretically be possible to prepare older children (4-year-olds) for the appearance and behavior of a crippled child. Younger children cannot be as well prepared; but they, on the other hand, often do not seem to notice differences. However, at any age, some children do question and do seem to mind. If so, then the teacher must meet their questions with matter-of-fact answers. Sometimes parents can help by talking about such differences at home.

But if a crippled child is not accepted socially in spite of all reasonable efforts by the teacher, then in our opinion attendance should probably be discontinued. The welfare of the total group should always be considered, and not simply the welfare of some special child.

The autistic child. This is a kind of child frequently met with in nursery schools and one who can usually be absorbed into the group without too much difficulty. This type of child can often be helped considerably by the school experience without too much expense to the group.

Leo Kanner was the first to describe this kind of difficulty, and we refer any serious students of personality deviation to his *Child Psychiatry*[1] for the best description and treatment of this deviation. Briefly, the autistic child is one who does not relate in the ordinary way to people and situations, from the beginning of life on. People say of him "He is in a shell" . . . "Happiest when left alone" . . . "Acts as if other people were not there."

1. Fourth ed. (Springfield, Ill.: C. C. Thomas, 1972).

Such children often treat other people as if the people were merely objects, and in part their relation to objects may be stronger than their relation to people. They also seem to have little defined sense of self or of who they are. One autistic boy we know, when asked if he could write his name (usually one of the first words a child can write), replied in the typically hollow, monotonous voice of the autistic child, "I don't know that word. That's just a middle-sized word and I only know big words and little words."

Their language, in the early years, often does not convey much meaning to other people, and their wish to communicate with others may be very slight. They often repeat things just as they hear them. Thus if someone says to them, "Say good-bye to Mrs. Jones," they will repeat, "Say good-bye to Mrs. Jones." Their surprising rote memory often encourages their parents, but their rigid demand that things be done always in the same way (like the 2½-year-old) can be extremely trying.

In dealing with a child of this type, it is important to recognize the fact that he was, in our opinion at least, born that way. Too many parents of autistic children have been counseled that the child acts as coldly and impersonally as he does because they, the parents, have rejected him. Too many are told that he is withdrawing from their own cold treatment of him. In our opinion, this is not the case. We do not believe that a child is "made" autistic by the way he has been treated. A parent's cold treatment—which he himself inspires—may exaggerate the child's behavior, but it does not cause his coldness. A warm approach, conversely, can help to "thaw him out," but it cannot change his basic personality. At he grows older, however, he may increasingly learn ways to manage his deviancy in social relations and self-awareness.

This kind of child, in order to effect a reasonably successful nursery school experience, requires very special handling. Since any discussion of this subject is virtually absent from the literature, we present here at some length special techniques for handling the autistic child in nursery school. Use of proper techniques facilitates his receiving optimum benefit from the experience, and helps to prevent him from disturbing the group.

First of all, teachers should recognize the basic qualities of autistic children and not expect too much. Lack of ability, of development, in personal-social relations should be accepted. Even the often-observed almost total lack of ego development must be fully appreciated before it can be dealt with successfully.

It is important to help the autistic child build up the knowledge that he is he, and that you are you. He may get the idea about another person before he gets the idea about himself. This is a first big step.

One special teacher should be assigned to each autistic child. She does not, of course, have to spend all her time with him, but she should always have her eye on him. It is difficult for such a child to shift teachers. He has such a slight concept of a teacher at best that to shift teachers will mean that he has to start all over again. His special teacher can help him by saying his name, over and over again.

The autistic child needs the teacher's protection in his inevitable rages over failure. When things do not go right, he may go into real rages. He needs to be protected from hurting himself, other people, and objects.

He needs the teacher's help in following routines. To some extent he may have to be allowed to stick to his own routines. There are often many things he needs to do which may seem silly or even undesirable to the teacher, but the rituals and rigidities of such a child should be respected. For instance, if he thinks he cannot walk but has to be carried over a particular area of the floor, he should be carried. He may ask the very same question every day. It should be answered. Or he may touch his cap to his throat before putting it on his head. Or count to twenty before doing something. The teacher will try to lessen his need for elaborate rituals but will accept those which are needed. She should go slowly in any effort to change his ways.

Sometimes such a child, on a walk with his teacher, will enjoy looking at cars and trucks. (Such children are often much interested in cars, or in the wheels of cars.) At first on such walks, autistic children may pay little attention to the teacher, but gradually may build up a slight relation with her.

If a teacher is to build up any relation with such a child, it will probably be through materials and manipulation, not through talking. A teacher's *hands* may be more important to him than the teacher's total personality. Or a teacher's garter or a hole in her stocking may be the thing to which such a child first relates.

It is usually best to start out by having the autistic child with children younger than himself, regardless of his intelligence, since he does not even know who he is at first and often does not even respond to his own name. In a 2-year-old group, other children do not pay much attention to him. Older children may need time to get used to him. Since he doesn't respond, others may give him up. Or they may give him an experimental shove to see what he is going to do, or to try to get some reaction from him.

The teacher can help him to experience himself through highly tactile materials such as water and sand. Later he can use paint and clay. The autistic child tends to prefer solitary activity, and needs to be protected from too much intrusion by others. (This is one of the reasons why he often gets on best in the parallel play situations of the 2-year-old group. Older children try to play *with* him, and then often become angry and aggressive when he does not respond.)

Some autistic children do their best in group music situations. They may respond to the music and may even sometimes imitate others. Music may bring out a type of cooperation impossible to achieve through any other medium. However, a teacher should try to cut down on such solitary activities as his sitting and continuously listening to records. An autistic child loves to do this, at home or at school, and such activity may not be particularly constructive. However, it may be very relaxing and satisfying to him.

The teacher should recognize that much of the time such a child will be asocial. He will just sit or stand, doing some funny little thing over and over. Then as time goes on, if he does start to be social, his first moves toward other children may be aggressive. (Thus parents may feel that he is going downhill or losing ground and that he is "worse" than when he started school. Actually even an aggressive approach to another child shows that he is developing. Just going up to somebody and hitting him may be quite a positive thing to do.) One must keep in mind that for the most part such a child, like the 18-monther only possibly more so, will treat others as if they were objects.

The teacher's problem is to help him build up a little response to some other child, as in water or sand play, or perhaps in some activity as on the rocking boat, where another person is necessary if rocking is to be effected. (Any such activity, however, would not be expected to come until after several school sessions, not at once.)

The autistic child may go around chanting something nonsensical. This should be expected. (One such child glimpsed a teacher's glasses—quite a triumph for him to look so far up on the teacher—and went around chanting, "Take the glasses on; take the glasses on.")

The autistic child needs bridges for any and all transitions. When he gets into one of his rages, a teacher may need to use rituals built up at home. Sometimes the parents can tell the teacher, in advance, what they do to calm him down. Or the teacher may be able to build up new transitions at school such as the singing of "Jingle Bells" or the use of some magic word or simple trick. Then she, in turn, can tell the parents about these new methods, for them to use as needed.

Eating may be patterned and unusual. The child may cling to baby foods, special-colored milk, no meat, or bacon that curls only in a special way. This is, of course, at home. At school at milk-and-cracker time, such a child may cooperate or not. If he does not want to eat or drink, he should not be forced to. Furthermore, toilet habits may be bizarre or he may resist toileting.

One of the school's most important tasks here is to help the parent recognize the seriousness and nature of the overall problem. Parents often think that the child acts as he does *because* of something that has happened to him, or because of the way they treat him. Or they think that he doesn't respond to other children because he has had little opportunity to be with other children. They should be helped to recognize the fact that *he acts the way he does because of his basic nature.*

Mothers ask over and over, *"Did he play with anybody today?"* They must be helped to realize that this will be one of the last things to develop, if it ever does. When this kind of behavior does appear the child will have come a long, long way, rather than just having taken the first step toward improvement.

We have discussed the autistic child at some length because helpful literature on this subject is still not plentiful. A somewhat technical but extremely good treatment of the subject is given by Bernard Rimland in his book *Infantile Autism*[2] and also by Carl Delacato in *The Ultimate Stranger.*[3]

The child who speaks only a foreign language. Now that people seem to be becoming ever more mobile, there are apt to be an increasing number of children who speak only a foreign language in any nursery school group. Such children can as a rule fit very well into the group, which can provide a most helpful learning situation for them, usually at little cost to the school.

A teacher will need to be extremely patient about such a problem, since for some children it may take many months before they begin to speak the group's language. It is usually best not to try to teach a new language word by word, except as such teaching may come naturally. Often, suddenly, such children begin to speak fluently and with no accent. It is almost as if during their preliminary silent period they have been storing up words for later use.

For an easy, comfortable, relaxed child, language inability

2. New York: Appleton-Century-Crofts, 1964.
3. New York: Doubleday, 1974.

may not be particularly disturbing. But for a tense, anxious child who may have just recently moved from another country and who may feel strange at home as well as at school, an inability to converse with other children may be disturbing. On occasion we have arranged for or agreed to having an inter-preter—perhaps a friend of the family—attend school with the child for at least some sessions, to make an acceptance of school easier. A book which can help introduce a child (and if need be, his family) to a new language is Richard Scarry's *Best Word Book Ever.*[4]

The hyperkinetic child. One special problem which is much talked of and much written about today, and one which is of concern to many parents and teachers, is the problem of so-called overactivity or hyperkinesis.

The chief characteristics of hyperactivity are that the child is super-energetic, never still, always in motion, constantly fidgeting. As an infant he is restless. As a preschooler he is always on the go, into everything, always touching things and breaking them. He cannot stay with any one activity for long. For instance, he may pull all toys off a shelf, play with each for a moment, then discard it. Attention is not well maintained.

This description, of course, is true of many preschoolers. The thing that best distinguishes the hyperactive child is that, even when requested, he cannot turn his motor off. He cannot inhibit his activity even when he tries. Such children not only are highly impulsive but have very poor impulse control. They tend to become highly upset when either things or people fail to behave as they want them to. There tends to be great emo-tional unevenness.

Hyperactive children tend to have both perceptual and learning difficulties. Though many are bright enough, endow-ment is often uneven. Even when a hyperactive child does not

4. New York: Golden Press, 1963.

have special perceptual problems, his lack of attention, constant activity, and emotional overreactivity can lead to school difficulties. When hyperactivity is combined with immaturity, as it often is, the child is in trouble indeed.

The hyperactive child often has difficulties in distinguishing right from left at an appropriate age, and in general coordination. He also tends to show extreme resistance to the usual social demands and prohibitions. People describe him as stubborn, negative, disobedient, bossy, "almost immune to direction."

Probably what the nursery school can best do for most parents is to help them get over their fears that their own child fits this new diagnosis of *hyperactivity*. One of the main ways that this can be done is by permitting the parent to watch all the children in school at play. She will in most cases quickly appreciate that her own child is no more active than any of the other preschoolers. It is very important to help a parent recognize the difference between a normally every-minute-on-the-go preschooler, and the child who is correctly described as hyperactive.

In those cases where a parent's suspicion that her child is hyperactive turns out, in the teacher's opinion, to be correct, there is, of course, more to be done. A nursery school teacher should not try to play the role of clinician in diagnosing any atypical behavior. But if in her opinion any given child actually *is* hyperactive, then she should suggest that the parent obtain a full diagnosis from a physician or psychologist qualified to give such a diagnosis.

Even here, since the line between normal overactivity and presumably true hyperactivity is a fine one, many children, even those diagnosed by the clinician as hyperactive, can be contained in a nursery school group. In such cases an experienced teacher can be of great practical help to a parent. She can discuss problems which occur at home, and give suggestions as to how they might best be handled. She can share with the parent, either by conversation or by encouraging observation, her own ways of helping the child calm down and behave more effectively.

She can demonstrate or explain not only that much patience is required in dealing with such a child, but that he will be helped most by a firm, consistent, explicit, and predictable environment and handling and often, curiously, by a stimulating physical environment. Medication is often helpful, though that, of course, will be determined by the physician and not by the school itself. And the experienced teacher can direct the parent to some of the helpful reading material now available on the subject of hyperactivity. Perhaps the most useful book for parents currently available is Dr. Paul Wender's *The Hyperactive Child: A Handbook for Parents.*[5]

School and parent both, in trying to determine whether what seems to be an extremely active child actually falls into the category "hyperkinetic," may be helped by a suggestion from Dr. Anthony Davids which appeared in the November 1971 issue of the *Journal of Learning Disabilities.* Dr. Davids lists seven areas of behavior which one might like to consider, and suggests making a rating of "Much less than most children," "Less," "Slightly less," "Slightly more," "More," "Much more than most children" for each. This may help to place the child in question in proper perspective.

The seven areas are general hyperactivity; short attention span; variability and unpredictability of behavior; impulsiveness and inability to delay gratification; extreme irritability; explosiveness; poor visual motor coordination and awkwardness of movement and gesture.

Minimal brain dysfunction. The above classification by Dr. Davids leads quite naturally to another kind of difficulty about

5. New York: Crown Publishers, 1973.

which one hears a very great deal today. This is the area of brain damage or minimal brain dysfunction.

It is often difficult for the layman, or even for the professional, to draw the line between mere hyperkinesis or overactivity, and minimal brain dysfunction. Often the terms are used almost synonymously. Among the primary symptoms of brain damage, listed by Dr. Richard A. Gardner in his excellent book *MBD: The Family Book about Minimal Brain Dysfunction.*[6]— a book to which any teacher or parent interested in this subject is referred—are the following. Immaturity, a lag in one or more of the usual developmental milestones; marked and continuous hyperactivity; distractability; coordination problems; perceptual problems (both auditory and visual) which may interfere directly with learning; poor retention of what is learned; poor concept formation; impulsivity; and generally disruptive behavior.

As will be seen, there is much similarity and overlap between hyperactivity and minimal brain dysfunction. In fact, the diagnosis may depend as much on the specialist's personal preference as on the child's behavior. However, it is generally considered that though a brain damaged child may be hyperactive, most children whose chief problem is hyperactivity are not brain damaged.

At any rate, children who fall under either classification, though certainly they will present special problems in nursery school, if their problem is not too extreme and if there are not too many in any one group, can often be helped, handled, and effectively included in a regular group. If the presence of such a child is too fatiguing for the teacher or too disruptive for the group, sometimes the child himself can be benefitted (and the group not too much disturbed) by planning for short and not too frequent sessions.

6. New York: Jason Aronson, 1973.

Learning disability. There is one further group of difficulties much talked about today. This is that very wide array of problems now grouped under the very general label "learning disabilities." Children who have had trouble in learning, especially in learning academic subjects, have always been with us. It may be only the intense interest in and concentration on these children, and the specific labeling of them, that is new.

This new interest is undoubtedly good in that it does make teachers, parents, and child specialists think a little more about children with school problems and what can be done for them. It has, perhaps, its unfortunate side in making some parents and some specialists believe that difficulty in learning is *a* thing, with *a* label, and that by so labeling one has actually done something toward solving a problem.

Since in many instances "learning disability" children are not discovered as such until they begin the formal academic work usually started in first grade, they are commonly not recognized during the preschool years and thus are probably not a major or special concern for most nursery schools. It is a part of the plan and purpose of the kind of school described in this book to note and adapt to any special problem which *any* of the children attending may exhibit, and to help them adapt to, and solve, such problems of personality, growth, or behavior as they may exhibit.

Many preschoolers have problems in learning that are merely transitory. Such problems should not be considered as true learning disabilities. A problem is serious only if it continues over an extended period of time and interferes with effective growth and learning in other areas.

Among the difficulties which children who later fall into the category of learning disability do display early are the following: poor perceptual-motor functioning, confused laterality, spatial confusion, difficulty in the processing of language, social or emotional problems.[7] Any teacher would be wise to be aware of and helpfully responsive to any such difficulties or deviations in any of the children in her group.

But if a child's behavior is not so atypical that his placement in a regular group is not in his best interest, there seems to be no reason why many children who may at later ages exhibit some difficulties in school or in other aspects of life, and who then may be labeled as having learning disabilities, cannot be included, *without any self-conscious or out-of-the-ordinary concentration on what may be or may later turn out to be their special problems.*

However, as a part of our present concern for children who are underprivileged in any respect, some states have passed legislation which requires, even though it may not actually provide, classes for children from three years of age *who are exceptional in any way.* This presumably includes children who are dull, physically handicapped, hyperkinetic, brain damaged, potential learning disability problems, or even exceptionally gifted.

Some communities have already set up special classes for "learning disability" preschoolers. Such classes need not be a primary concern of the ordinary nursery school or of its teachers, though if available they might well provide that special facility to which some children felt not to be potentially good members of a regular group could be referred.

The gifted child. It is surprising to some to see the gifted child considered along with other kinds of exceptional children. Yet a little reflection tells us that either the high or the low range of any human endowment—in language, motor skills,

7. Two publications about learning disabilities which both teachers and parents may find useful are Milton Brutten, S. O. Richardson, and C. Mangel, *Something's Wrong with My Child* (New York: Harcourt, Brace Jovanovich, 1973), and Margaret Golick, *Strictly for Parents: A Parent's Guide to Learning Problems* (Quebec Association for Children with Learning Disability, P.O. Box 22, Cote St., Luc Postal Station, Montreal, Quebec, Canada).

personal-social or adaptive behavior—is indeed exceptional.

The truly gifted child may indeed be superior in all these areas. Like a diamond with many facets, he shines splendidly in a number of ways. It is true that he is exceptional; yet he does not present an educational problem in the sense of the other kinds of exception just discussed. He has many resources to enjoy and develop; his presence can be a delight to others. He finds pleasure and opportunity for growth in almost any situation—because he always has a talent and interest to bring to that situation.

There are, however, children unusually "gifted" in just one area of their development, to such an extent that their abilities are extremely lopsided. For example, some children are especially talented in the use of language, can verbalize about almost any subject with anyone, with an unusual degree of understanding. Such children often seem to their parents to be geniuses and unsuited to such unchallenging academic programs as most nursery schools provide.

Yet these same children can be very clumsy in the use of their hands, for example, so that they take no pleasure in doing anything but talking. They often wear adults out in their constant demands for conversation, and they are bored if left to their own devices. The nursery school can help such children develop manual skills (though they may never be really good at them) and can help them find ways to participate in better-rounded experiences.

Many such children, thought by their parents to be extremely superior, may fall in the classification of "superior immature." Such children are usually very good talkers, have a reportedly high measured IQ, are often much interested in letters and numbers, and may read at a very young age. But on a test of total behavior rather than of mere intellect, they usually rate well below their chronological age and tend to be quite babyish in many ways.

Such a child at four years of age, for instance, may actually not be mature enough to fit in with the play of other 4-year-olds. His parents then often attribute this lack of adjustment to the fact that he is "too bright" for the group and needs more of a kindergarten type of schooling. Actually it is more that he is not up to the group in many ways, rather than that he is beyond it, which causes his difficulty.

Precocious abilities in music, with numbers, with physical agility are similarly remarkable singly, but when they are extremely out of line with other areas of development, can present problems of adjustment both to a group and to the child's own range of happy opportunities for growth.

It is important so far as possible to try to see each child as a total individual, with high points and low points as well, and not to be too much impressed by his highs or too greatly discouraged by his lows.

GENERAL SUGGESTIONS APPLYING TO ALL KINDS OF EXCEPTIONAL CHILDREN

As we have emphasized, it often is not so much the kind of handicap or even the degree of handicap which must be considered when questioning the advisability of nursery school attendance, as it is the total personality of the child in question, his level of intelligence, his drive, the way he sees himself, and the way he relates to others. Some atypical children obviously fit into a group much better than do others.

The way in which the group reacts to the child is also of utmost importance. With all handicapped children, a teacher or director must ask herself, To what extent does this child's presence penalize the group? Any benefit to the individual child must always be weighed against what it may cost the group.

Not only how much his presence penalizes the group, but

the group's reaction to the child must be considered. Sometimes in spite of a teacher's most skillful efforts, a specially handicapped child is not being helped. If this is the case, his attendance may need to be discontinued. Nursery school probably should not—unless set up for that purpose—be thought of as a place for handling atypical children.

Thus the question is primarily: Can the school give a good educational experience to the child with special needs and still maintain its ongoing program?

Teachers can, of course, be helped by reading all available literature dealing with any handicap in question and should be as fully informed as possible about the special characteristics, problems, and needs of atypical children.

It is well to remember that in the ideal nursery school the purpose is to give every child a good school experience. This is one of the reasons why the school should accept the full range of its commitment and its responsibilities when it includes any child with special needs.

FIVE

The Parent

14

Parents and School

CHOOSING A SCHOOL

Any parent of a preschooler who is thinking about sending the child to nursery school will quite naturally have several major concerns. To begin with, will the child benefit from school? How will the parent know that the school chosen is really a good school? And what can the parent reasonably expect to get, for child and for self, from the school?

As discussed earlier, there are certain exceptional cases where attendance may not be in the best interests of the child. Some extremely immature and dependent children find it just too hard to leave their mothers. Some children are so extremely susceptible, physically, or find school so fatiguing, that the drawbacks of attendance outweigh the advantages. For some, transportation presents too difficult a problem. An occasional child has such a rich, full life at home, such adequate play equipment, so many friends, and such good supervision from mother, that school does not seem particularly necessary.

For the majority, however, nursery school can offer a tremendous and exceptional opportunity for play, learning, developing social and motor skills, and all-around enjoyment. We can say without hesitation that in the majority of cases, a child will benefit from preschool attendance.

Once a parent has decided to send a child to preschool, how

can she or he decide which one to choose, or whether the one being chosen will benefit the child? We suggest that a parent visit the school while it is in session. The following characteristics of what we consider a good preschool may be some of the things a parent will wish to look for.

1. The children seem to be having a good time. Work and play are indistinguishable, in the general spirit of fun.

2. The children are given reasonably free expression. There is no spirit of coercion or pushing.

3. The children are getting on with each other with only a minimum of fighting and/or crying.

4. The teachers seem to like the children; relationships are warm yet unsentimental.

5. The school room is bright, clean, and reasonably orderly.

6. There is a reasonable amount of order in setting and in schedule, yet no undue rigidity, and no abdication of responsible adult authority.

7. The classroom is equipped with a diversity of materials that afford opportunities for firsthand sensory experiences and investigation. There are no sets of materials for the whole class.

8. There is both outdoor and indoor activity, and alternating times of quiet and active play.

9. Children are encouraged in attitudes of active questioning, not passive acceptance or conformity. They do not always depend on the teacher.

10. Activities arise from the children's interests and responses; teachers are not constrained by predetermined programs. There is no grouping of children through standardized tests.

11. Children feel free to express their feelings and sense of self through dance, graphic art, literature, music, dramatic play.

12. Although letters and numbers may be used in the class-

room, they are not presented as symbols for rote memory, but are closely related to the child's experience and activity.

13. The approach to learning is interdisciplinary. The child is not expected to confine himself to a single subject. The teacher avoids whole class "assignments."

14. Children have time to work through the completion of any problem or mastery of a skill.

15. The teacher respects every child's way of thinking, feeling, and acting; she rarely commands.

16. The teacher accepts mistakes as part of learning, not as signs of failure.

Also, it seems important to stress that no single approach to educating children can be ideal for all children at all times. Each new educational methodology is not the answer for all. Each has values and limitations, but in a good nursery school it is hoped that the staff will be not only well informed and flexible, but sensitive to the needs of each individual child.

A final question which a parent might ask about nursery school is: What can she expect to get out of it for her child and for herself? What can be expected depends to some extent on what a parent wants and what kind of school has been chosen. It is very important to make up one's mind in advance whether one is looking for heavy academic emphasis or seeks merely a situation in which a child can live and learn—about self and others—and grow and play. The choice is available in most communities.

If you choose a school which offers a heavy academic program, you have a right to expect rather formalized teaching, and can quite easily measure how much your child is "learning." If you choose a school more along the lines described in this book, you have a right to expect first of all that your child will enjoy school. Most do. You may also find that his enjoyment of school carries over into home life. Many parents do discover, often somewhat to their surprise, that the child who has his own rich, full, exciting school life has less need than he may have expressed before for getting emotional satisfaction from fighting with siblings, refusing to eat "properly," stalling at bedtime, becoming emotionally entangled with mother.

For herself, a mother will probably find that there are many, many advantages. Almost any mother entangled in life with a preschooler will welcome a few hours' respite. Almost any mother of a preschooler, with an often too busy pediatrician, will welcome a chance to talk over her child's personality and his problems and his learnings with a qualified professional person who is genuinely interested in, knowledgeable about, and friendly toward her child.

Any mother can set some of her own anxieties at rest when she sees that many of the ways her child is behaving occur in other children. She can get clues as to how her child's behavior compares with that of other children by seeing him in group action. And she will benefit immeasurably from the fact that school attendance adds something extra to her child's existence and thus, very often, makes him happier and easier to live with at home.

PARENT GUIDANCE

The concept of *guidance* has to quite an extent replaced the concept of *training* in child rearing. It is indeed rewarding when parents, in the process of understanding what they consider to be the bad and the good in a child, realize their obligation to the child in a new way. When responsibility is accepted for both good and bad, parents sometimes learn to enjoy both aspects of a child's behavior in a new way. "Most people do not approve of anyone else in all respects, not even themselves" is a statement that often helps parents in their acceptance of all aspects of their child—and of themselves.

Parents may need help, too, in seeing the distinctive features in each of their children, so that they can treat each child in his own right. Parents often create difficulties for themselves and their families by comparing children too much with one another, rather than thinking of each child as a separate entity who needs individual consideration.

Although the more enlightened guidance for parents may appear at first glance to be *easier* than the old nostrums which said absolutely what was right and what was wrong to do, actually this type of guidance is much more difficult though far more rewarding. In this creative method of guidance both the individual parent and the individual child must be considered. If the difficulties and complexities of communication are considered too closely, many are inclined to despair. But that the way is difficult is no reason to withdraw completely from attempts at guidance which at least have a good direction. And such attempts come very naturally in a nursery school which has also the facilities to be a guidance center.

Parents of the preschool child seem to be especially eager for guidance. Perhaps this is the golden time to reach parents, not only because their children are young, but because parents themselves are generally delighted with their young offspring and touched by their dependence. Yet they are often bewildered and anxious when they are confronted with the child's confusing and unreasonable behavior. Many parents have had little or no experience with young children. Sometimes they are far away from friends or relatives to whom they can turn for advice. And the child changes so rapidly in the first years that the parent may feel he or she is writing on sand insofar as being able to observe any consistent effect he or she may be having on the child.

But platitudes will not help parents to relax, enjoy, and accept their child. Usually the parent is reached as he or she asks specific questions and receives specific answers. Meaning-ful help can be given parents only in an individualized way. Such help takes time; the same bit of information or advice must be presented in a number of different ways on a variety of occasions. Parents may gain insight from observing other children as well as their own child in the nursery school. They may have this reinforced by a statement they hear in a confer-ence. Reading may further deepen perception. Learning thus may take time, and may remain only fragmentary unless the parent has the good fortune to put what is learned into mean-ingful concepts and, perhaps with the help of a teacher in the school, to relate one bit of learning about children to an overall philosophy of child rearing. But the philosophy usually will be the end, not the beginning.

In the chapter on "Adjustment" we have already drawn attention to the very different approaches of mothers in bring-ing their children to school for the first time. Such differences in individuality as we have pointed out apply to parents as well as to children—and of course to the teachers who might be offering guidance as well! Parental handling of children may be excessively rigid or permissive; parents may be insecure, or too aggressive. They may be naturally friendly and warm in rela-tions with people, or cold and withdrawn. The discerning per-son in guidance will accept the parents as they are and will help them to work at their problems with their children even while basic weaknesses may remain.

Furthermore parents can be helped to avoid situations that are too hard for them. A parent who cannot stand a messy child at the family table (more often a father) can be encouraged that this situation need not be made a moral issue—that it is quite all right for the child to eat alone. A parent who is irritated by the disorder in a child's room might well be encouraged to have someone else tend to its cleaning occasionally. Parents with such problems, of course, need in addition to this simple expedient of meeting some problems by avoiding them, some concomitant help in understanding themselves and their child in relation to one another.

Parents should be met and talked to in informal and formal ways. Sometimes meetings of groups of parents may be arranged with a view to imparting some of the information parents want. We have found such meetings of about eight mothers at a time most rewarding. Customarily, the parents meet in the late afternoon at the home of a teacher, or one of the mothers, and discuss such general topics as eating, sleeping, or elimination. The teacher in charge guides the discussion with leading questions and appropriate comments. Sometimes the teacher offers herself as a person whom the parents may question about these topics if they wish, or parents themselves may organize a mothers' group which meets monthly.

Parents (fathers as well as mothers) seem to like to have an orientation meeting in the fall, when nursery school commonly begins, to discuss what is going to happen in the course of the year, to help them get acquainted with one another, and to emphasize that they can ask for help from the school staff at any time. Parents enjoy becoming acquainted with the teachers with whom their children will be so intimately associated during the year.

It is advisable to have a general meeting for parents early in the year at which teachers discuss with them any evaluations of their children which have been arrived at, explaining any assessment techniques used. This is a good time also to talk about various research projects under way so that parents will be more interested in what is going on. In some instances parents may complain that they do not want their children used as "guinea pigs." Such comments tend to come from parents who are uninformed about the nature of any research that is being conducted. In general, parents greatly enjoy being a part of a study in child development.

Films and lectures of general interest stimulate parents' thinking about their children and afford good reason for arranging meetings of the group. Family picnics for parents and children are excellent. Parents bring their own food, and as many other children in their families as would enjoy such an outing. Often the older children have attended nursery school themselves and enjoy reexperiencing with the present nursery school group an afternoon picnic in a public park or some suitable outdoor place of recreation.

Finally, it is helpful for the nursery school to have available to parents a well-stocked library of books in the field of child development. The parents waiting at school can have the use of books from such a library, or teachers can refer parents to suitable books which they may borrow, as discussion with the parents suggests that such books might be of interest.

However, the most important parent guidance is given individually, either informally at school, or by means of a guidance interview. At school the head teacher frees herself from other tasks at the beginning and end of each morning so that she can greet each parent as he or she brings the child. Since it is unwise to make comments about the child in his presence, when problems are suggested the parent may make an appointment to talk with the teacher at some other definite time, or the teacher may call the parent on the telephone to talk about the child.

At the end of the morning, either the head teacher or one of the other teachers tries to make some positive statement to each parent about the child's play during the morning. We emphasize that statements at occasions of brief encounter should be positive, since it is extremely difficult to communicate to a parent something that may be unpleasant. Communication that may threaten a parent's preconceived ideas about a child presents a very delicate problem in education and should be handled only by a head teacher, or a person especially trained in such communication, at a time when there is freedom for both parent and teacher to explore one another's ideas. A teacher trained in guidance comes to know that unraveling of specific situations and problems which the parent presents helps most.

PARENT OBSERVATION IN THE NURSERY SCHOOL

In addition, parents should be encouraged to visit the nursery school and to watch their children in the group. All parents should do this the first days of school, in the process of adjusting their children to coming to school. Thereafter, the teacher can suggest that parents come to observe. A one-way vision screen, when available, allows the parent, unobserved by the child, to watch his child play. Such observation very often prompts the parent to ask a number of questions—often he has never before had the experience of watching his child so objectively, nor has he compared his child's behavior with that of a number of other children of his own age. If no screen is available, parents can come, one at a time, to sit in the playroom. Questions that parents ask after such observation are excellent points of departure for further conferences.

When *Marsha's* mother came to observe, the teachers already knew that she was a highly directive parent, subjected to many pressures to conformity, and very much set in her ways. Her daughter, a trim-looking little girl with a serious-looking face, with thin lips usually tightly drawn and bright blue eyes that blinked excessively, had rigidities in behavior that were probably not distressing to the mother, since Marsha's meticulous, directive behavior was very much a reflection of her own.

So Marsha's officiousness alone would probably not have disturbed the mother even though Marsha scolded her friend Barney when he colored in inappropriate places, and grabbed him and attempted to hold him down and undress him when he did not take off his snowsuit as soon as he came inside. Marsha also reported misdemeanors constantly: "Barney hit me"; "They're calling me ugly names"; "Someone was in my way when I was coming down the slide!" She also instructed the teachers in the right deportment: "When I say 'Pardon me,' you should say 'Surely.' "

But Marsha showed, too, her aggressiveness and hostility toward others. She went to the clay table and some of those at the table called out "Hi!" "Stinky," she replied, very sullen about the whole matter. She also attacked others without warning and for no apparent reason kicked Martin when he was happily coming down the slide, pushed Sara over as she was playing with blocks. These were the actions that disturbed the mother, and the difficult task in meetings that followed was to present the child's behavior as being all of one piece. That is, her officiousness and directive behavior were as characteristic of her as her aggressiveness. This mother needed a better understanding of young children in general, and her daughter in particular, so that she might improve her handling of Marsha and might relax her own rigid demands.

It must be emphasized that conferences between teacher and parent involve two-way communication. It is not just a matter of the teacher giving the parent words of wisdom. The parent informs the teacher, too, telling about her own personality and about the child's personality. Very often, too, a parent can make valuable suggestions to the teacher as to the handling of her child.

Such was the case with *Ellen,* a 3-year-old whose problems were similar to those of Marsha, although she expressed them in quite different ways. In the beginning, Ellen apparently adjusted to nursery school with no trouble at all. At least she made no fuss when her mother left her. Although she did not participate in activities at first, it was considered that she might be a "watcher"—a child who likes to observe a long time before she finally joins the others in play. So her nonparticipation was at first respected, especially since her mother said this was her usual pattern in new situations. The teachers, however, made advances to Ellen, encouraged the overtures of other children to her, and saw to it that she was exposed to a variety of materials.

But it soon became apparent that Ellen had a more complicated problem in adjustment than at first had appeared. Not only did she refrain from playing, she refrained from speaking. On the day her mother came to observe at nursery school, she did not say a word, although her mother said she talked all the time at home. Further conference with the mother revealed also that she was highly aggressive at home, especially so with her baby sister, toward whom she was ruthless in her attacks, and over whom she exercised complete power.

Ellen's withdrawal lasted so long that it became clear that it was more than shyness or a cautious approach to a new situation. The mother at length gave an extremely helpful suggestion to the teachers that Ellen be permitted to bring her baby sister, age two, to nursery school. "She could not possibly be aloof with the baby around," the mother said, "and perhaps this will help her adjust to the school in a normal way."

The mother's suggestion was good, for Ellen became a changed personality with her sister at school. She scolded and bossed and ran around in great excitement, eager to display her prowess to her sister and to tell her what to do. Through this technique suggested by the mother, the teachers gained a new insight into Ellen's personality.

A question remained which needed to be clarified: Why did Ellen need to be thus in power before she could relax? Were her silence and nonparticipation in reality a weapon by which she showed her power? Through numerous conferences the teacher and mother reexamined all the routines at home to see whether too much pressure was being put on Ellen there, and found that standards had been held much too high for her. Ellen, with two younger siblings, had missed out in being a baby and needed much more attention and time to experience the dependency and power of infancy.

This type of excessive demand on the part of the parent is fairly common, but the opposite can also be true. *Bobby's* mother, for example, seemed to us to be too indulgent. She was not permissive because of any theory about the matter. This was just her natural way to behave toward children. She said she "just dissolved" when they wanted something, nothing was too much trouble, and she was their constant and loving servant. But she had three other small children, and her tendency to permissiveness was taking all her time and energy, so that with increasing exhaustion she realized that she was desperately in need of help, but did not know what to do.

Since this mother really felt she was in trouble, and was seeking aid, it was easier to help her in her difficulties than it is to provide help in those cases when the parents do not recognize that they have any difficulty.

But again we must emphasize that it is not just through difficulties that guidance is given. Many parents, especially parents of young children, just seem to have a driving curiosity to know their child, to be informed about children in general. And this desire for information is often the happy basis for good relationships between teachers and parents in the nursery school.

15

The Guidance Interview

One of the most rewarding methods of communication between the teacher and the parent is the meeting scheduled once each year. We call this meeting the guidance interview. Such an interview is a formal situation for giving and receiving information about the child. It is different from the introductory interview which comes before the child starts school. At the earlier interview, parents and teacher simply get acquainted. The teacher is not ready to give, or the parent to receive, much guidance.

In this beginning interview, in addition to getting acquainted, the teacher learns as much as possible of the child's developmental history; and the parent learns about the school hours, the program, lunch (if any), fee, system of billing, health regulations, observational facilities, induction system (how and when children come to school), whether the parent should stay with the child and, if so, how long, and what she should do while she stays.

At this time the teacher also gives the parent the names of all the teachers, so that she can refer to them by name as she talks about school with her child. The teacher may also acquaint the parent with the names of the other children in the school and where they live, since parents often wish to form car pools at the outset of the year or to think in terms of providing playmates from the nursery school for their children.

The guidance interview is a rather special experience. Both the father and the mother are encouraged to come to talk with the head teacher or the director of the nursery school about their child. The interview usually lasts between one and a half and two hours. The meeting should take place in pleasant, informal surroundings, free from interruptions. Occasionally, in addition to the teacher who is interviewing, a student teacher who knows the child and parents is also present, with the parents' previous knowledge and consent. (The best way to teach seems to be to have the student sit in on actual interviews. And when she has been acquainted with the child in the nursery school, she can sometimes contribute some special information about his behavior in the school.)

The value of such an interview depends a great deal on the skill and warmth of the teacher interviewing. The guidance interview is not an instrument for use by untrained nursery school teachers. The teacher using it must know a good deal about child behavior. She must be a sympathetic, sensitive, and well-informed listener. And she must have special awareness and good judgment as to the readiness of the parent to receive certain information.

She must know how long to wait for the parent to recognize danger areas, problems, difficulties of the child himself, or difficulties in the parents' relationship with the child. For example, although she may feel even early in the year that a child and parent are much too dependent on each other, she will not try to get this problem faced and discussed immediately or too directly. When parents do not feel that they need help, she will not make an abrupt issue of the fact that in her opinion they do. She will not try to make them accept "facts" unless they are ready or at least somewhat ready.

Almost any parent finds a discussion of his or her child's personality and problems endlessly fascinating. Though parents should feel free to talk with teachers about their children throughout the year, the formal guidance interview comes as a sort of bonus for all concerned. At this time the teacher can share with the parents the things she has learned about their child. They in turn can fill her in on the many things which only they know about him. Questions can be asked and answered to mutual benefit.

It is hoped that, if a good relationship has been established and if the child has seemed to benefit from his school experience, the participants in this interview will not be in an adversary relationship. Neither should feel defensive. Rather, together they should aim to explore the fascinating topic of the child being discussed.

Sometimes it does seem difficult for a young teacher to interview an experienced mother of several children. Teacher or mother might feel that the interview should be the other way around. Both should appreciate that the teacher does have a good deal of importance to share with the mother, since she has had a special view of the child which the mother does not have. Also, even if childless herself, she will quite possibly have worked with more children than the mother has. And if her training has been adequate, she may be more familiar with literature on child behavior than will the mother.

Almost any mother, no matter how experienced, will have some questions she would like to ask of an impartial but friendly person outside her immediate family. Even a rather young teacher can often answer these questions effectively. Many parents actually know the answers to their *own* questions about their children—but this knowledge often comes out only in frank and open discussion. It is good to have one's own conclusions confirmed. In such cases a teacher may serve more as a sounding board than as a mere informant.

One warning which we have always given to teachers is that they should not try to serve the role either of psychiatric consultant or of clinical psychologist. It is not the teacher's responsibility to point out to the parents what may be wrong with them, or to give a psychological diagnosis of the child's personality problems if any.

Helping parents to see their child objectively, and as a whole, is perhaps the most important general aim of the interview. Added value comes when it helps them to start thinking about their child from a new point of view, or to reexamine their own methods of dealing with him.

But the teacher should always take pains to make any parental interview as enjoyable as possible. Her manner should be friendly and not too official. Her approach should be that together she and the parents are going to have an interesting time discussing an attractive and intriguing subject. She should, as far as practical, focus the interview on the child; should avoid prying into personal affairs of parents. If and when parents express differences of opinion with any degree of animosity, she should as tactfully as possible shift the conversation to more neutral topics.

Most parents like to talk about their children, but some parents are more appreciative of this sort of interviewing than others. Some are not very much interested in individuality and want, rather, specific advice about problems that concern them. When such instances occur, the teacher must adapt herself to the needs of the parents as much as possible.

Some parents haven't much to say, answering in monosyllabic terms to the subjects the interviewer brings up. Such a parent challenges the interviewer's skill in finding some topic of interest. She needs often to discuss some general topic—such as siblings, school, playmates—and to offer considerable "warm-up" material to encourage the parents to friendly conversation. Other parents may ramble away from the subject of the child to talk about relatives, friends, their own childhood, etc., and the interviewer has the task of bringing them gently back to the point.

Some parents are defensive about their child; some are clearly troubled; some have feelings of inadequacy; and some have great self-confidence. With all these parents the teacher must find a way to establish rapport; the teacher must be sensitive to and sympathetic with all kinds of persons, even though they differ from her in many significant ways.

The guidance interview as we use it concerns itself with a set of carefully prepared *areas* of questioning—not just a haphazard series of questions and answers. Such a standard number of topics for discussion gives some assurance that the major problems in child rearing will be considered, and gives the interview form. It keeps the parent from running away with the interview, in anecdote and unrelated information. It provides for general, yet definite subjects for discussion for parents who have trouble getting started. The discussion of these areas tells the teacher a great deal about the parents' child-rearing practices, although she does not need to ask directly the abrupt and paralyzing question, "What is your philosophy of child rearing?"

The various areas which the interview covers include feeding (schedule, weaning, solids, appetite, preferences, refusals, self-help); sleeping (quality, nap, night, inducement, waking); elimination (bowel and bladder control, words used, self-help); habits (thumb sucking, masturbation, nail biting, temper tantrums, etc.); play (alone, with others, materials); development—motor (sitting, creeping, walking, etc.); development—language (length of sentences, pronunciation, questions); development—personal-social (self-help, behavior with siblings); ethical concepts, discipline, and health. With some parents, too, it is rewarding to get an opinion about the child's general personality by asking, "Which side of the family does he resemble, if either?" And very often parents enjoy discussing suitable books, records, toys, and plans for the child's future schooling.

As the teacher explores each of these areas, interpreting the child's behavior in terms of his age and his sex, she explains to the parent, when it seems helpful, characteristic norms of behavior. She may also project ahead and tell the kinds of behavior the child may show next. In order to do this, of course, she must be keenly sensitive to the child's individuality; she must utilize every opportunity in the course of the discussion to make the parent aware of any special individual characteristics of behavior which this particular child may be likely to bring to every age.

Ann, for example, was a child rich in creativity, highly emotional and dramatic. She was much stimulated by her environment and expressed her feelings constantly and loquaciously in extraordinary flights of imagination. She lacked self-discipline, however, and was apt to ramble and to respond to stimuli without much reference to the correctness of her response. She bogged down in her own rambling creativity and often forgot what she had set out to do. Helping her involved not only being very much interested and appreciative of what she was doing, but exercising a rather strong control and giving renewed directions to help her terminate activities, keep her mind on her original task, and lead her to the next step in what she needed to do.

Debbie, on the other hand, tended to placidity and conformity. It never seemed to occur to her to do the opposite of what was asked—but neither did it occur to her to explore her environment in any more than the easiest way, or the way she was told to explore it. Although she was a very intelligent little girl, she needed prodding and encouragement to utilize her opportunities. She had very little enthusiasm or warmth and tended to show the same bland reaction of mild pleasure whatever the situation. Her motions were deliberate and cautious. She rarely got very much excited or challenged about anything. She did just what was required of her age, and no more, in most instances. She seemed to have no drive to succeed, and once she made a mistake she was not inspired to correct her error or to try another method or approach.

Her parents needed suggestions as to how they might encourage her enthusiasms and expressions of emotion. They themselves needed to be more expressive with this child, quicker to praise, more open in appreciation. They also needed help in finding her a friend who could be stimulating to her.

Another child, *Stevie,* was a boy of unusual sensitivity and self-criticism. Failure was for him a most unfortunate experience. Yet he frequently made errors, and seemed to have a rigidity in perception that made him unable to correct his errors. Once he did a thing the wrong way, he seemed to be stuck with that way of doing it; yet he knew it was wrong.

Increasingly, fear of failure interfered with joyous self-abandon. His problem was made worse when his older brother made fun of his errors and of his inferior activities or productions. Stevie, increasing in willfulness, tried to cope with his problems by controlling his environment. He seemed to need to compensate for his feelings of inadequacy by asserting himself in troublesome ways. For example, he would suddenly refuse to eat lettuce, which he would then accept several days later. Clothes, toys, decisions about outings were subject to this same kind of arbitrary behavior.

Stevie's parents needed to learn ways to communicate to Stevie that everyone makes mistakes, that it is all right to have a wrong idea. He, more than others, needed to be provided with situations in which he could experience success.

Judy, on the other hand, was not at all bothered by failure. A child high in social interest, with a peripheral, distracted approach to problems, she counted on coquetry and guile to carry her along, cared very little about whether what she did was right or wrong, so long as she could get a smile or attention from someone. Judy was likely to try anything, to say "Oh, sure" with great geniality to all directions, and to give an affable response of some sort even when she had no knowledge of what she was asked. Judy never concentrated on any endeavor; she had such a keen interest in people and in her surroundings that it was extremely difficult for her to pay attention to problem solving in any task. She had a high degree of that component so characteristically feminine, an interest in persons more dom-. inating and pervasive than any other interest.

Judy's parents needed to understand better her extraordinary sociability and social sensitivity, and to plan for ways in which this could be used to advantage.

There are as many patterns of individuality as there are children. The four children just described suggest the range of differences in personality. Some children seem outstanding in the clarity and speed of their thoughts and actions, so much so that they often get tripped in their own speed. Sometimes such children, however, seem to lack in depth, in the rich overtones of personality.

Some are so overwhelmed by energy that they are constantly overstimulated; they seem to lack restraining mechanisms in any area. Others seem meticulous, calm, thoughtful, reserved in their approach to everything, highly self-contained. Such children often do not manifest in the usual way the tensions characteristic of the various ages.

Some children set too high standards for themselves. Some make daring and important efforts which fail. Some know their limitations very well and are not tempted to try anything too difficult. There are children who seem to be habitually clever in achieving their own needs. There are "born leaders" who usually have a plan, a creative idea of their own in almost every situation; they must work out their own impulses before they can settle down to any kind of conformity.

Some children put everything they have into a situation at once, respond fully as they give their "all." Others, highly dependent on praise and acceptance, tend to make slow beginnings at a low level of achievement; they may have trouble following directions initially; they may be insecure; they may see too much in a situation and be unable to discriminate among possible responses.

The teacher explores with the parent all such possible differences as these, as well as constitutional differences, patterns of abilities, and the pattern of growth in these abilities. As the parent better understands and accepts his child, he can help him grow and can enjoy him for what he is. Such exploration is helped by the more structured areas of the interview that have already been set forth, and which will now be considered in greater detail.

SPECIAL AREAS FOR GUIDANCE INTERVIEW

Although the teacher usually approaches each of the areas of the interview with at least some sort of introductory remark or question, for some children some whole areas may not need to be explored. The teacher must not be rigid in staying too close to the structure outlined. Thus, if parents report that a child accepts his bed immediately at night, sleeps without waking, and has a two-hour nap with no trouble, this area of sleeping is not one she will need to spend much time discussing. Some area may seem much more important to parents and teacher than others. When this is so, as much time as seems necessary should be spent with this, even if other areas are neglected.

At the outset of the interview a friendly, positive relationship should be established. Therefore it is usually a good plan if the teacher can begin with some appreciative remarks about the child—either about his behavior in school or, if the interview follows the developmental examination, about some aspect of his performance in the examination.

After this, a topic of the interview which is generally easy for parents to talk about, and which is not threatening to them in their role as parents, is the subject of play. "What does your child play with at home; how does he spend his time?" is a good beginning question. Parents usually enjoy answering this question, and most can easily talk about play.

For the rest, it is good for the teacher to try not to ask questions too directly, but to give the parent a number of face-saving opportunities. For example, in discussing the matter of discipline, rather than asking, "Do you spank?" it is better to say, "What methods of control work best with your child— talking to him, confining him to a special place, spanking him, bribing him, or what?"

To illustrate the range of inquiry in the interview, we present possible questions that might be involved in the areas of eating, sleeping, and toilet training. The questions are not in any special order; not all these questions would necessarily be asked; and questions other than these will often be used.

However, such sample questions indicate what may be asked of parents and suggest the significance of what is asked. For, in answering such questions, the parent not only tells a great deal about his child—he reveals much about his own attitudes. And such an extensive review of his child's behavior, and his method of handling it, often affords new insights about the child to both parents and teacher, and permits the teacher to point up the child's individuality.

Questions About Feeding

Does the child eat well? (The response to this question sometimes tells a great deal about the child's feeding, without need of many more questions. Some parents are much disturbed about the topic, and it is apparent at once. Others are casual and unworried. But even if the parent says, "He's O.K.," or "No trouble at all," it is often rewarding to go on with a few more questions, since it is possible to learn a lot from this area of investigation.)

What are his favorite foods? What does he dislike or refuse? (The teacher can consider and point out possible constitutional reasons for refusals. She can ask if he is imitating someone else in his refusals. The possibility of minimal allergies should definitely be considered.)

Will he eat anything, or is he discriminating? If discriminating, what special foods does he like?

How much does he eat? Does he eat all kinds of foods? Does he have a large or small appetite?

Does he eat between meals? How much? Does he get hungry just *before* mealtime, and if so has the parent considered moving mealtime up a little? How many meals does he have a day? (Some children do better with five small meals a day.)

Does the parent make the best possible use of food to avoid fatigue, prevent quarreling, induce sleep, etc.?

Which is the child's best meal? Does he eat all three meals well or one much better than others? What is a sample breakfast, lunch, dinner?

Does the child have food jags? What foods? Does he like highly spiced foods or bland foods? (This may be an important question, especially if the child doesn't eat well. He may be a child who likes spicy food, and the parents may not have realized this and may have been feeding him only bland foods. Some parents, oddly, feel that spicy foods are not proper for little children.)

What is his liquid intake? Is he a good milk drinker? Does he get milk in other ways?

Does he have real, obvious allergies, foods that he just can't eat? Does the parent know the excellent food value of bananas for the child with allergies?

Does the child have a great craving for sweets? When does he eat sweets? How many sweets a day?

How do mealtimes go? Rituals? Refusals? (There are many instances where the child has dominated parents at mealtimes, and parents need guidance. Often every meal is a fight, and the parent dreads it. Parents may be emphasizing nutrition too much. They may be too demanding in their set notions of what a child ought to eat, when he ought to eat, how much he ought to eat.)

Does the child eat with parents at the family meal, or separately? (Many parents think children and parents should eat together, no matter how badly it goes. A possible compromise worth suggesting is that the child eat first, then have dessert with the family.)

How are his manners? (The teacher may point out at how late a stage manners usually come in.)

Does the child have patterns and rituals in eating? (Does this go along with other rituals and rigidities?)

How much does the child help himself at meals?

Will he eat foods which need chewing?

How is he about new foods? Has he color preferences, an aesthetic interest in food, dishes, etc.?

How does his eating compare with that of his siblings?

Is he a messy eater?

Does he stay at the table well? (Some parents are relieved to realize that children are not "abnormal" if they prefer to eat on the run.)

Does he need TV, a book, or other entertainment or distraction while eating?

Does he still have a bottle? If so, how does the parent feel about this?

How does the child act in a restaurant or when eating away from home? (Parents may be surprised to hear that some children eat better away from home, and that meals away from home are often good times to introduce new foods or break up rituals.)

If the child does seem to be a feeding problem, what has the parent tried?

Questions About Elimination

(The interview here varies with the age of the child. At the earlier ages, the questioning may be more detailed than at later ages. By the time the child is four, and very likely reasonably well trained, the initial question may well be "Was it difficult to toilet-train him?")

At 2-3 Years

Is he toilet-trained? For bowel? For bladder?
(This initial question usually brings out any problems which are present. Actually, if there is a daytime problem, the teacher may know about it. Sometimes, however, children can stay dry at school, but not be dry at home. If the parents' answer to the initial question is "No," the teacher can encourage them to talk about their attitude in the matter. If the answer is "Yes," she can ask when the child was trained and how it was accomplished. The teacher may question separately for the two toilet functions, or the parent may discuss both more or less at the same time.)

Questions About Bowel Training (If There Is Still Difficulty)

Is he aware of failure? Is he distressed at failure?
Does he have just an occasional accident, or is he completely untrained?
Does he seem to be using withholding (or soiling) as a weapon? Is he too busy to be bothered?
Does he have unusual toilet habits? Any stool smearing?
Is he still in diapers, or in training pants?
Is he showing some indication of wanting to succeed? Does he tell? Does he have a regular time? Does he use toilet facilities at all, or does he function only when his diaper is put back on? Does he hide when he functions? Does he prefer to function standing up?
Are you doing anything to help things along, or do you think he is still not ready for help?

Questions About Bladder Training Are Often Similar to Those for Bowel Training

Is he dry now, and how long has he been dry? What did you do to promote this?
Does weather make any difference? Does he have accidents when he

is overexcited, ill, overfatigued, or under some special stress? Does he interrupt meals to urinate?

What is his attitude about any daytime accidents?

Is he independent or do you have to help? If independent, does he still have to tell before and/or after?

Is he social or solitary about toilet habits?

How long is his span? Is he sometimes too busy to stop and function on the toilet? Can he function on strange toilets?

How about naptime?

How about night? If he wets, when does he do so? Do you pick him up? If so, when? If you pick him up, does this keep him dry, or is he nevertheless wet in the morning? Does he awaken when you pick him up? If he wets the bed, how does he feel about it? Is he independent—could he get out of bed and get to toilet facilities?

If training seems delayed, have you checked with your doctor to see if there is any physical basis for the delay?

What are you doing about this training, or do you think he is still not ready?

Questions About Sleep

What time does he go to bed? Does he still take a nap? Does he sleep as much as he "should"? Does the amount of sleep he has affect his behavior? Does his time of going to bed affect his time of waking?

How long does it take him to get to sleep? How deeply does he sleep?

Does he have a room of his own, or does he sleep with a sibling? Can he sleep in strange places? Can you leave him with a sitter to put him to bed?

What is the procedure about putting him to bed—any rituals? Does he take toys to bed with him? Does he need a night light?

How is his sleep pattern influenced by upsetting situations: do these put him to sleep in exhaustion, or keep him from sleeping?

Does he wake in the middle of the night? What does he do when he wakes? How do you get him back to sleep? Does he get into your bed? Does he wander around the house? Does he need you? Will food quiet him? If he does not stay in his crib, do you use any restraining devices?

Does he have night fears? Does he dream? Does he rock, bang his head, take his crib apart? Does he sleep quietly or restlessly? Does he sleep in odd positions?

Is he still in a crib, or has he moved to a bed?

In the morning, what does he do when he wakes up? Does he stay in his own room, come to parents' room, go downstairs, get into things?

Does he have a nap every day, or just when he's tired? How long? Does he accept it readily? Is it a real sleep, or a playtime? Does a nap affect night sleep? Do you wake him if he is sleeping too long? When you do go in to wake him, can you just go right into his room, or do you have to make noises outside the room before you go in? What is his mood on waking? What happens if he skips his nap?

The above questions are only samples of questions asked in three of the areas that occupy so much of the young child's time and attention. The next chapter will deal with some of the questions parents themselves ask as they search both for immediate answers and for sources of information.

16

Questions Parents Ask

Using questions such as those listed in the preceding chapter, teachers will be able to steer a parent interview into channels that should lead to rich interpretation of the child being discussed. Parents, of course, will ask a lot of questions of their own during the course of such an interview, or merely in daily contact with the teacher.

The teacher in a nursery school should be well provided with a great deal of specific information about child behavior in general and especially about problems in child rearing. In many instances many of the usual questions likely to arise will be discussed with the teachers by the director, during daily or weekly sessions, after the children have gone home. Teachers in training should expect to learn a good deal not only about nursery school teaching, but also about child behavior in general during their training period.

Also, answers to the usual questions parents ask can be found in any of the many books for parents currently available in such profusion. Teachers can obtain much useful information from these books and will also wish to bring them to the attention of parents, who will in many instances enjoy and benefit from reading them. Books which we currently recommend are listed on pages 300 to 304.

Ideally we might give such information here. But that would be another book in itself. Of our own books, those which con-

288

tain most specific answers to the usual parent questions are *Child Behavior, Infant and Child in the Culture of Today, Parents Ask, Don't Push Your Preschooler,* and *Helping Young Children Learn.*[1] Books by others which we have found especially helpful include *How to Parent* and *How to Father* by Fitzhugh Dodson; *Understanding Children* by Richard Gardner; *How to Raise Children at Home in Your Spare Time* by Marvin Gersh; and *Guiding Your Child to a More Creative Life* by Fredelle Maynard.[2]

We list in this chapter some of the more customary questions which parents are likely to ask. This listing, we hope, will alert both the teacher in training and the more experienced teacher as well to some of the questions which she may be expected to answer.

Routines—Feeding, Sleeping, etc.

What do you do about a poor eater? What do you do when your child refuses to eat certain foods?

If a child doesn't eat his meal, should you refuse him any food until the next meal and then make him eat the refused food?

Should a child be required to finish his main course before he gets dessert?

Are sweets really bad for the teeth?

What do you do if your child really can't eat some foods?

How do you induce a child to sleep at naptime?

1. Louise B. Ames and Joan A. Chase, *Don't Push Your Preschooler* (New York: Harper & Row, 1974); Arnold Gesell, Frances L. Ilg, and L. B. Ames, *Infant and Child in the Culture of Today,* rev. ed. (New York: Harper & Row, 1974); F. L. Ilg and L. B. Ames, *Child Behavior* (New York: Harper & Row, 1955), and *Parents Ask* (New York: Harper & Row, 1962); Evelyn G. Pitcher et al., *Helping Young Children Learn,* 2d ed. (Columbus, Ohio: Charles E. Merrill Publishing Co., 1974).

2. Fitzhugh Dodson, *How to Father* (Los Angeles: Nash Publishing Corp., 1974), and *How to Parent* (Los Angeles: Nash Publishing Corp., 1970); Richard Gardner, *Understanding Children* (New York: Jason Aronson, 1973); Marvin Gersh, *How to Raise Children at Home in Your Spare Time* (New York: Stein & Day, 1966); Fredelle Maynard, *Guiding Your Child to a More Creative Life* (Garden City, N.Y.: Doubleday & Co., 1973).

What do you do if a child lies in bed for a long time and can't get to sleep?

What can parents do when the child wakes in the night and cries, won't go back to sleep, and keeps everybody awake?

How about the child who wanders around the house in the night? Should you tie his door?

What do you do when the child wants to come into your bed?

How do you keep a child in bed in the morning?

Is it all right for him to take a bottle to bed?

What do you do with a 4-year-old who still wets his bed?

Questions about Age: "Is It Normal?"

How do you cope with the oppositional tendencies of Two-and-a-Half?

How do you get a 2½-year-old to share?

How about the uncertainty and insecurity of the 3½-year-old?

Should typical 4-year-old "out-of-bounds" behavior be allowed, or should the parent put his foot down?

Is this (any of a number of ways of behaving) a stage, or should we worry about it?

What are the best toys for a child of a given age?

Is it true that many toys now on the market are totally unsafe for child use?

What are the best books, the best records, for each age?

Fears, Bad Habits, Health

How do we handle nervous habits? (Head banging, picking sores, nail biting, thumb sucking, rocking)

What do we do about eye blinking? Stuttering?

How do we handle fears? (Dogs, noises, storms, dark, water)

What do you do when a child wakes up frightened?

Sex, Masturbation

What do you do about sex play? About exhibitionism?
How do you tell a child about the birth of a baby?
What do you do about masturbation?

Discipline

How do you handle hostile reactions and deliberate badness? (Wets
pants on purpose, dumps potted plants onto floor, etc.)
Am I spoiling my child?
How do you regard morbid conversation about cutting people's heads
off, throwing them into the garbage, shooting, stabbing, etc.?
How much shouting, name calling, is permissible? How could you
stop it?
What are effective methods of discipline? What about spanking?
How much can you reason with a child when he seems to understand,
but then disregards what has been said?
How about the so-called new Behavior Modification method of disci-
pline?

Conflicting Theories of Discipline

How do you cope with conflicting philosophies of grandparents and
parents? Of visiting relatives? Others who live in the home?
How do you cope with conflicting philosophies of mother and father
—one lax and one demanding?
Should parents always agree about discipline?

Nursery School Behavior and Adjustment

How long should a parent have to stay at school with a child?
Should children play out of doors in all weather?
How well should a child play with others?
If a child doesn't want to go to school, should he be forced to do so?

What prompts a child to like the friends he does?

Is the child happy at school?

Does the child ask for his mother when she is away? Does he miss her? Need her?

Does he share his toys? Does he play nicely? Should he play nicely?

How can departures from school be expedited when child doesn't want to leave?

How does it happen that he behaves so well at school and so badly at home?

Is it usual for a child to adjust well to school at first, then have a period of backsliding? What do you do about it?

Does he paint at school? What is the significance of the colors he uses? Why does he seem to feel the need of keeping his hands clean?

Is a car pool a good idea?

How about safety? Should the teachers be watching each child all the time?

Does a child have more colds when he goes to school? How can we prevent colds?

Does the school snack take away appetite for lunch?

Related Problems about School

Won't he be bored by kindergarten if he goes to nursery school?

At what age should a child start kindergarten? First grade?

He is interested in letters—should we teach him to read?

Can a parent increase a child's intelligence by teaching him in the preschool years?

Can you make a child ready for school earlier by doing just the right things in the preschool years?

Should the child go to public or to private school?

What activities outside school should be encouraged?

What is the best method for teaching music to young children? What instrument? At what age should one start?

Relation to Siblings

What can one do about constant fighting between siblings?
How do you handle it?
How do you prevent dangerous aggression of an older child toward
    a younger?
Is it good to send a child to nursery school when there is a new baby,
    or might he get jealous?
Do you have to get two of everything to keep siblings happy?
How far should you go trying to keep things "fair"?
When the older sibling brings a friend home to play, must he be
    required to include the younger sibling in their play?
Should there be a gradation of privileges with respect to age?

Neighborhood Problems

How do you cope with constant fighting of children in the neighbor-
    hood, and with complaints of mothers?
What do you do when your child acts badly when visiting, or when
    company comes to the house?
What should you do if children in the neighborhood tease your child
    badly?
Should a child, especially a boy, be expected to "stand up for him-
    self"?
Should you interfere if other children are always ganging up on your
    own?

Movies and TV

How can you regulate TV watching? How much *should* you regulate
    it? Should children be allowed to see exciting programs? Programs
    showing violence?
Should children be allowed to watch TV while they are eating?
Does TV watching hurt their eyes? Will watching TV interfere with
    their interest in books?

Does seeing aggression on television make children aggressive?
At what age can you take a child to the movies and be assured it does
him no harm?

Special Family Problems

How can traveling be made easier and more enjoyable for a child?
Does it harm a child if mother and father go away together, without
him, on a vacation?
How can a child be prepared for hospitalization? How can he be
helped when his mother is away because of illness?
Should mother stay with a child who is being hospitalized?
If parents are going on an extended trip, should they try to explain
this to the child beforehand? Should they communicate with the
child while they are gone?
What play areas or play equipment can be set up in a home where
there is little space and little money?
When there are special problems, what are some sources of help in the
community? (Psychiatric, visual, auditory, etc.)

Religion and Death?

How do you explain death to a young child?
What do you say about God?

Epilogue

In an ideal educational situation, the child is taught at a level of learning which his own level of readiness permits. The nursery school for this reason provides what may well be the ideal educational opportunity.

Even in the early primary grades, flexible as a teacher may be, the curriculum of any given grade requires that certain subject matter be covered during the course of a school year, and to that extent the child has to adapt to the requirements of the school.

But in the nursery school, if it is flexibly run within a developmental philosophy, the school adapts to the child. Certainly he makes his adaptations, too, even as does the infant who follows a self-regulation feeding schedule. We have always taken pains to term such a schedule "self-demand *and* self-adaptation." Even the young infant does his share of adapting. Equally so with the nursery school child. There are certain rules which he must follow; certain adaptations he must make to the wishes of the teacher and to the needs of his fellow students. But in general, the nursery school is the educational situation par excellence in which the child's needs can be considered and adapted to.

As in all good educational and disciplinary situations this does not mean that no rules prevail, or that the child does just as he pleases. It does mean, however, that the teacher starts where the child is and proceeds only as rapidly and as far as his true abilities permit.

That is, an effective nursery school always deals with the child at his current behavior level. This can go so far as to have him put into an older group should he prove too mature for his contemporaries; or, conversely, might suggest his need, temporarily, for being in a group of children somewhat below his own age. Similarly, a truly flexible schedule might permit a child to have fewer or more days of school a week than others in his group.

In the best nursery schools a relaxed teacher, skilled in appraising individual differences in rapidly growing minds and bodies, avoids any stereotyped program, or at least she is ready to modify her program to suit the needs of any individual girl or boy. Knowing the wide span of a child's development in any year, and the variety in different children's interests and motivations to learn, she will keep groups small and will provide them with numerous types of activities which they can explore freely: those involving music, science, numbers, literature, people, and physical skills. She will value the process of learning whereby the child can develop such traits as independence, resourcefulness, curiosity, creativity, and responsibility.

The best in early childhood education will not be achieved by more rigidity, technology, or gadgets. Nothing can take the place of skilled teachers who are fully aware of each child's individuality and also able to recognize his present developmental level and to provide experiences which fit this level.

As we have indicated in earlier chapters, we do not consider that the preschooler is wasting his time when he "just plays." Nor do we favor a rigid presentation of academic subjects such as reading and arithmetic during the preschool years. Rather, we agree with those who consider that play *is* the young child's work. Dr. Gesell commented as long ago as 1912:

The normal child's acute powers of attention, observation and perception, impelling him to the closest scrutiny and investigation of each new thing, and his countless experiments in physics, *all of which we call play,* are the means adopted by Nature to exercise and develop his faculties. . . . One of the threatening evils of education is over-sophistication. It is easy to philosophize and to become mysteriously didactic, to surround the everyday natural interests and characteristics of childhood with impenetrable psychological analysis.[1]

As to giving preschoolers formal instruction in reading, it is true, certainly, that some very young children are ready and eager for experiences with letters and numbers. Before formal instruction is given, however, a teacher should see to it that the child has meaningful experiences in his contacts with the environment which will make meaningful the printed words he finally comes to read. In the last analysis, the presentation of language symbols is a useless trick unless the child has enough experience to comprehend the meaning of these symbols.

Teachers working in early childhood education need a broad base for their teaching experience. Ideally they should be well informed in all there is to know about children from infancy through age six. Nursery school should never be considered as an isolated experience. Rather, the school experiences of nursery school, kindergarten, and first grade should be considered as a unit.

Within this unit the behavior of children is extraordinary in its variety. Any first-grade class composed of children chronologically aged six contains children who have a wide range of developmental ages. (In fact, it is for this very reason that we are urging primary schools to give up the present practice of entering all children who are chronologically six years of age into first grade, and to substitute a practice of basing decisions

1. Arnold and Beatrice C. Gesell, *The Normal Child and Primary Education* (New York: Ginn and Co., 1912), p. 334.

about school entrance and grade placement on the child's actual behavior age, rather than on his age in years.)

Similarly, in nursery school as in primary school, developmental levels may range from two to five years, even though children in attendance may all be three or four years old in birthday age.

A good nursery school teacher must be aware of the irregular nature of growth in children in terms of their motor, adaptive, personal-social, and language behaviors, as well as of their different developmental levels. She must realize that slow development in one area of behavior does not necessarily or even usually imply what is technically called retardation. She must also be able to support the child who is immature for his age level as well as be able to challenge the gifted child with a creative, meaningful program.

Thus a teacher of young children needs to have a concept of growth that will prompt her to introduce a wide variety of experiences into any school program for the young child. She must know how to accept a child where he is, regardless of his level, and how to stimulate his potentialities. She will appreciate the fact that play is creative work for the young child.

She must also come to grips with a number of theoretical considerations in child psychology. She must be acquainted with theories of learning, with the findings of constitutional psychology, and with known facts and current research in the field of child development. Yet it is important that her philosophy should not be rigidly conceived or held to. Rigidity has no place in early childhood education. At best, a good teacher should have what she considers working hypotheses, including a provision for reading, listening, examining new points of view from every available source.

A successful program in early childhood education does not exist without effective communication with parents. A school program for the young child which does not consider parent education fully as important as the education of the child is inadequate. At no other time in the child's educational career is the parent so close to him and to the school as in the pre-school years.

This makes the teacher's interpretation of the child and his needs to the parent both possible and fruitful; and the teacher has much to learn from the parents' interpretation of the child to her. The teacher of the young child has an extraordinary opportunity to help parents understand their child both as to his individuality and his level and rate of development, and to be happy with the child and to relax in this early, close relationship.

In conclusion, what do we hope that this earliest educational experience will do for the child? In any dynamic progress, an integrated beginning is the most important stage. The bases for successful and effective adult living are not taught by precept in later years. They should be built into the character of the child during his earliest years. Those who overemphasize the early learning of specific academic skills, in our opinion, have little idea of, or respect for, what the young child is like or what the education of young children really involves.

Early childhood is a time for education in living and for approaching life with the freedom to explore, to ask questions, to create. Later education in information and in the development of intellectual skills will be fully effective only if the child has learned first to live with himself, his parents, and his fellows, and to approach his environment with curiosity and creativity.

A truly flexible nursery school can provide an invaluable supplement to a good home in promoting all of these opportunities. A good school experience in these early years is as important as any which comes later.

References

Books About Nursery School and School in General

Ames, Louise B.; Gillespie, Clyde; and Streff, John. *Stop School Failure.* New York: Harper & Row, 1972.

Ashton-Warner, Sylvia. *Teacher.* New York: Simon & Schuster, 1963.

Berson, Minnie P. *Kindergarten: Your Child's Big Step.* New York: E. P. Dutton & Co., 1959.

Beyer, Evelyn. *Teaching Young Children.* New York: Pegasus, 1968.

Braun, Samuel, and Edwards, Esther. *History and Theory of Early Childhood Education.* Worthington, Ohio: Charles A. Jones Publishing Co., 1972.

Brown, George. *Human Teaching for Human Learning: An Introduction to Confluent Education.* New York: Viking Press, 1970.

Burgess, Helen Steers. *How to Choose a Nursery School.* Public Affairs Pamphlet No. 310, 1961. 22 East 38th Street, New York, N.Y.

Burnett, Dorothy K. *Your Preschool Child: Making the Most of the Years from Two to Seven.* New York: Holt, Rinehart & Winston, 1961.

Christianson, Helen M.; Rogers, Mary M.; and Ludlum, Blanche A. *The Nursery School: Adventure in Living and Learning.* Boston: Houghton Mifflin Co., 1961.

Delacato, Carl. *The Ultimate Stranger: The Autistic Child.* New York: Doubleday, 1974.

Dinkmeyer, Don, and Dreikurs, Rudolf. *Encouraging Children to Learn.* Englewood Cliffs, N.J.: Prentice-Hall, 1963.

Doak, Elizabeth. *What Does the Nursery School Teacher Teach?* (Pamphlet) New York: National Association for Nursery Education, 1955.

Fletcher, Margaret I. *The Adult and the Nursery School Child.* Toronto: University of Toronto Press, 1958.

Frost, Joe L., ed. *Early Childhood Education Rediscovered.* New York: Holt, Rinehart & Winston, 1968.

Furth, Hans. *Piaget for Teachers.* Englewood Cliffs, N.J.: Prentice-Hall, 1970.

Gesell, Arnold, et al. *The First Five Years of Life.* New York: Harper & Row, 1940.

Gesell, Arnold; Ilg, Frances L.; and Ames, Louise B. In collaboration with Janet Learned Rodell. *Infant and Child in the Culture of Today: The Guidance of Development in Home and Nursery School.* Rev. ed. New York: Harper & Row, 1974.

Golick, Margaret. *Strictly for Parents: A Parent's Guide to Learning Problems.* Quebec Association for Children with Learning Disability. P.O. Box 22, Cote Street, Luc Postal Station, Montreal, Quebec, Canada.

Green, Marjorie M., and Woods, Elizabeth L. *A Nursery School Handbook for Teachers and Parents.* Sierra Madre, Cal.: Sierra Madre Community Nursery School Association, 1961.

Hart, Harold H., ed. *Summerhill: For and Against.* New York: Hart Publishing Co., 1970.

Hymes, James L. *Effective Home-School Relations.* Englewood Cliffs, N.J.: Prentice-Hall, 1953.

Landreth, Catherine. *Education of the Young Child: A Nursery School Manual.* New York: John Wiley & Sons, 1942.

Langford, Louise M. *Guidance of the Young Child.* New York: John Wiley & Sons, 1960.

Leavitt, Jerome E., ed. *Nursery-Kindergarten Education.* New York: McGraw-Hill Book Co., 1958.

Leeper, Sarah H., et al. *Good Schools for Young Children.* 2d ed. New York: Macmillan & Co., 1968.

Logan, Lillian M. *Teaching the Young Child.* Boston: Houghton Mifflin Co., 1960.

Miller, Mabel E. *A Practical Guide for Kindergarten Teachers.* New York: Parker Publishing Co., 1970.

Montessori, Maria. *The Montessori Method.* New York: Schocken Books, 1964.

Parker, Ronald K., ed. *The Preschool in Action: Exploring Early Childhood Programs.* Boston: Allyn and Bacon, 1972.

Pitcher, Evelyn G., Lasher, Miriam; Feinburg, Sylvia; and Braun, Linda. *Helping Young Children Learn.* 2d ed. Columbus, Ohio: Charles E. Merrill Publishing Co., 1974.

Read, Katherine. *The Nursery School.* Rev. ed. Philadelphia: W. B. Saunders & Co., 1971.

Spodek, Bernard. *Teaching in the Early Years.* Englewood Cliffs, N.J.: Prentice-Hall, 1972.

Stant, Marg. *The Young Child: His Activities and Materials.* Englewood Cliffs, N.J.: Prentice-Hall, 1972.

Weber, Evelyn. *Early Childhood Education: Perspective on Change.* Worthington, Ohio: Charles A. Jones Publishing Co., 1970.

Weber, Lillian. *The English Infant School and Informal Education.* Englewood Cliffs: Prentice-Hall, 1965.

Wylie, Joanne, ed. *A Creative Guide for Preschool Teachers.* Racine, Wis.: Western Educational Services, 1965.

Background Reading for Teachers and Parents

Ames, Louise B. *Child Care and Development.* Philadelphia: J. B. Lippincott Co., 1970.

————. *Is Your Child in the Wrong Grade?* New York: Harper & Row, 1967.

Ames, Louise B., and Chase, Joan A. *Don't Push Your Preschooler.* New York: Harper & Row, 1974.

Axline, Virginia H. *Dibs in Search of Self.* Boston: Houghton Mifflin Co., 1964.

Beasley, Jane. *Slow to Talk.* New York: Teachers College Press, 1956.

Beck, Helen. *Don't Push Me, I'm No Computer.* New York: McGraw-Hill Book Co., 1973.

Bley, Edgar S. *Launching Your Preschooler.* New York: Sterling Publishing Co., 1955.

Brazleton, T. Berry. *Infants and Mothers.* New York: Delacorte Press, 1969.

————. *Toddlers and Parents.* New York: Delacorte Press, 1974.

Briggs, Dorothy Corkille. *Your Child's Self-Esteem.* Garden City, N.Y.: Doubleday & Co., 1970.

Brutten, Milton; Richardson, Sylvia O.; and Mangel, Charles. *Something's Wrong with My Child.* New York: Harcourt, Brace Jovanovich, 1973.

Burnett, Dorothy K. *Your Preschool Child: Making the Most of the Years from Two to Seven.* New York: Holt, Rinehart & Winston, 1961.

Capa, Cornell, and Pines, Maya. *Retarded Children Can Be Helped.* New York: Channel Press, 1957.

Caplan, Frank, and Caplan, Theresa. *The Power of Play.* Garden City, N.Y.: Doubleday & Co., 1973.

Cass, Joan. *The Significance of Children's Play.* London: B. T. Batsford, 1971.

Chess, Stella; Thomas, Alexander; and Birch, Herbert G. *Your Child Is a Person.* New York: Viking Press, 1965.

Chukovsky, K. *From Two to Five.* Berkeley: University of California Press, 1963.

Coffin, Patricia. *1,2,3,4,5,6.* New York: Macmillan & Co., 1972.

Coleman, Lester L. *Visit to the Hospital.* New York: Grosset & Dunlap, 1957.

Dodson, Fitzhugh. *How to Father.* Los Angeles: Nash Publishing Corp., 1974.

———. *How to Parent.* Los Angeles: Nash Publishing Corp., 1970.

Edwards, Vergne. *The Tired Adult's Guide to Backyard Fun with Kids.* New York: Thomas Y. Crowell Co., 1957.

Gardner, Richard A. *The Boys and Girls Book about Divorce.* New York: Science House, 1970.

———. *Understanding Children.* New York: Jason Aronson, 1973.

Gersh, Marvin J. *How to Raise Children at Home in Your Spare Time.* New York: Stein & Day, 1966.

Gesell, Arnold; Ilg, Frances L.; and Ames, Louise B. In collaboration with Janet Learned Rodell. *Infant and Child in the Culture of Today.* Rev. ed. New York: Harper & Row, 1974.

Ginott, Haim. *Between Parent and Child.* New York: Macmillan & Co., 1965.

Grollman, Rabbi Earl, ed. *Explaining Death to Children.* Boston: Beacon Press, 1967.

———. *Explaining Divorce to Children.* Boston: Beacon Press, 1969.

Harrison-Ross, Phyllis, and Wyden, Barbara. *The Black Child: A Parent's Guide.* New York: Peter H. Wyden, 1973.

Hartley, Ruth, et al. *Understanding Children's Play.* New York: Columbia University Press, 1952.

Hymes, James L. *The Child Under Six.* Englewood Cliffs, N.J.: Prentice-Hall, 1963.

Ilg, Frances L., and Ames, Louise B. *Child Behavior.* New York: Harper & Row, 1955.

———. *Parents Ask.* New York: Harper & Row, 1962.

Kraskin, Robert A. *You CAN Improve Your Vision.* Garden City, N.Y.: Doubleday & Co., 1968.

Levine, Milton I., and Seligman, Jean H. *The Parents' Encyclopedia of Infancy, Childhood and Adolescence.* New York: Thomas Y. Crowell Co., 1973.

Liepmann, Lise. *Your Child's Sensory World.* New York: Dial Press, 1973.

McIntire, Roger W. *For Love of Children.* Del Mar, Cal.: CRM Books, 1970.

Mayle, Peter. *Where Did I Come From?* New York: Lyle Stuart, 1973.

Maynard, Fredelle. *Guiding Your Child to a More Creative Life.* Garden City, N.Y.: Doubleday & Co., 1973.

Murton, Alice. *From Home to School.* New York: Citation Press, 1973.

Neisser, Edith. *Brothers and Sisters.* New York: Harper & Row, 1951.

Pitcher, Evelyn, and Prelinger, Ernst. *Children Tell Stories: An Analysis of Fantasy.* New York: International Universities Press, 1963.

Porter, J. D. R. *Black Child, White Child: The Development of Racial Attitudes.* Cambridge, Mass.: Harvard University Press, 1971.

Putnam, Tracy J. *Epilepsy: What It Is and What To Do About It.* Philadelphia: J. B. Lippincott Co., 1958.

Salk, Lee. *What Every Child Would Like his Parents to Know.* New York: David McKay Co., 1972.

Sheldon, William H. *Varieties of Temperament.* New York: Hafner, 1969.

Siegel, Ernest. *Helping the Brain Injured Child: A Handbook for Parents.* New York: Association for Brain Injured Children, 1961.

Smith, Lendon H. *The Children's Doctor.* Englewood Cliffs, N.J.: Prentice-Hall, 1969.

Swartz, Harry. *The Allergic Child.* New York: Coward, McCann & Geoghegan, 1954.

Todd, V. C., and Heffernan, Helen. *The Years Before School: Guiding Preschool Children.* New York: Macmillan & Co., 1970.

Wenar, Charles. *Personality Development from Infancy to Adulthood.* Boston: Houghton Mifflin Co., 1971.

Wender, Paul H. *The Hyperactive Child: A Handbook for Parents.* New York: Crown Publishers, 1973.

Wunderlich, Ray C. *Allergy, Brains and Children Coping.* St. Petersburg, Fla.: Johnny Reads Press, 1973.

Books for Children

Alexander, Martha. *Babies Are Like That.* New York: Golden Press, 1967. (3–6)

Aliki. *Hush, Little Baby.* Englewood Cliffs, N.J.: Prentice-Hall, 1968. (15 mos.–2 yrs.)

Anglund, Joan. *A Friend Is Someone Who Likes You.* New York: Harcourt, Brace Jovanovich, 1958. (3–6).

Bennett, Rainey. *The Secret Hiding Place.* New York: World Publishing Co., 1960. (3–6)

Berger, Terry. *I Have Feelings.* New York: Behavioral Publications, 1970. (4–8)

Brenner, Barbara. *Barto Takes the Subway.* New York: Alfred A. Knopf, 1961. (4–6)

Brown, Margaret Wise. *Goodnight, Moon.* New York: Harper & Row, 1947. (2–3)

———. *The Important Book.* New York: Harper & Row, 1949. (3–5)

———. *The Little Fireman.* New York: William R. Scott, 1952. (2–5)

———. *The Noisy Book.* New York: Harper & Row, 1939. (3–5)

———. *The Runaway Bunny.* New York: Harper & Row, 1942. (3–5)

———. *Shhh . . . Bang!* New York: Harper & Row, 1943. (4–6)

Brownstone, Cecily. *All Kinds of Mothers.* New York: David McKay Co., 1969. (4–8)

Buckley, Helen. *Grandfather and I.* New York: Lothrop, Lee & Shepard Co., 1959. (3–6)

———. *Grandmother and I.* New York: Lothrop, Lee & Shepard Co., 1961. (3–6)

———. *My Sister and I.* New York: Lothrop, Lee & Shepard Co., 1963. (3–6)

Burton, Virginia Lee. *Choo-Choo.* Boston: Houghton Mifflin Co., 1943. (3–5)

———. *Mike Mulligan and his Steam Shovel.* Boston: Houghton Mifflin Co., 1939. (4–7)

Chalmers, Mary. *Kevin.* New York: Harper & Row, 1957. (3–4)

Ciardi, John. *I Met a Man.* Boston: Houghton Mifflin Co., 1961. (3–5)

Cook, Bernadine. *The Little Fish that Got Away.* New York: Scholastic Book Services, 1959. (4–6)

Darrow, Whitney, Jr. *I'm Glad I'm a Boy; I'm Glad I'm a Girl.* New York: Simon & Schuster, 1970. (4–7)

Davis, Daphne. *The Baby Animal Book.* New York: Golden Press. (15 mos.– 2 yrs.)

DeBeanlien, G. *Baby's First Book.* New York: Platt & Munk Co. (15 mos.– 2 yrs.)

DeBrunhoff, Jean. *The Story of Babar.* New York: Random House, 1933. (3–6)

Duvoisin, Roger. *The Crocodile in the Tree.* New York: Alfred A. Knopf, 1973. (3–6)

———. *Day and Night.* New York: Alfred A. Knopf, 1960. (4–7)

———. *Jasmine.* New York: Alfred A. Knopf, 1973. (4–7)

————. *Our Veronica Goes to Petunia Farm.* New York: Pantheon Books, 1973. (4–6)

————. *Petunia.* New York: Alfred A. Knopf, 1950. (3–5)

————. *The Rain Puddle.* New York: Lothrop, Lee & Shepard Co., 1965. (3–6)

Ets, Marie Hall. *Another Day.* New York: Viking Press, 1953. (3–4)

————. *Gilberto and the Wind.* New York: Viking Press, 1963. (3–6)

————. *Just Me.* New York: Viking Press, 1965. (3–5)

————. *Play with Me.* New York: Viking Press, 1955. (3–5)

Fassler, Joan. *Don't Worry, Dear.* New York: Behavioral Publications, 1971. (3–7)

Fatio, Louise. *The Happy Lion.* New York: Whittlesey House, 1954. (4–6)

Flack, Marjorie. *Angus and the Cat.* Garden City, N.Y.: Doubleday & Co., 1931. (2–3)

————. *Angus and the Ducks.* Garden City, N.Y.: Doubleday & Co., 1939. (2–4)

————. *Ask Mr. Bear.* New York: Macmillan & Co., 1958. (2–5)

————. *The Restless Robin.* Boston: Houghton Mifflin Co., 1951. (4–6)

————. *The Story about Ping.* New York: Viking Press, 1933. (3–6)

————. *Tim Tadpole and the Great Bullfrog.* Garden City, N.Y.: Doubleday & Co., 1934. (3–6)

Freeman, Don. *Corduroy.* New York: Viking Press, 1968. (3–5)

Gag, Wanda. *Millions of Cats.* New York: Coward, McCann & Geoghegan, 1928. (3–6)

Grollman, Earl, ed. *Talking about Death.* Boston: Beacon Press, 1970. (4–8)

Hample, Stoo. *The Silly Book.* New York: Harper & Row, 1961. (4–6)

Heide, Florence, and VanClief, Sylvia. *That's what Friends Are For.* New York: Scholastic Book Services, 1968. (3–6)

Hoban, Russell. *Bedtime for Frances.* New York: Harper & Row, 1960. (3–5)

————. *Best Friends.* New York: Harper & Row, 1969. (3–5)

————. *A Birthday for Frances.* (A series.) New York: Harper & Row, 1968. (3–5)

————. *Bread and Jam for Frances.* New York: Harper & Row, 1964. (4–8)

Hoban, Tana. *Push-Pull, Empty-Full.* New York: Macmillan & Co., 1972. (2–4)

Johnson, Crockett. *Harold and the Purple Crayon.* New York: Harper & Row, 1955. (4–7)

Justus, May. *New Boy in School.* New York: Hastings, 1963. (5–7)

Kesselman, Wendy. *Angelita.* New York: Hill, 1970. (4–7)

Kessler, Ethel. *Do Baby Bears Sit on Chairs?* Garden City, N.Y.: Doubleday & Co., 1961. (3–4)

Kessler, Ethel, and Kessler, Leonard. *The Day Daddy Stayed Home.* Garden City, N.Y.: Doubleday & Co., 1959. (3–5)

Klein, Norma. *Girls Can Be Anything.* New York: E. P. Dutton & Co., 1973. (3–6)

Krasilovsky, Phyllis. *The Man who Didn't Wash his Dishes.* Garden City, N.Y.: Doubleday & Co., 1950. (3–6)

Krauss, Ruth. *The Backward Day.* New York: Harper & Row, 1950. (3–6)

_____. *The Birthday Party.* New York: Harper & Row, 1957. (3–5)

_____. *The Carrot Seed.* New York: Harper & Row, 1945. (2–4)

_____. *The Growing Story.* New York: Harper & Row, 1947. (3–5)

_____. *I Want to Paint My Bathroom Blue.* New York: Harper & Row, 1956. (4–6)

_____. *Somebody Else's Nut Tree.* New York: Harper & Row, 1958. (4–6)

Kruglovsky, P. *The Very Little Boy.* Garden City, N.Y.: Doubleday & Co., (15 mos.–2 yrs.)

_____. *The Very Little Girl.* Garden City, N.Y.: Doubleday & Co., 1953. (15 mos.–2 yrs.)

Kunhardt, Dorothy. *Junket Is Nice.* Boston: Houghton Mifflin Co., (4–6)

_____. *Pat the Bunny.* New York: Simon & Schuster, 1962. (15 mos.–2 yrs.)

Kuskin, Karla. *All Sizes of Noises.* New York: Harper & Row, 1962. (4–6)

Langstaff, Nancy. *A Tiny Baby for You.* New York: Harcourt, Brace Jovanovich, 1955. (2–5)

Leaf, Munro. *Ferdinand.* New York: Viking Press, 1962. (4–6)

Lear, Edward. *The Nonsense Alphabet.* Garden City, N.Y.: Doubleday & Co., 1962. (3–6)

Lenski, Lois. *Animals for Me.* New York: Henry Z. Walck, 1941. (2–5)

_____. *Cowboy Small.* New York: Oxford University Press, 1949. (2–4)

_____. *The Little Auto.* New York: Henry Z. Walck, 1934. (2–4)

_____. *Little Baby Ann.* New York: Henry Z. Walck. (15 mos.–2 yrs.)

_____. *The Little Family.* Garden City, N.Y.: Doubleday Doran, 1932. (2–5)

Lexau, Joan. *Benjie.* New York: Dial Press, 1964. (4–6)

_____. *Benjie on his Own.* New York: Dial Press, 1970. (4–6)

Lionni, Leo. *The Biggest House in the World.* New York: Pantheon Books, 1973. (4–6)

_____. *Fish Is Fish.* New York: Pantheon Books, 1970. (4–6)

_____. *Little Blue and Little Yellow.* New York: Astor-Honor, 1959. (3–6)

————. *Swimmy.* New York: Pantheon Books, 1963. (4–6)

Lobel, Arnold. *A Zoo for Mister Muster.* New York: Harper & Row, 1962. (3–6)

McCloskey, Robert. *Blueberries for Sal.* New York: Viking Press, 1948. (3–6)

————. *One Morning in Maine.* New York: Viking Press, 1952. (4–8)

McGovern, Ann. *Black Is Beautiful.* New York: Four Winds Press, 1969. (4–7)

————. *Too Much Noise.* Boston: Houghton Mifflin Co., 1967. (3–5)

Martin, Mary Steichen. *The First Picture Book.* New York: Harcourt, Brace Jovanovich, 1930. (15 mos.–2 yrs.)

Merriam, Eve. *Boys and Girls: Girls and Boys.* New York: Holt, Rinehart & Winston, 1972. (4–6)

Miller, Edna. *Mousekin's ABC.* Englewood Cliffs, N.J.: Prentice-Hall, 1937. (15 mos.–2 yrs.)

Milne, A. A. *Christopher Robin Book of Verses.* New York: E. P. Dutton & Co., 1967. (4–6)

————. *When We Were Very Young.* New York: E. P. Dutton & Co., 1961. (4–6)

Minarik, Else. *Little Bear.* New York: Harper & Row, 1957. (3–6)

Moffett, Martha. *A Flower Pot Is Not a Hat.* New York: E. P. Dutton & Co., 1972. (3–5)

Nakano, Hirotaka. *Elephant Blue.* Indianapolis: Bobbs-Merrill Co., 1970. (2–5)

Nodset, Joan L. *Go Away, Dog.* New York: Harper & Row, 1963. (4–6)

————. *Who Took the Farmer's Hat?* New York: Harper & Row, 1963. (4–7)

Parsons, Ellen. *Rainy Day Together.* New York: Harper & Row, 1971. (3–7)

Piper, Watty. *The Little Engine that Could.* New York: Platt & Munk Co., 1930. (3–5)

Preston, Edna Mitchell. *The Temper Tantrum Book.* New York: Viking Press, 1969. (4–7)

Reich, Hanns. *Baby Animals and Their Mothers.* New York: Hill & Wang, 1965. (15 mos.–2 yrs.)

Rey, H. A. *Curious George.* (A series.) Boston: Houghton Mifflin Co., 1941. (4–6)

Ringi, Kjell. *The Magic Stick.* New York: Harper & Row, 1968. (4–6)

————. *The Sun and the Cloud.* New York: Harper & Row, 1971. (3–6)

Rodgers, Mary. *The Rotten Book.* New York: Harper & Row, 1969. (4–8)

Schick, Eleanor. *A Surprise in the Forest.* New York: Harper & Row, 1964. (3–6)

Schlein, Miriam. *Fast Is Not a Ladybug.* New York: William R. Scott, 1953. (3–5)

_____. *Heavy Is a Hippopotamus.* New York: William R. Scott, 1954. (3–5)

Sendak, Maurice. *Where the Wild Things Are.* New York: Harper & Row, 1963. (4–8)

Seuss, Dr. *And to Think that I Saw it on Mulberry Street.* New York: Vanguard Press, 1937. (3–5)

_____. *The Cat in the Hat.* New York: Random House, 1957. (4–8)

_____. *The 500 Hats of Bartholomew Cubbins.* New York: Vanguard Press, 1938. (3–5)

_____. *Green Eggs and Ham.* New York: Random House, 1960. (4–8)

Showers, Paul. *Your Skin and Mine.* New York: Thomas Y. Crowell Co., 1965. (4–7)

Simon, Norma. *What Do I Say?* New York: Whitman Publishing Co., 1967. (15 mos.–2 yrs.)

Skaar, Grace. *What Do Animals Say?* New York: Young Scott Books, 1968. (15 mos.–2 yrs.)

Slobodkina, Esphyr. *Caps for Sale.* New York: William R. Scott, 1947. (3–6)

Steiner, Charlotte. *My Slippers Are Red.* New York: Alfred A. Knopf, 1957. (2–3)

Tenggren, Gustav. *The Tenggren Mother Goose.* Boston: Little, Brown & Co., 1956. (2–4)

Thompson, Blanche. *The Silver Pennies.* New York: Macmillan & Co., 1967. (3–6)

Tudor, Tasha. *Pumpkin Moonshine.* New York: Henry Z. Walck, 1962. (3–5)

Udry, Janice. *A Tree Is Nice.* New York: Harper & Row, 1956. (3–5)

Ungerer, Tomi. *The Beast of Monsieur Racine.* New York: Farrar, Straus & Giroux, 1971. (4–8)

_____. *Crictor.* New York: Harper & Row, 1958. (4–8)

Wildsmith, Brian. *Brian Wildsmith's ABC.* New York: Franklin Watts, 1963. (15 mos.–2 yrs.)

Williams, Margery. *The Velveteen Rabbit.* Garden City, N.Y.: Doubleday & Co., 1958. (3–6)

Wright, Blanche. *The Real Mother Goose.* Chicago: Rand McNally & Co., 1966. (15 mos.–2 yrs.)

Wright, Ethel. *Saturday Walk.* New York: William R. Scott, 1954. (3–5)

Zaffo, George. *Airplanes and Trucks and Trains.* New York: Grossett & Dunlap, 1968. (4–7)

Zion, Gene. *Dear Garbage Man.* New York: Harper & Row, 1957. (4–6)

———. *Harry the Dirty Dog.* New York: Harper & Row, 1956. (4–8)

———. *No Roses for Harry.* New York: Harper & Row, 1958. (4–8)

———. *The Plant Sitter.* New York: Harper & Row, 1959. (4–8)

———. *Really Spring.* New York: Harper & Row, 1956. (3–6)

Zolotow, Charlotte. *Big Sister and Little Sister.* New York: Harper & Row, 1966. (4–8)

———. *Do You Know What I'll Do?* New York: Harper & Row, 1958. (3–5)

———. *A Father Like That.* New York: Harper & Row, 1972. (4–6)

———. *The Hating Book.* New York: Harper & Row, 1969. (4–6)

———. *The Quarreling Book.* New York: Harper & Row, 1963. (4–6)

———. *The Sky Was Blue.* New York: Harper & Row, 1969. (4–8)

———. *Someday.* New York: Harper & Row, 1965. (4–8)

———. *William's Doll.* New York: Harper & Row, 1972. (2–5)

Index